D0160536

LATINO AMERICA

Dynamic Population is
Poised to Transform the Politics of the Nation

LATINO AMERICA

MATT BARRETO
AND GARY M. SEGURA

With contributions from
Elizabeth Bergman, Loren Collingwood, David Damore,
Justin Gross, Blanca Flor Guillen, Sylvia Manzano,
Adrian Pantoja, Francisco Pedraza, Gabriel Sanchez,
and Ali Valenzuela

PUBLICAFFAIRS
New York

Published in the United States by PublicAffairs™,
a Member of the Perseus Books Group

Book Design by Jeff Williams

Library of Congress Cataloging-in-Publication Data
Barreto, Matt A.

Latino America : how America's most dynamic population is poised to transform the politics of the nation / Matt Barreto and Gary M. Segura ; with contributions from Elizabeth Bergman, Loren Collingwood, David Damore, Justin Gross, Blanca Flor Guillen, Sylvia Manzano, Adrian Pantoja, Francisco Pedraza, Gabriel Sanchez, and Ali Valenzuela.—First edition.

pages cm

Includes bibliographical references and index.

ISBN 978-1-61039-501-4 (hardcover : alk. paper)—ISBN 978-1-61039-502-1 (electronic : alk. paper) 1. Hispanic Americans—Politics and government. 2. United States—Politics and government—2009-I. Segura, Gary M., 1963- II. Title.

E184.S75B367 2014
320.973089'68—dc23

2014015544

First Edition

10 9 8 7 6 5 4 3 2 1

CONTENTS

We dedicate this book

To Juan and Catalina, Enrique James, Ana Victoria, Itati, and Fiby,

And to Daniel Javier and Clara Victoria

Who represent the future Latino America we study here. . . .

Chapter 1

LATINO AMERICA: AN INTRODUCTION

Sometime in April 2014, somewhere in a hospital in California, a Latino child was born who tipped the demographic scales of California's new plurality. Latinos displaced non-Hispanic whites as the largest racial/ethnic group in the state. And so, 166 years after the Treaty of Guadalupe Hidalgo brought the Mexican province of Alta California into the United States, Latinos once again became the largest population in the state.

Surprised? Texas will make the same transition sometime before 2020, and Latinos have had a plurality in New Mexico for some time. Latinos are already over 17% of the population of the United States, and that number will grow toward a national plurality over the course of this century. The America that today's infants will die in is going to look very different from the nation in which they were born. Oh, and by the way, more than half of today's children under age five are nonwhite.

The pace of demographic change and its impact on both the racial structure of American society and the future makeup of the electorate are illustrated clearly in Table 1.1. In the 1950 census, the white share of the population reached its peak at just under 90%. And in 1980, when Ronald Reagan was elected president, nearly 80% of all Americans were white. Meanwhile, in 1970, just 4.7% of Americans identified themselves as being of Hispanic ancestry. These populations were concentrated in New York and Chicago (Puerto Rican), Miami (Cuban), and the Southwest,

TABLE 1.1 Historical Trends in White Identification in the US Census

Year	*White*	*Non-Hispanic White*	*Hispanic (Any Race)*	*Non-Hispanic, not in Combination*	*Non-Hispanic, Two or More Races*
1800*	81.1%	--	--	--	--
1850	84.3%	--	--	--	--
1900	87.9%	--	--	--	--
1950	89.5%	--	--	--	--
1960	88.8%	--	--	--	--
1970	87.5%	83.2%	4.7%	--	--
1980	83.1%	79.6%	6.4%	--	--
1990	80.3%	75.6%	9%	--	--
2000	77.1%	70.9%	12.5%	70.4%	1.6%
2010	74.8%	65.3%	16.4%	63.7%	1.9%

Source: US Bureau of the Census. For 1800, see US Bureau of the Census, "Table 1. United States—Race and Hispanic Origin: 1790 to 1990," available at: www.census.gov/population/www/documentation/twps0056/tab01.pdf. For 2010, see US Census Bureau, "Overview of Race and Hispanic Origin 2010 Census Briefs," March 2011, available at: http://www.census.gov/prod/cen2010/briefs/c2010br-02.pdf (accessed June 1, 2011).

from Texas to California (Mexican). Since 1980, however, the share of all Americans identifying themselves, unambiguously, as white has fallen precipitously, and Latinos, at 17%, are now present in every state and are the largest minority group in more than half of them. Nationally, the Latino population includes not just Mexicans, Puerto Ricans, and Cubans but also large numbers of Salvadorans, Guatemalans, Dominicans, Hondurans, Colombians, and countless others.

The ethnicity question in the census allowed us to count Hispanics separately from others answering "white" to the race question. It is ironic in the extreme that Latinos had been previously classified as "white" since that nominal status did not prevent them from being sent to segregated schools, kept off juries, being refused burial in local cemeteries, and other indignities historically reserved for the nonwhites in American society. White privilege clearly did *not* extend to Latinos.

The rapid growth of the Latino population will change America in profound ways. In the 1990s, Latino activists were fond of citing the 1992 report that salsa had displaced ketchup as America's most frequently purchased condiment, but that change really just scratches the cultural surface. Latin food, music, and dance have gone fully mainstream. Lin-Manuel Miranda won the Tony Award for Best Musical in 2008 for *In the Heights,* a story set in the largely Dominican community of Washington Heights, New York, almost exactly fifty years after *West Side Story* introduced Americans to Puerto Ricans living in the same city. Yet at the same time, English-language television continues to feature very few Latino lead characters. And although Latinos outnumber African Americans overall in the United States (and in more than half the states), African Americans are far more visible, both culturally and politically. Latinos may have restructured the race discussion in this country, once so powerfully dominated by the black-white dyadic relationship, but it is clear that the Latino story is very much a work in progress.

The central argument of this book is that in the twenty-first century American politics will be shaped, in large measure, by how Latinos are incorporated into the political system. The Latino electoral history of significant inter-election movement over time suggests that Latino population growth will combine with growth in the Latino electorate to present both political parties with new opportunities in their approaches to Latino voters. Such opportunities are not, of course, without precedent—the large-scale incorporation of urban immigrants in the early twentieth century played a significant role in realigning the American electorate and establishing the New Deal coalition, which dominated national politics for two generations.

If the past is prologue, the more than 53 million souls who make up this (mostly) new American community may well rewrite the political history of the United States. The demography is relentless—live births contribute more to population growth among Latinos now than immigration does, and over 93% of Latinos under age eighteen are citizens of the United States. More than 73,000 of these young people turn eighteen and become eligible to vote every month! There will be no stunning reversal of these numbers—there will be neither a sudden surge in white immigration and live births nor a Latino exodus. Each day every congressional district in the United States, and nearly every census tract, becomes more Latino than it was the day before.

If these new Americans represent political opportunity, they also represent political peril. For Republicans, the current numbers look grim. These new Americans enter the electorate two-to-one Democratic. In 2012 they voted nearly three-to-one Democratic. It wasn't always so. Ronald Reagan and George W. Bush both performed significantly better among Latinos in their reelection fights. But those days appear to be long gone, and as we discuss later in this book, it's high time for the GOP to get to work on rebuilding its brand with the Latino electorate.

The Democrats face perils of their own. The party's failure to provide meaningful outreach and effectively mobilize voters has led Democrats to leave millions of votes on the table, and they will continue to do so if nothing changes in their approach. Moreover, with the Democratic Party's reliance on minority voters—most notably African American voters—and rainbow racial coalitions, it must carefully nurture policy agreement and strategic partnerships between the minority groups. Rivalry—or worse, direct conflict—could undo the Democratic demographic advantage.

The complexity of Latinos as a group makes for a politics more nuanced and less lockstep than the political behavior often described by the media and casual observers. Nevertheless, over the last several elections there can be little question that Latinos have become a political force—a force whose potential may not yet have been realized, but a force nonetheless. Latinos have been moved to political action by different issues at different times. In 2006 immigration reform and hostile GOP-sponsored legislation dominated the headlines, just as would happen again in 2010. But in 2008 immigration was all but missing from the electoral agenda while Latinos focused their attention on the economy, which was hurting them far worse than other American racial/ethnic groups, and on the Iraq War, for which Latinos were paying a terrible price. In 2012, though the economy was still important, immigration was once again the moving issue.

As the Iraq War demonstrated, Latinos are not just a one-issue constituency. In the 1990s, when Cruz Bustamante became California's first Latino State Assembly speaker in the modern era (and later lieutenant governor), he liked to say that the "Latino agenda is the American agenda." For most Latinos, good jobs, good schools, and safe neighborhoods are the dominant issues. More recently, health care and environmental issues have begun to play an important (and related) role in the "Latino agenda." Latinos are among the most underinsured populations in America (although their health outcomes are not as bad as we might expect looking at average incomes), and many live in neighborhoods that present significant environmental challenges, such as particulate pollution, which increases the incidence of asthma.

Latinos, like all other Americans, have a lot of worries, a lot of goals, and strong views about the country and its government. Our hope is that this book will serve as a broad introduction to at least some aspects of modern Latino life and aspirations in the United States.

THE AUTHORS ASK: WHO ARE WE? WHY ARE WE HERE?

In some respects, the two of us represent several characteristics of the group we describe. One of us is Peruvian, the other Mexican, and both of us are of mixed parentage. Neither of us grew up in a Latino-intensive locale, at least not at the time of our upbringing—Matt Barreto was born in San Juan, Puerto Rico, but raised from age two in Topeka, Kansas, and Gary Segura is from New Orleans, Louisiana. Like most of America, both Topeka and New Orleans have experienced rapid recent increases in the size of their Latino populations.

Both of us are the sons of veterans. The connection between the Latino community and military service is strong and long-standing, and as we discuss in Chapter 6, it played an important role in Latino opposition to the Iraq War and in the 2008 election. Matt Barreto's dad came to the United States at age seventeen and was drafted into the Vietnam War by age nineteen, as a legal resident but not yet a US citizen. He refined his English skills in the Army and would earn both a bachelor's and master's degree after his military service. More than ten years later, right after Matt was born, he became a naturalized US citizen. Gary Segura's dad was a generation older, born in the United States during the First World War. He joined the US Army Air Corps before the Second World War broke out and served as a tail-gunner in the South Pacific before being grounded and hurt. He never went to college—in fact, during the Depression he left school at thirteen to go to work in a furniture factory to help support his eight siblings. His youngest brother, Lloyd, died in the Korean War.

We came to know one another at the Tomás Rivera Policy Institute (TRPI) at the Claremont Colleges, where Segura joined the academic staff in 1996. He began polling there during the 1996 presidential election, working with the late Harry Pachon, Rudy de la Garza, Louis DeSipio, Jongho Lee, Adrian Pantoja, Nathan Woods, and others. Barreto came aboard as a research assistant in 1999, working with Segura and other TRPI researchers on a pre-election poll of Latinos prior to the 2000 presidential election; he subsequently began graduate studies at Claremont Graduate University in 2000. Barreto and Segura continued to collaborate on polls of Latino voters with Pachon, de la Garza, and DeSipio in 2000, 2002, and 2004. These early TRPI polls represented some of the very few political polls of Latino voters in the 1990s and early 2000s. When Segura left Claremont, Barreto transferred to the University of California at Irvine, where he earned his PhD in political science.

We continued to work together, and in 2004 we published the first piece on Latinos in the *American Political Science Review* in over seventy years.[1] In 2005 we found ourselves together on the faculty of the University of Washington, where we again polled both the general population and Latinos—the former by founding the Washington Poll, a statewide poll of the Evergreen State, and the latter through membership in the Latino Policy Coalition alongside Fernando Guerra of Loyola Marymount University. In 2007, with Mark and Andrew Rosenkranz of Pacific Market Research, we founded the partnership now known as Latino Decisions.

This book, like Latino Decisions, is a collective enterprise. We received fine and important contributions from the rest of the Latino Decisions team and our contributing analysts, each of whom is a successful social scientist in his or her own right. We note those contributions throughout.

Everything we have to say in the coming chapters—much of which is based directly on our work over the last seven years—reflects two core commitments that both Latino Decisions and we ourselves have made to define our research approach. First, Latino interests are best served if the data collection—and thus the claims made on the basis of the data—is indisputable. Scientific rigor in the pursuit of public opinion and community engagement is of no use if data are poorly collected. Second, we never say anything as pollsters that we do not believe is true as scholars. This principle has not always won us political friends, but we believe that our commitment to it has been the right thing for Latinos and for Latino Decisions.

To ensure the accuracy of what we say in our polling, we combine the finest current social scientific techniques with cultural competency so that our bilingual interview teams can ask the right questions in a manner that our community will understand, using the right format, question design, and sampling strategy. In 2012, amid our extensive polling of Latino voters, an article in *Time* magazine called Latino Decisions "the gold-standard in Latino American polling," and we were named to Politic365's list of "The 30 Latinos & Latinas Who Made the 2012 Election." We stand behind every result we present in this book.

AN OVERVIEW OF THE BOOK

We begin, in Chapter 2, by examining some of the characteristics that complicate any narrative of Latinos as an identifiable electoral and social bloc, such as differences in generation, nativity, and national origin. Those differences notwithstanding, there is a growing sense of Latino identity that bridges these differences and is becoming increasingly palpable and politically relevant.

In Chapter 3, we examine three critical aspects of the question: what do Latinos think about government? First, we demonstrate that, despite a strong commitment to norms of self-reliance, Latinos (and other racial/ethnic minority groups) repeatedly express a preference for a government that acts to improve the lives of its citizens and reduce inequality. Second, we explore Latino religiosity and its impact, if any, on the political beliefs of Latinos. We discover that religion is experienced very differently among different groups: as it turns out, Latinos are neither as socially conservative as popularly conceived nor as susceptible, through their perceived social conservatism, to the arguments of modern conservatism. Finally, we show that on matters both big and small, Latinos vote consistently as economic pragmatists—liberal pragmatists—who favor tax increases to balance spending cuts and generally prefer Democrats to steer the economy while blaming the GOP for economic ills. These views stem from the economic and social vulnerability of Latinos in the face of low-income parentage, weak educational opportunity, and bias in the mortgage market.

In Chapter 4, we introduce several people we had a chance to talk with in-depth. Rafael, David, Juanita, and Anita, all residents of metropolitan Houston, shared something in common with Catalina and Alfredo M., who lived in the Los Angeles area: none of them voted. For economic reasons among others, Latinos don't vote as frequently as other Americans. Some don't vote because they are not registered, while others are registered but have chosen of late not to go to the polls. Our interviewees' answers to our questions about this voting behavior allow us in this chapter to explore the frustrations and opportunities in Latino voter turnout.

In the second part of the book, we look at Latinos at the polls by exploring in detail the 2008 presidential primary contest between Hillary Clinton and Barack Obama and the 2008, 2010, and 2012 general elections. In Chapter 5, we explore the claim made by Hillary Clinton's Latino pollster that Latinos would not vote for black candidates. We show that, in fact, race had little to do with the Latino primary vote, and in Chapter 6 we show that this remained true in the general election. What really made the difference at the polls was Clinton's far deeper and longer ties to the Latino community.

Latinos overwhelmingly supported Barack Obama in the 2008 election, and in Chapter 6 we provide several of the reasons why. We show clearly that neither immigration nor race was particularly important to Latinos in that contest, despite immigration's importance in 2006 and 2010 and the general importance of race to white voters. Rather, the Iraq War and the collapse of the economy—and Senator John McCain's lack of credibility on both issues—set the stage for a Democratic landslide among Latino voters. In examining this election, we offer several novel ways to think about the importance of Latino voters to elections.

In 2010 Democrats suffered a big setback in the congressional elections. Latino voters, however, played a critical role in preserving the Senate for the Democrats and keeping Harry Reid (D-NV) in his job. In

Chapter 7, we offer a detailed account of the evolution of Latino enthusiasm across the 2010 electoral cycle and the key roles played by immigration politics, Arizona's SB 1070, and the Dream Act.

The 2012 presidential election looked very different from the 2008 election. The incumbent administration had been very disappointing on immigration, which was now a major campaign issue, and the national economy remained weak. Nevertheless, that election would prove historic for the Latino electorate: for the first time ever, Latino votes provided the margin of victory for the winning candidate. Chapter 8 examines the role of Latinos in that election and extends our thinking from Chapter 6 about how best to estimate Latino influence.

The third and final section of the book examines key issues in the Latino community beyond the economy. We start by delving deeply into immigration politics. In Chapter 9, we look at the experience of California in the 1990s, when Proposition 187 (and later 209 and 227) played a key role in moving the state from politically competitive (and even leaning Republican in presidential and gubernatorial elections) to one of the safest Democratic strongholds in the country. California's experience in the 1990s, we suggest, has much to show us about how the politics of the nation will evolve in the coming years. If past is prologue, we can only conclude that in continuing to allow short-term strategic calculations and the outspoken voices of xenophobia within their coalition to shape Republican policy and political actions, GOP leaders are courting politically catastrophic consequences for their party over the long term.

In Chapter 10, we look at the current environment through the same lens and identify districts where immigration politics may begin to reshape the House of Representatives, if not in the election of 2014, then in elections to come. Although a majority of Latino voters report having voted GOP at least once, the reputation of the Republican Party continues to suffer in ways that may tarnish its brand for a generation. There are certainly things the GOP could do to increase its Latino vote share, as we show in this chapter, but currently it is doing none of them.

However important the issues of the Iraq War, the economy, and immigration have been in the last few electoral cycles, a variety of other concerns also have an important impact on the lives of Latinos, and those concerns significantly influence their political orientations and voting behavior as well. In Chapter 11, we examine the Patient Protection and Affordable Care Act, or Obamacare, which has so dominated the political landscape since it was passed in March 2010; Latinos have consistently favored Obamacare and opposed its repeal. In Chapter 12, we look at environmentalism. Although environmental problems are often constructed as white, middle-class issues, Latinos show themselves to be acutely aware of them, both immediate issues like local air pollution and global issues like climate change. Defying conventional wisdom, Latino registered voters demonstrate strong environmental attitudes and a considerable willingness to act politically on the basis of those views.

So here we go. As with any good story, we start at the beginning, and so we ask that most basic question: exactly who are Latinos?

Part I

UNDERSTANDING LATINOS AND THEIR PLACE IN THE POLITY

Chapter 2

UNITY AND DIVERSITY

Coauthored with Adrian Pantoja

The rapid growth of the share of Latinos in the US population in the last decade is now widely recognized in academic and political circles.* Just over 12% of the US population in 2000, Latinos accounted for 16.3% in the 2010 census—a 33% increase in ten years. A majority of that growth came from native births rather than immigration. According to US Census Bureau projections, Latinos will make up one-quarter of the national population by 2050.

Although the Latino share of the electorate has significantly lagged the population share, it too has grown substantially. In 2008 Latinos were an estimated 9% of the national electorate, up considerably from 5.4% in 2000 and dramatically from 3.7% in 1992, when Bill Clinton was first elected president.[1] Disadvantages in education and income are generally associated with lower rates of voter registration and turnout, but Latinos have nevertheless been closing the gap, largely by overperforming for their socioeconomic status. And in reported voter participation, Latinos trail non-Hispanic whites with the same levels of both education and income by a mere 4%.[2]

---

*Portions of this chapter appeared in earlier form in Gary M. Segura, "Latino Public Opinion and Realigning the American Electorate," *Daedalus* 141, no. 4 (Fall 2012): 98–113.

The remainder of the lag can be attributed to two factors, both of which will become less significant with time. First, Latinos in the United States are a very young population; among those who are citizens, only 57.7% are over the age of eighteen (compared with 79.1% of non-Hispanic whites), according to the American Community Survey. Second, noncitizens make up around 40% of the adult Latino population. Although many of them are undocumented residents whose future in the country is uncertain at best, in time these noncitizens will be replaced in the population with their US-born offspring.

The growing Latino electorate has already significantly reshaped politics in the Southwest and California and is beginning to do so in Texas, Florida, and even Georgia and North Carolina. As the Latino population and electorate continue to grow, so will the impact of Latino public opinion on the national conversation—and on political outcomes in particular.

JUST THE FACTS

Much of the discourse on Latino politics in the United States is filled with myths and misperceptions based on anecdotal accounts gathered by news reporters or self-designated experts. Moreover, many observers assume that what is true for the Mexican-origin population is also true for Puerto Ricans or for other Latin American ancestry groups. But considering that over twenty countries in Latin America and the Iberian Peninsula are represented in Latino ancestries, generalizing from the experiences of one nationality group overlooks important differences between them. Differences between Latino immigrants and those who are non-immigrants or who have been living in the country for many generations are also significant but often ignored. And the political differences between Latinos who are Democrats and those who are Republicans are often significant. In this book, we address many of the myths surrounding Latino politics and identify many of the similarities as well as the differences across varying types of Latinos.

Before we delve into the diverse and dynamic world of Latino America, it is important to establish some baseline demographic information on the 53 million Latinos presently living in the United States. Longtime

FIGURE 2.1 The Latino Population in the United States (in Millions)

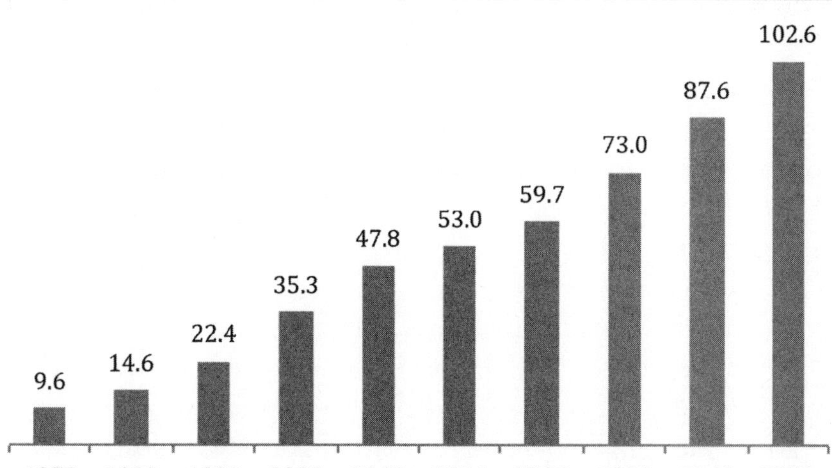

observers of Latino politics can recall a time when Latinos flew under the political radar because they were considered demographically and politically insignificant. The rapid growth of the Latino population in the late twentieth century, however (see Figure 2.1), coupled with a political awakening in the mid-1990s, propelled them into the national spotlight.

Although Mexican Americans and Puerto Ricans, the two largest Latino groups, were active in the 1960s civil rights struggles, by and large Latinos were not significant nationwide political actors in the 1970s and 1980s. But by the 2000 census, Latinos had grown to over 35 million (or 12.5% of the US population; see Figure 2.2) and were on the verge of becoming the nation's largest minority. In the last decade, their size and growing political clout have come to the notice of political pundits and politicians, many of whom proclaim that the "sleeping giant" has finally "awakened." No doubt, Latinos' political strength will only continue to surge in the coming decades, given the population growth forecasts shown in Figures 2.1 and 2.2.

Immigration is a critical factor behind Latino growth rates and a pivotal policy issue for Latinos, as we will see in this book. The foreign-born

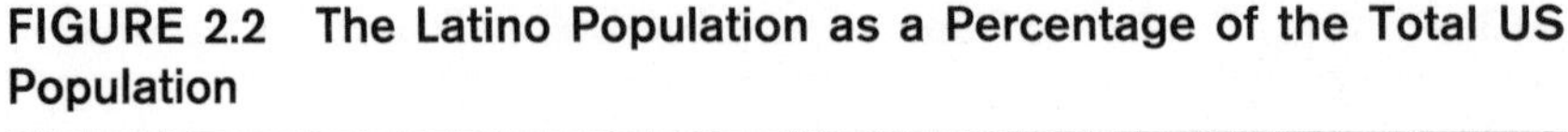

FIGURE 2.2 The Latino Population as a Percentage of the Total US Population

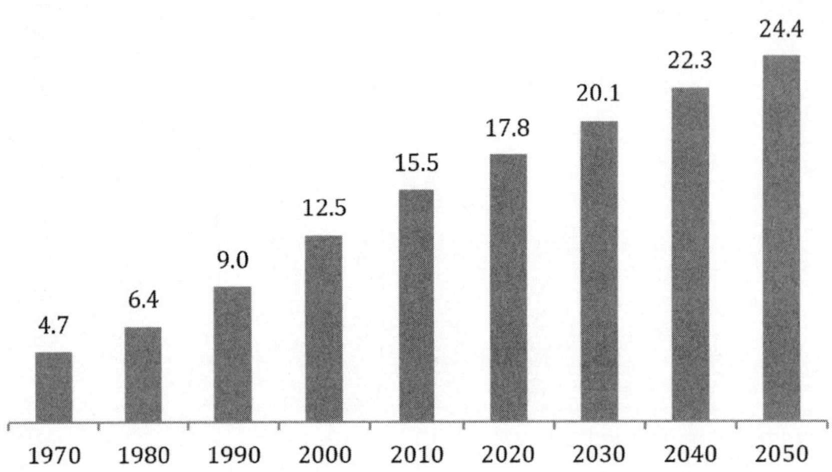

Latino segment has more than doubled in the last forty years, from 20% in 1970 to 40% by the 2000 census, to an estimated 43% today (see Figure 2.3).

The doubling of the number of foreign-born Latinos can be directly attributed to changes in US immigration law, beginning with the Immigration and Nationality Act of 1965. Essentially, the 1965 act eliminated the preference categories for Northern and Western Europeans in favor of a preference system that emphasized family reunification. The 1965 act facilitated immigration not only from Latin America but also from Asia and other parts of the globe, leading to a so-called fourth wave of mass immigration. In fact, immigration patterns from Latin America closely follow changes in US immigration laws and migration patterns from other parts of the world. In contrast to previous immigration waves, however, Latin Americans constitute the largest segment of contemporary immigrants, at 53%.[3] Not surprisingly, the backlash that followed this wave was largely directed at immigrants from Mexico, since that country was the single largest source of immigrants from Latin America in 2010 (55%), as well as from around the world (29%). In effect, immigration became

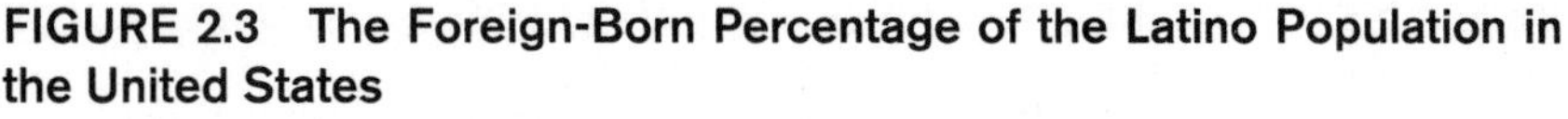

FIGURE 2.3 The Foreign-Born Percentage of the Latino Population in the United States

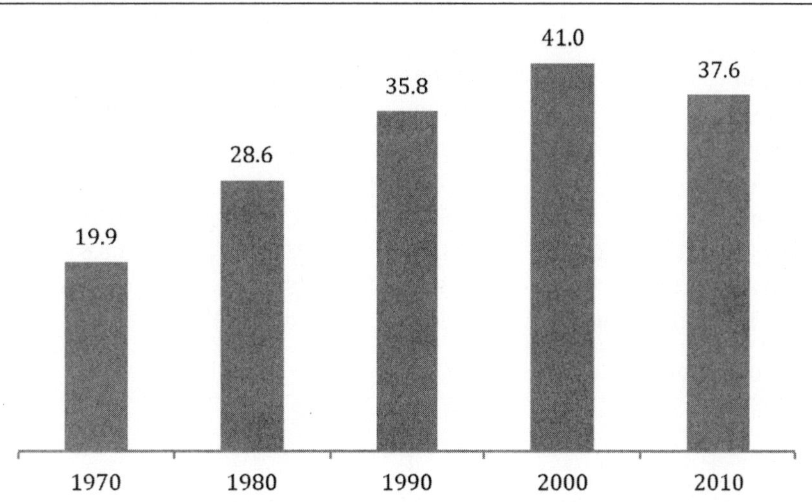

synonymous, in the minds of the American electorate, with "Latino" in general, and with "Mexican" in particular. As popular dissatisfaction with all forms of immigration—and particularly undocumented immigration—grew and was stoked by political provocateurs, it is not surprising that Mexican-origin people were most often identified, targeted, and disparaged.

Before we look at the states with the largest concentration of Latinos, it is important to examine the differing sizes of the national-origin groups that make up the Latino population. Then, given that Latino settlement patterns in the United States are driven by history, geographical proximity to the country of ancestry, employment opportunities, and the social networks established by transnational ties, we can establish where and why particular ancestry groups reside where they do.

Mexican Americans are the largest segment of the Latino population, at 29 million, or 65% of Latinos in the United States. The second-largest group, Puerto Ricans, make up a mere 9%. Cubans constitute less than 4%, Salvadorans 3.6%, and Dominicans 2.8% of all Latinos in the United States. When we consider the distribution between native- and foreign-born populations across each group (see Table 2.1), what is most

TABLE 2.1 The Latino Population in the United States, by Nativity, 2007

Ancestry	*Total Population*	*Native-Born*	*Foreign-Born*
Latino	45,378,600	56.3%	43.7%
Mexican	29,189,300	59.5	40.5
Puerto Rican	4,114,700	64.8	35.2
Cuban	1,608,800	37.5	62.5
Salvadoran	1,473,500	33.3	66.7
Dominican	1,198,800	37.9	62.1
Other Central American	2,059,100	31.2	68.8
South American	2,500,800	28.9	71.1
Other Hispanic or Latino	3,233,500	80.9	19.1

Source: Garcia (2012), 30.

striking is that for most Latinos the foreign-born population is a considerably larger portion of their total numbers than the native-born population. That Mexican Americans and Puerto Ricans are the exception may seem odd, given that Mexico is the single largest source of immigration to the United States. Yet a closer look at the history of the population reveals that Mexican Americans have a long and continuous presence in the United States. Some Mexican Americans can trace their ancestry to the time when the American Southwest belonged to Mexico (thus the adage, "I did not cross the border, the border crossed me"). A significant portion also arrived at the turn of the twentieth century, following the Mexican Revolution (1910–1920). Many more came as braceros during World War II to fill labor shortages brought about by the war. The fact that an estimated 500,000 Mexican Americans served in the US armed forces during World War II shows the size of the population even before the passage of the 1965 Immigration and Nationality Act. Settling in the American Southwest was natural given its geographic proximity to Mexico, the economic opportunities it offered, and the long-standing presence of Mexicans in the region.

Migration from the US Commonwealth of Puerto Rico was also significant prior to the 1965 act. In fact, because Puerto Ricans have been US citizens since 1917, the immigration act had little impact on their migration patterns. Puerto Rican migration can be traced back to Operation Bootstrap, an economic development program initiated in 1952 by the Commonwealth's first elected governor, Luis Muñoz Marín. Operation Bootstrap had a profound impact on Puerto Rican migration. In the 1940s there were 69,967 Puerto Ricans in the United States, but by the 1960s the population had grown to 887,662. The primary destination point for Puerto Ricans was New York, which is home to the largest concentration of Puerto Ricans on the mainland to this day.

Cubans and Salvadorans migrated as a direct result of turmoil brought about by revolutions in their homelands. With the ousting of President Fulgencio Batista's regime by Fidel Castro on January 1, 1959, political and economic elites fled from the island of Cuba; geographic proximity and long-standing networks made Miami their natural destination. Because Cubans were fleeing a Communist regime, they were easily able to enter the country because they were considered political refugees. This experience stands in sharp contrast to what happened in the 1980s to Salvadorans who were fleeing political violence initiated by a regime that was an ally of the United States. Salvadorans were treated as economic refugees and summarily returned to El Salvador if they were caught at the border or within the United States. After a series of legal challenges, Salvadoran refugees were finally granted temporary protected status. Los Angeles became a primary destination for Salvadorans given its proximity to El Salvador and the established communities of Mexican and Central American immigrants.[4]

Among the top five Latino groups in the United States, Dominicans have been the greatest beneficiaries of the 1965 Immigration and Nationality Act. The easing of immigration restrictions combined with the overthrow of the Trujillo dictatorship (1930–1961) to dramatically increase migration from the Dominican Republic to the United States. The first wave of Dominican migrants came to escape the civil strife following Trujillo's assassination and the bloody political vacuum that ensued. Only 9,897 Dominicans had come to the United States in the 1950s, but that figure jumped to 93,292 in the 1960s. Many of those leaving in the 1960s were middle-class Dominicans seeking to avoid becoming victims of the political violence, and the US government, in an effort to stabilize the

FIGURE 2.4 Latino Population Size, by State

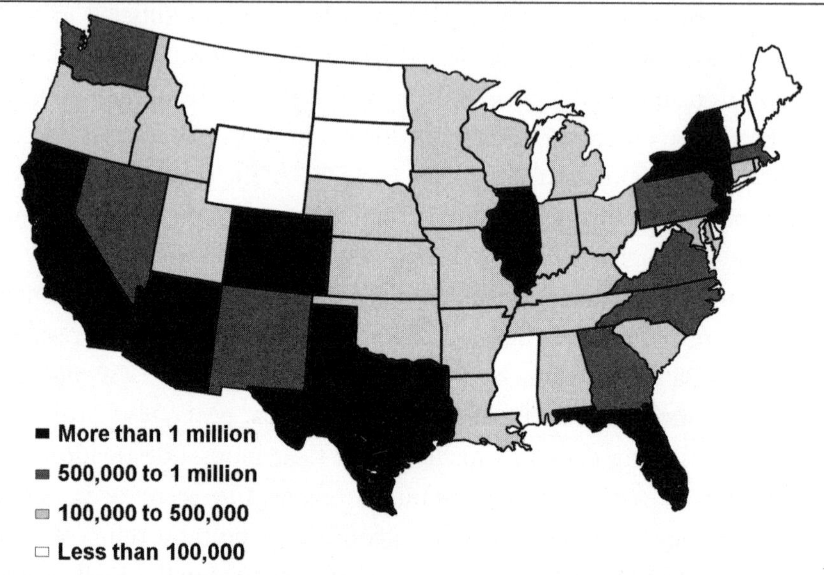

country, granted US visas even to potential opponents of the US-backed regime. Since that era, Dominican emigration, largely motivated by the push and pull of economic factors, has risen dramatically. Between 1961 and 2000, 828,713 Dominicans legally immigrated to the United States. Like Puerto Ricans, Dominicans have primarily settled in New York City.[5]

From the map in Figure 2.4 showing the geographic distribution of the Latino population in the country, we can observe that more than half (55%) of US Latinos reside in three states: California, Texas, and Florida. California is home to the nation's largest Latino population, with about 14.4 million Latinos. California's Latino population alone accounts for more than one-fourth (28%) of US Hispanics.[6] When it comes to the four largest ancestry groups, more than half (61%) of the Mexican-origin population in the United States reside in California (11.4 million) and Texas (8 million) alone. About two-fifths (41%) of the Puerto Rican population live in two states: New York (1.1 million) and Florida (848,000). More than two-thirds (68%) of all Cubans live in one state: Florida (1.2 million). Dominicans are highly concentrated in the state of New York, with nearly half residing there in 2010 (675,000, or 48%). Nearly half (48%) of the Salvadoran population is concentrated in California (574,000) and Texas (223,000).[7]

TABLE 2.2 Selected Demographic Characteristics of the Top Five Latino Groups in the United States

Group	English Fluency	Median Age (Years)	BA Degree (at Age 25 or Older)	Median Household Income (in 2008 US Dollars)	Homeownership Rate	Catholic
Mexican	61.6%	25	9%	40,736	50.5%	75%
Puerto Rican	80.5	29	16	40,736	40.3	60
Cuban	58.3	41	25	43,587	59.7	66
Salvadoran	44.2	29	5	43,791	46.0	58
Dominican	53.4	29	8	35,644	28.3	72

Source: Pew Hispanic Center, Statistical Portrait of Hispanics in the United States, 2008 survey. Data on identification as Catholic are from the 2006 Latino National Survey.

Despite the differences in their migration and settlement patterns, the various ancestry groups share many sociodemographic characteristics, though of the five largest Latino ancestry groups, Cubans have a distinctive sociodemographic profile (see Table 2.2). Cubans on average are older, they are more educated, and they have higher incomes and homeownership rates. The sociodemographic differences between Cubans and the other Latino ancestry groups stem largely from the demographic characteristics of the immigrants who fled the Cuban revolution. Now living in exile in this country, those immigrants, for the most part, represented the upper strata of Cuban society—in sharp contrast to the sociodemographic status of immigrants from the other Latino groups.

Cubans aside, the other groups are more alike than different in their demographic profiles. Across these and other Latino groups, Catholicism remains the dominant religion. Some geographic and socioeconomic differences have an impact on Latino political beliefs and behaviors, however, and there are key social factors we must consider as well.

POINTS OF DIVERSITY AMONG LATINOS

The Latino population of the United States is diverse in several important ways. Not only does the diversity of this population complicate any analysis of Latino public opinion, but its effect—that is, the degree to which it yields meaningful differences in Latino views or behavior—varies considerably. Three particular characteristics are especially important to understanding Latino opinion and behavior: national origin, nativity (including differences by age), and generation in the United States. These demographic facts capture the differences between the children of immigrants, the grandchildren of immigrants, and subsequent generations.

National Origin

Among the myriad complications of examining Latino public opinion and political participation is the definitional question: who exactly is a Latino? As simplistic as that question may sound, the issue of identity has important social and methodological implications. For one, Latino residents of the United States migrated or are descended from migrants from over twenty Latin American nations (including the US Commonwealth of Puerto Rico). Second, while the ethnic histories of the Iberian Peninsula and Southern Europe are complex enough, the varied racial histories of Latin America add another layer of complexity to definitions of "Latino" and account for the significant apparent variation in Latino phenotype across the United States. Think about Univision anchor Jorge Ramos, talk-show host Cristina Saralegui, actors America Ferrara and Jimmy Smits, baseball players Alex Rodriguez and Sammy Sosa, and singers Jennifer Lopez and the late Celia Cruz: all are Latinos, but they exhibit a wide array of physical characteristics reflective of the unique racial histories of their national-origin groups.

Indigenous, European, and African ancestral origins combine in each Latin American nation in ways that make Latino identity racially complex.[8] Although 51.2% of the 8,634 respondents in the 2006 Latino National Survey (LNS) believed that Latinos constitute a distinct racial category, the reality in fact varies across national origins. Mexicans, many Central Americans, Peruvians, and Bolivians are of mestizo and indigenous ancestries; Colombian, Venezuelan, and Caribbean national origins more directly reflect the African diaspora in the Western Hemisphere; and individuals from Argentina, Chile, Uruguay, and Paraguay better represent Spanish (and other European) colonization. Yet despite these differences, anyone with Latin American origins is considered, in the context of American politics, "Latino" or "Hispanic." Research suggests that this racial complexity has an effect in the American political environment.[9]

That said, we should not overstate the diversity of national origins in the Latino population. More than 65% of all Latinos are Mexican or Mexican American, and another 9.1% are Puerto Rican. Salvadorans make up 3.6%, Cubans 3.5%, and Dominicans 2.8%.[10] Almost 86% of the Latino population in the United States is from one of those five national-origin groups. Guatemalans (2.2%) and Colombians (1.9%) are by far the largest of the remaining groups. More than a dozen other Latin American nations are represented in the US populace, but their population shares are tiny. Mexicans and Mexican Americans, and to a lesser extent Puerto Ricans, dominate the conversation.

Though these national-origin groups have distinct cultural characteristics and racial histories, the Spanish language, Roman Catholicism, and entertainment and media cultures that have become highly integrated over the course of decades have knitted all these Latino communities more closely together.[11] Nevertheless, several characteristics specific to certain national-origin groups can, and do, shape public opinion and political participation.

The most politically distinct are Cuban Americans in South Florida, many of whom are refugees (or offspring of refugees) of the Cuban revolution. Stereotypically Republican, Cubans have been influenced by the unique circumstances of their arrival in the 1960s; by the privileged legal immigration regime that they and no other Latino immigrants have enjoyed; and by their economic circumstances relative to other Latinos. Many who arrived in the 1960s and 1970s came with some resources and received considerable assistance from the United States. Their Republicanism is rooted in both these resource differences and their experience of the Cold War. Moreover, under the 1995 revisions to the Cuban Adjustment Act, Cuban migrants who reach US soil are given nearly automatic asylum and status, which removes immigration status as a barrier to the growth of their communities and their political incorporation.

Cuban distinctiveness appears to be eroding, however. Younger Cubans who are several generations removed from the Castro experience, as well as those descended from the "Marielitos" who arrived in the Mariel Boatlift in 1980 (and who came with fewer resources and faced some within-group bias from the longer-established population), are far less likely to be Republican. Their opinions and political characteristics more closely reflect those of other US Latinos.

The Puerto Rican experience is also distinct. Because Puerto Rico is part of the United States, Puerto Ricans, including those born on the island, are US citizens from birth—a provision of the Jones Act of 1917. Citizenship for Puerto Ricans and the lack of any legal consequences to their migration to and from the island highlight two key distinctions between Puerto Ricans and other Latinos: immigration is not an immediate issue for Puerto Ricans, and their access to the political process is straightforward.

Nevertheless, and for reasons that remain underexplored, political participation among mainland Puerto Ricans lags considerably behind other Latino national-origin groups, and more curiously, behind voters on the island as well. As Louis DeSipio noted in 2006, "Despite these relatively equal opportunities to participate politically in the United States or in Puerto Rico, turnout in Puerto Rican Elections is approximately twice as high as Puerto Rican participation in mainland elections."[12] DeSipio cites the differences between the island and the mainland in electoral institutions (including different political parties) and the absence of meaningful party mobilization on the mainland; he also points out that politics on the island is based in different issues, including most obviously the future status of the island as a US state or an independent nation. The effect is significant: Puerto Rican turnout hovers around 40% on the mainland but is more than twice that on the island. The undermobilization of Puerto Ricans remains a missed opportunity in terms of Latino impact on the US political system.

Nativity and Generation

Approximately 40% of all Latinos in the United States are foreign-born. This number understates, however, the role of nativity in Latino political life. About 34% of the Latino population is under the age of eighteen, but

93% of those young people are US citizens, with just 1% naturalized and 92% native-born. By contrast, 52% of adult Latinos are foreign-born, less than one-third of whom (31% of the total) have naturalized to US citizenship.[13] While these percentages vary significantly by state, they point to two important facts about the Latino population: only 64% of the adults are citizens of the United States, and naturalized citizens make up just 25% of the total. An additional share of this population, island-born Puerto Ricans, may not be US citizens through naturalization but have still experienced the economic, social, and linguistic challenges of migration.

Place of birth can shape attitudes and engagement in American politics in three important ways. First, embarking on the path to migration and citizenship is a profoundly self-selecting choice. Those who migrate are arguably different from their countrymen who do not, and moving from immigrant status to citizenship is even more demanding. In the past, the naturalization process was primarily driven by life events—marriage, childbirth, and the like—and naturalized immigrants voted less often than native citizens.[14] More recently, however, there is considerable evidence that immigrants choose to naturalize in response to political events, particularly rhetoric, initiatives, and legislation that target immigrants. Among the consequences of politically driven naturalization may well be a higher propensity to turn out for elections.[15]

Second, foreign-born citizens may hold beliefs and expectations about politics that are rooted in their home-country experience. Sergio Wals has demonstrated that variations in nation of birth can shape turnout propensity and that foreign-born citizens' experience with democracy (or lack thereof) may affect both their expectations of the US political system and their orientation toward it.[16]

Finally, for obvious reasons, immigrants who arrive after school age become familiar with the US political system as adults. Melissa Michelson has observed a curious process of adverse socialization: foreign-born citizens have a more favorable view of US politics than their US-born children and grandchildren, a finding confirmed elsewhere with regard to efficacy.[17] Foreign-born citizens are also more likely to identify as independents than as partisans.[18] In addition, they are less likely to see what they have in common with African Americans. "Becoming" American

TABLE 2.3 Selected Markers of Latino Assimilation and Acculturation, by Generation, 2006

	(Generation)			
	First	*Second*	*Third*	*Fourth or Later*
Roman Catholic	73.8%	69.7%	66.8%	58.1%
Social capital (group participation)	14.1	25.0	29.4	33.4
Military service, self or family	16.1	48.9	68.6	72.3
Less than high school education	49.7	22.9	17.6	16.2
Annual household income below $35,000	53.4	34.9	29.2	33.4
Percentage married to a non-Latino	13.3	32.2	42.6	53.3
Proficient in English	38.3[a]	93.2	98.6	99.0
Proficient in Spanish	99.2	91.6	68.7	60.5

Source: Authors' calculations using data from the Latino National Survey, 2006.
a. Includes noncitizens.

seems to bring with it a growing familiarity with US political coalitions, an increasing awareness of racial hierarchies in American society, and decreasing satisfaction with American institutions and processes.

The passage of generations, in theory, has the potential to erode the political distinctiveness of Latino citizens across national-origin groups and between Latinos and non-Latinos. As data from the Latino National Survey reveal (see Table 2.3), Latinos in later generations are significantly more likely to marry non-Latinos (as reflected in the declining frequency of Hispanic surnames) and to experience substantial economic and educational mobility; they are also less likely to retain their Catholic identity and significantly less likely to speak Spanish.

It is certainly the case that assimilation and acculturation produce changes in the political behavior of later generations. These changes can vary in form and function over time. For example, while self-reported electoral participation increases monotonically over generations, participation in ethnically based political activities—including attendance at protests and rallies and membership in organizations—increases through the first two generations but decreases thereafter.[19]

The Effects of In-Group Variation

There are at least as many similarities as differences among national-origin groups, generations, and nativities. For example, speaking Spanish and retaining Latino cultural practices are widely shared commitments across cohorts. Community and identity are enormously unifying factors.

A critical dynamic in maintaining such commonalities is the ongoing debate over immigration and policy toward undocumented immigrants. It has become increasingly clear that political views are substantially unified in response to perceived attacks on the community, notwithstanding the impact of nativity and generation. A perfect example is the Latino community's reaction to the passage of SB 1070 in Arizona, the "papers please" law that allows police to identify undocumented aliens during virtually any contact with the public. Just a week after the bill was signed into law, opposition among Latino registered voters transcended generational boundaries: a poll conducted by the National Council of La Raza, the Service Employees International Union, and Latino Decisions showed that supermajorities of all generations opposed the law (see Figure 2.5). Two especially revealing facts are worth noting from the poll. First, all respondents were citizens and registered voters—that is, they were the most secure and incorporated Latino members of Arizona society. Second, the fourth-generation respondents were limited to individuals whose *grandparents* were US-born and who would thus have been long established as members of American society.

How were the citizens polled interpreting this law, which ostensibly is aimed at undocumented immigrants? Their consensus probably arose from a widespread expectation that transcended generation: that enforcement would involve racial profiling and therefore could threaten all Latinos (see Figure 2.6). These 2010 findings from Arizona are deeply reminiscent of the impact of Proposition 187 in California and other anti-Latino or anti-immigrant actions, which appear to have had large-scale

FIGURE 2.5 Support for, and Opposition to, SB 1070 among Arizona Latino Registered Voters, May 2010

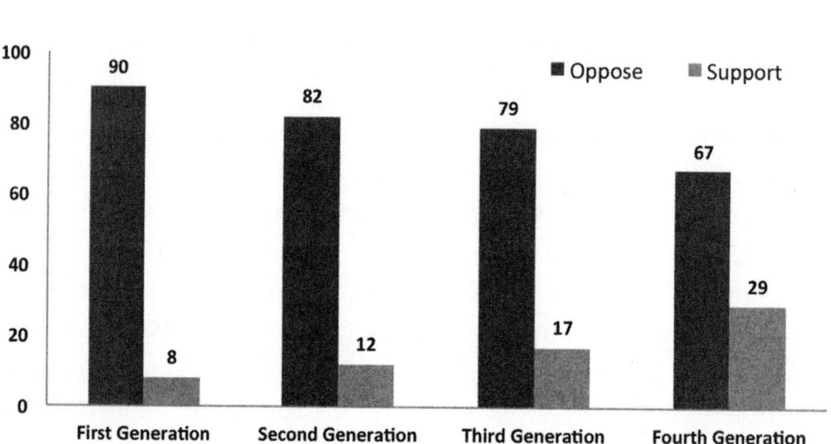

Respondents answered the following question: "Arizona has passed a law that will require state and local police to determine the immigration status of a person if there is a reasonable suspicion he or she is an illegal immigrant, and would charge anyone with trespassing who is not carrying proof of legal status when questioned by the police, and also prohibit immigrants from working as day laborers. From what you have heard, do you [rotate: support or oppose] the new immigration law in Arizona?" *Source:* Figure created by authors using data from National Council of La Raza/Service Employees International Union (SEIU)/Latino Decisions Arizona Poll, April–May 2010.

and significant political effects on Latinos across generations.[20] Issues that cut to the heart of ethnic identity are particularly likely to transcend differences in nativity, generation, or national-origin group.

~

Though there is plenty of evidence of substantial similarity across what is in many ways a diverse population, Latinos have until recently been a step shy of establishing a sense of group identity—that is, an awareness of commonality that in the electoral arena could provide the political coherence required for mobilization and collective action. However, as suggested by the cross-generational Latino reaction to some issues, such as anti-immigrant initiatives, Latino commonalities are now gelling into such an identity.

FIGURE 2.6 The Estimation of Arizona Latino Registered Voters of the Likelihood that Non-Immigrants Would Be Caught Up in Enforcement of SB 1070, May 2010

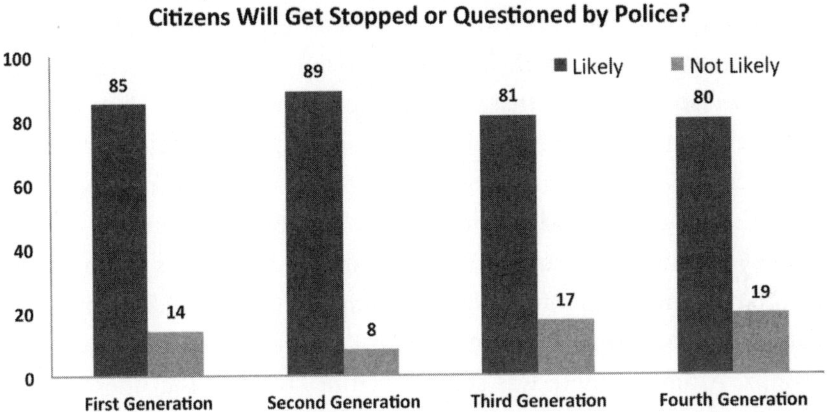

Respondents answered the following question: "How likely do you think it is that Latinos who are legal immigrants or US citizens will get stopped or questioned by the police? Is it very likely, somewhat likely, not too likely, or not likely at all?" *Source:* Figure created by authors using data from National Council of La Raza/SEIU/Latino Decisions Arizona Poll, April–May 2010.

When the Latino National Political Survey (LNPS) was completed in 1989, it revealed little evidence for the possibility that Latinos saw themselves as a "group" in any meaningful sense of the word.[21] The vast majority of LNPS respondents understood themselves in terms of separate national identities and had little sense of a politically significant pan-ethnic identity.[22] However, a mountain of evidence now suggests that this social reality has changed. The Latino National Survey completed in 2006 found very high levels of identification with pan-ethnic terminology: at least 87.6% of respondents said that they thought of themselves in these terms "somewhat strongly" or "very strongly." Moreover, when asked to choose between national-origin identifiers, the pan-ethnic term, or merely "American" (an arbitrary, forced choice that only an academic could devise), more than one-third of the respondents chose the pan-ethnic identifier (38.3%). One of us, as part of the LNS team, has argued that this forced choice was artificial, that identities are multiple and simultaneous.[23] Nevertheless, the change between 1989 and 2006 reflects a significant shift in how Latinos or Hispanics envision themselves as part of the national fabric.

Moreover, in 2006 Latinos from all groups perceived significant commonality and linked fates with other Latinos, even those from national-origin groups other than their own. Surprisingly, when the LNS assessed whether respondents felt that they and their national-origin group shared political, economic, and social conditions with other Latinos, an overwhelming 71.9% said that they had "some" or "a lot" in common with other Latinos in "thinking about issues like job opportunities, educational attainment or income." When the question was posed with respect to the respondent's national-origin group, 74.6% said that their group had "some" or "a lot" in common with Latinos of other national-origin groups. Although there was some variation, the fact that these results were largely consistent across national-origin groups suggests that this pan-ethnic identification may have social and political relevance.

When the LNS focused on political concerns, the level of perceived commonality was again high, though lower than on the social dimension. In "thinking about things like government services and employment, political power, and representation," 56.1% of respondents felt that as individuals they had "some" or "a lot" in common with other Latinos, and 64.4% felt the same when assessing what their own national-origin group had in common with others.

Finally, respondents were asked whether their fate and their group's fate were linked to the fate of other Latinos—the "linked fate" measure first described by political scientist Michael Dawson.[24] At the individual level, 63.4% said that their fate was linked "some" or "a lot" to the fate of others. When asked about the fate of their national-origin group relative to other Latino groups, 71.6% said that the two were linked "some" or "a lot." Thus, huge majorities of Latinos believe that their own futures and those of their coethnics are intrinsically linked.

~

The belief that Latinos and their futures are linked is very likely to have motivated recent group-based mobilization. Most major national organizations, political and otherwise, use pan-ethnic terminology and view the Latino constituency as being composed of the entire Latino population—both across generations and, most important, across nationality groups. The National Council of La Raza, the Hispanic Chamber of Commerce, the Congressional Hispanic Caucus, the National Association of Latino Elected and Appointed Officials, and the Univision and Telemundo television networks all define their constituency as the pan-ethnic Latino or Hispanic population.

It is not clear why Latinos increasingly identify with pan-ethnic descriptors, but scholars have offered a variety of explanations. Pan-ethnic identity may emerge in contexts where population diversity and political cooperation would give pan-ethnic groups political power unavailable to individual national-origin groups.[25] Similarly, such an identity may have been created by politicians seeking to empower Latinos through coalition and running roughshod over important community, cultural, and social distinctions in the process.[26] Or it may be that a pan-ethnic identity develops as the cultural and media establishment, as mentioned earlier, increasingly addresses Latinos as a somewhat undifferentiated whole. Whatever the case, we can now say with confidence that Latinos are a group: they see themselves as such, and they use a shared identity to act politically.

And when they act politically, they act progressively. Latinos prefer more government engagement in solving society's challenges, not less. Despite their embrace of values based in self-reliance, they see a critical and decisive role for government in the lives of individuals. The result is a supermajority that votes Democrat, with a political effect that is likely to grow as the Latino share of the electorate continues to rise rapidly. If the recent past is prologue, and if there is no substantial change in their current preferences and opinions, this increasingly unified and empowered population has the potential, almost by itself, to realign American politics.

Chapter 3

RONALD REAGAN WAS WRONG: LATINO IDEOLOGY AND BELIEFS ABOUT GOVERNMENT

For most of the last thirty years, Latinos have given a preponderance of their votes to Democrats at both the state and national levels, with the exception of South Florida Cubans.* The Democratic ticket has taken between 65% and 70% of the two-party vote in national elections since the 1980s, with the notable exception of 2004, when George W. Bush secured approximately 40% of the Latino vote in his quest for reelection.[1] For some time, GOP strategists have expressed frustration with this state of affairs, largely—so the story goes—because they believe that a churchgoing and entrepreneurial group should naturally be Republican. Ronald Reagan best expressed this sentiment when he reportedly told GOP Latino pollster Lionel Sosa, "Hispanics are Republicans, they just don't know it yet."

Was Reagan right? And if so, what evidence is there? The answer is: somewhere between little and none. Latinos are significantly to the left of non-Hispanic whites on virtually every issue of public policy. This is

* Portions of this chapter appeared in earlier form in Gary M. Segura, "Latino Public Opinion and Realigning the American Electorate," *Daedalus* 141, no. 4 (Fall 2012): 98–113.

FIGURE 3.1 Selected Policy Liberalism of Latinos and Non-Hispanic Whites, 2008

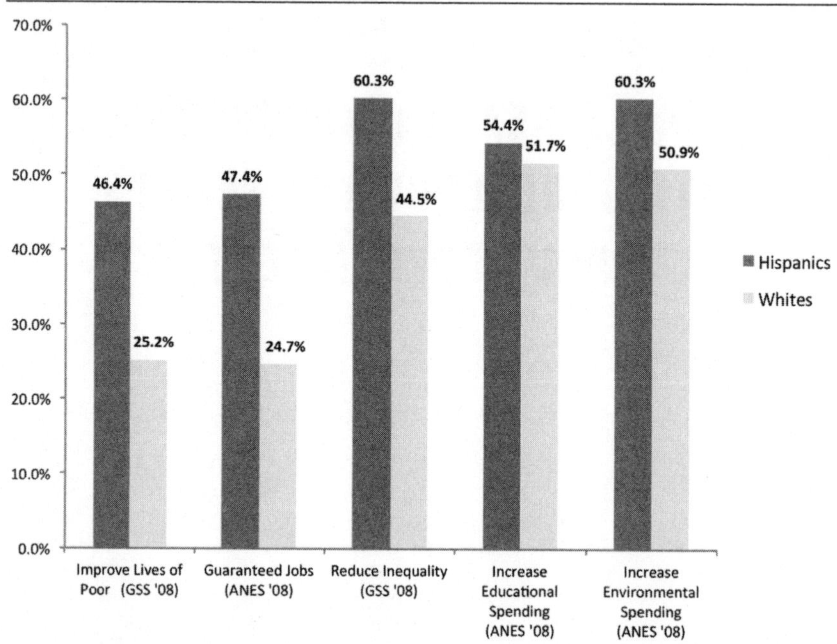

The bars in the figure represent the total share of respondents holding "liberal," or left of midpoint, views on each issue. *Source:* Figure created by the authors using data from the American National Election Study (ANES), 2008, for guaranteed jobs and increased educational and environmental spending; and the General Social Survey (GSS), 2008, for improving the lives of the poor and reducing inequality.

hardly surprising when the issue is minority- or race-specific, such as immigration or affirmative action. Latinos are significantly more pro-immigrant, more supportive of affirmative action, and less enthusiastic about the death penalty than non-Hispanic whites. As Donald Kinder and Nicholas Winter first noted, this liberalism extends to redistributive policy.[2] And as one of us reports, Latinos can lean systematically liberal even on issues with no implicitly racial content.[3] Figure 3.1 illustrates that Latinos are also more liberal than their non-Hispanic white fellow citizens when it comes to government guarantees on standards of living, education, and the environment. Even on matters of relative consensus, such as education, the difference between groups is meaningful.

FIGURE 3.2 Views Regarding Whether Minorities Should Be Self-Reliant

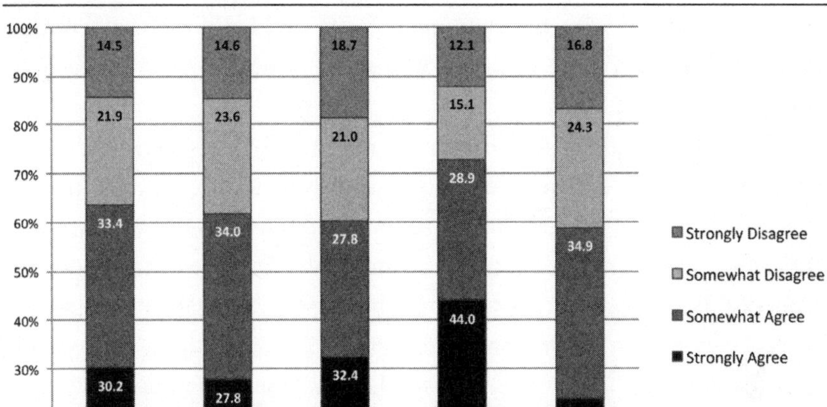

Respondents answered the following question: "If racial and ethnic minorities don't do well in life, they have no one to blame but themselves. Do you . . . strongly agree, somewhat agree, somewhat disagree, or strongly disagree?" *Source:* Figure created by the authors using data from the National Politics Study, 2004.

But policy preferences are not the same as an overall approach to government. The fact that Latinos are more liberal than whites on specific issues does not necessarily mean that they are philosophically pro-government. The high levels of entrepreneurial activity among Latinos and a stereotypic perception of their strong work ethic have encouraged conservatives to argue on behalf of Latinos' "natural," albeit unrealized, Republicanism. Indeed, significant evidence suggests that, consistent with conservatives' claims, Latinos embrace the core individualist norm of self-reliance.

Figure 3.2 shows an across-group comparison on a key indicator of self-reliance: specifically, respondents were asked: "If racial and ethnic minorities don't do well in life, they have no one to blame but themselves. Do you strongly agree, somewhat agree, somewhat disagree, or strongly disagree?" Latinos held the most "conservative" position on this question of any major racial or ethnic group. A significantly higher percentage of Latinos—higher than among non-Hispanic whites—somewhat agreed or strongly agreed with the statement. Certainly, Latino citizens' enthusiasm for a norm of self-reliance casts some doubt on their underlying liberalism.

Adherence to norms of self-reliance is generally associated with more conservative views on the role of government, including a preference for limited government. If Latinos share this preference, that would seem to undermine the claim of Latino liberalism. However, the evidence does not support this supposition. In fact, though a significant majority of Latinos express support for self-reliance, supermajorities of Latinos also reliably embrace a greater role for government. Latino Americans evidently see no contradiction in the two views.

In the 2012 American National Election Study (ANES), citizens were asked three questions designed to capture their core feelings about the role of government, distinct from any particular policy area. Figure 3.3 reports on their responses to the question: "Which of two statements comes closer to your own opinion: ONE, the less government, the better; or TWO, there are more things that government should be doing?" This question juxtaposed the core contention of movement conservatism—that government is better when it is smaller—with a desire for government to do more, not less. Given this stark choice, the responses were revelatory. Among all Americans the answers were evenly divided, and almost 60% of non-Hispanic whites chose the "less government" approach. But more than 71% of Latino respondents said that they would like government to do more, a more than thirty-point difference compared with non-Hispanic whites. (African Americans were even more liberal.)

The second question asked in the 2012 ANES to try to get at respondents' core feelings about government was this: "Which of two statements comes closer to your own opinion: ONE, the main reason government has become bigger over the years is because it has gotten involved in things that people should do for themselves; or TWO, government has become bigger because the problems we face have become bigger?" Like the first question, this question offered a choice between quite different attitudes toward the growth of government, thereby tapping a

FIGURE 3.3 Views on Government Action to Solve Problems, by Race and Ethnicity

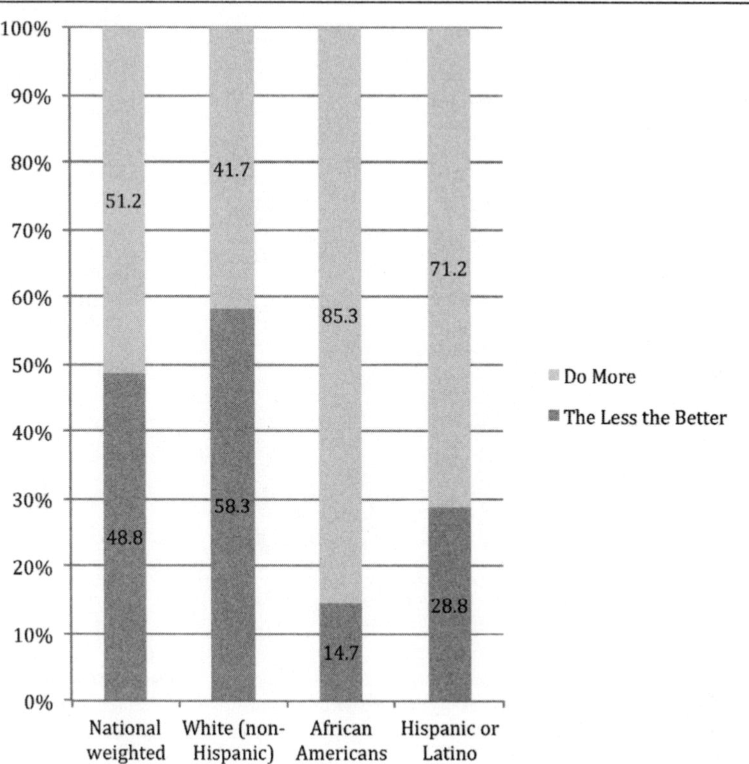

Respondents answered the question: "Which of two statements comes closer to your own opinion: ONE, the less government, the better; or TWO, there are more things that government should be doing?" *Source:* Figure created by the authors using data from the American National Election Study, 2012.

core element of ideology. And once again, Latinos were significantly more liberal than non-Hispanic whites, more than half of whom believed that government has become involved in matters of personal responsibility. By contrast, almost two-thirds of Latinos believed that government growth has been justified by the scope or size of the problems they expect it to address—twice the share who thought that government has expanded where it should not have.

Finally, ANES respondents were asked a question aimed at discerning their enthusiasm for the free market, the most frequently identified

FIGURE 3.4 Attitudes toward Government Growth, by Race and Ethnicity

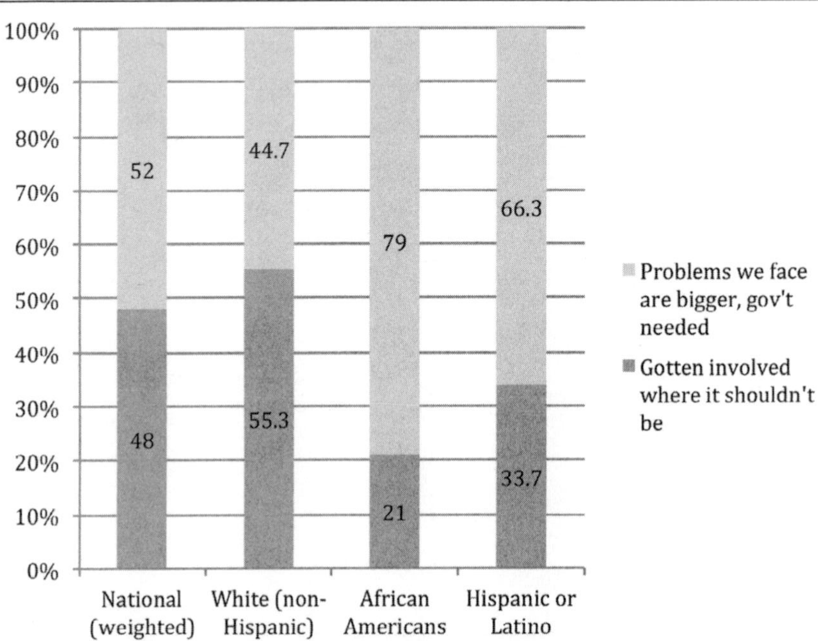

Respondents answered the question: "Which of two statements comes closer to your own opinion: ONE, the main reason government has become bigger over the years is because it has gotten involved in things that people should do for themselves; or TWO, government has become bigger because the problems we face have become bigger?" *Source:* Figure created by the authors using data from the American National Election Study, 2012.

alternative to government action: "Which of two statements comes closer to your own opinion: ONE, we need a strong government to handle today's complex economic problems; or TWO, the free market can handle these problems without government being involved?" The choice offered again captured ideology in terms that resonated with the public debate. And once again, Latinos were significantly to the left of non-Hispanic whites. Just over 21% of Latinos saw the free market as the preferred instrument of social change, whereas almost twice that percentage of non-Hispanic whites preferred to leave problems to the free market. Almost 80% of Latino respondents in the ANES saw the need for a strong government to solve problems. And it is worth noting that even among

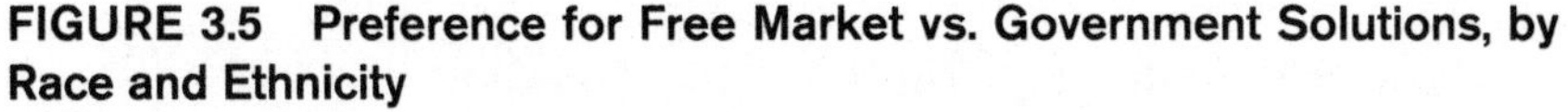

FIGURE 3.5 Preference for Free Market vs. Government Solutions, by Race and Ethnicity

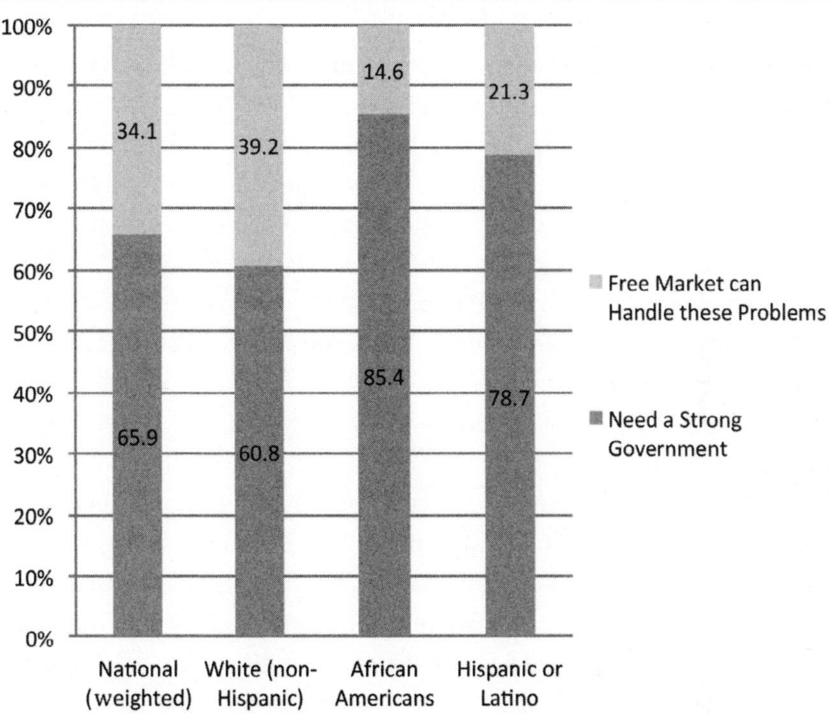

Respondents answered the question: "Which of two statements comes closer to your own opinion: ONE, we need a strong government to handle today's complex economic problems; or TWO, the free market can handle these problems without government being involved?" *Source:* Figure created by the authors using data from the American National Election Study, 2012.

whites the free market lost out to government action by over twenty percentage points.

Overall, among Latino citizens, there is general enthusiasm for an active, growing, and problem-solving government and little enthusiasm for the alternative as described by the right: a shrinkage of government and reliance on the free market. Despite their embrace of a norm of self-reliance—a clear belief that individuals are for the most part responsible for their own outcomes—Latinos' underlying ideology appears to be solidly progressive. This finding is directly reflected in their policy preferences, which are uniformly to the left of views held by non-Hispanic whites.

ECONOMIC OPINION: PREDOMINANTLY WORKING-CLASS LATINOS ARE NOT FREE-MARKETEERS

Latinos, like most Americans, worry about money. And economic opportunity and mobility have been problematic for them. Latino median income is significantly below the national average and below that of non-Hispanic whites. The 2010 Current Population Survey (CPS) shows that Hispanic household family income was just below $31,000, while the comparable figure for non-Hispanic whites was above $42,000.[4] Such income differences have substantial impacts on quality of life. For instance, Hispanics are less likely to reside in homes they own. In 2010 (according to the American Community Survey), 77.9% of non-Hispanic whites lived in homes that they or their family owned. Only 58.1% of Latinos owned rather than rented their home.

Likewise, Hispanic educational attainment is significantly below the national average and below that of non-Hispanic whites. Using the 2010 CPS, only 15.7% of Hispanic adult citizens had a college degree or greater, compared with 31% of non-Hispanic whites. Foreign-born Latinos are significantly disadvantaged here since free, compulsory education did not extend after eighth grade in Mexico until very recently. Not surprisingly, then, many Mexican immigrants to the United States have lower-than-average levels of formal education.

As a consequence, the Latino population expresses considerable concern about making ends meet, and their concerns are reflected in their opinions on what government ought to be doing. For example, an extensive study on housing undertaken by Latino Decisions in April 2011 showed that the housing crisis—which was the principal factor underpinning the great recession of 2008—was acutely felt by Latinos. By some estimates, Latinos were 70% more likely than other Americans to have received subprime mortgage loans, and 71% more likely than white mortgage holders to have faced foreclosure.[5] The result has been devastating. By some estimates, Latinos lost as much as 66% of their net wealth in the 2008 crisis.[6] The comparable number for non-Hispanic whites was 13%.

Mortgages and rent represent a significant strain on Latino resources (see Figure 3.6). Over half of Latino registered voters reported having

FIGURE 3.6 Latino Economic Stress and Costs of Housing, April 2011

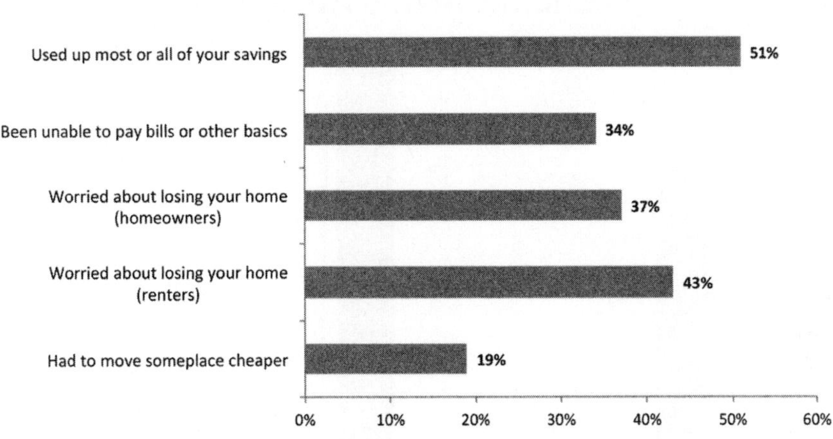

Source: Latino Decisions–ImpreMedia poll of Latino registered voters, April 2011 (N = 500; +/-4.3).

spent down all their savings, more than a third reported being late with other bills, and nearly one in five had to move to a cheaper place to live. It should not be surprising, then, when this level of financial strain results in considerable enthusiasm for government action. When asked about specific policy responses, Latinos were supportive of mortgage relief for those who had lost their job (75%) and direct mortgage reductions, rather than foreclosure, for those who couldn't pay their existing obligation (79%). There was also strong support for reforming the practices they thought might have been hurting Latinos, such as requiring banks to provide documents in English and Spanish if the customer needs it (87%) and providing greater tax incentives for home buyers (83%). These actions and proposed reforms, it is fair to say, did not enjoy conservative support during this last housing crisis.

In November 2011, just as the GOP primaries were about to get under way, we asked all voters, Latinos and other Americans, who they blamed for the economic troubles in the country and who they trusted to solve them. As shown in Figure 3.7, former President George W. Bush, rather than President Barack Obama and the Democrats in Congress, took the

FIGURE 3.7 Registered Voters' Attribution of Blame for US Economic Problems, November 2011

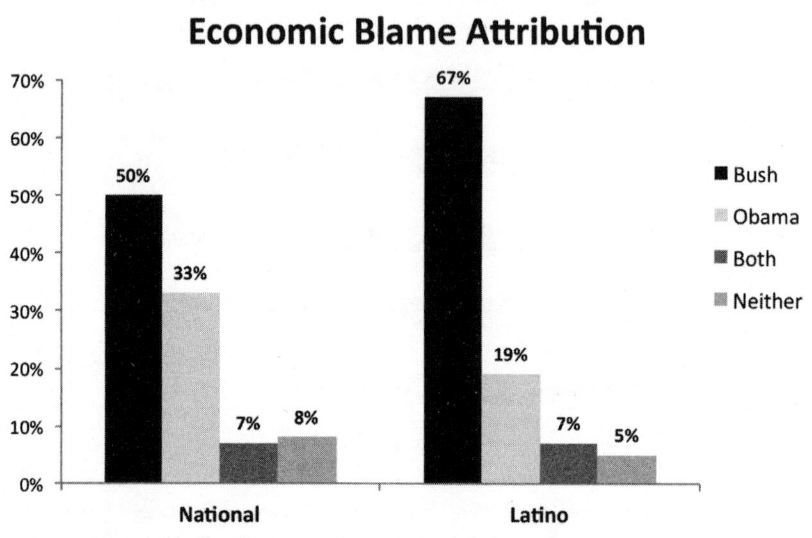

lion's share of the blame for economic performance among the general electorate (50%), and particularly among the Latino electorate (67%). These numbers track the 2008 general election results very closely.

When we looked to the future, in anticipation of the 2012 race, the news was less sunny for Obama and the Democrats (see Figure 3.8). Among all voters, a slight plurality (43%) trusted the GOP more than Obama and the Democrats (42%), though these results were inside the margin of error. Among Latinos, Obama did better (57%) compared with the GOP (24%), though by a smaller margin than the one we observed in how Latinos attributed blame for US economic problems.

On fiscal policy, the story of Latino viewpoints remains consistent—Latinos are roughly pragmatic progressives when it comes to taxation and spending. During the high-stakes standoff in the summer of 2011 between Republicans and President Obama over extending the government's borrowing authority and solving the budget deficit, we asked Latinos about their preferred solutions. We found that 46% of Latino registered voters

FIGURE 3.8 Trust among Registered Voters in Republicans or Democrats to Shepherd the Economy, November 2011

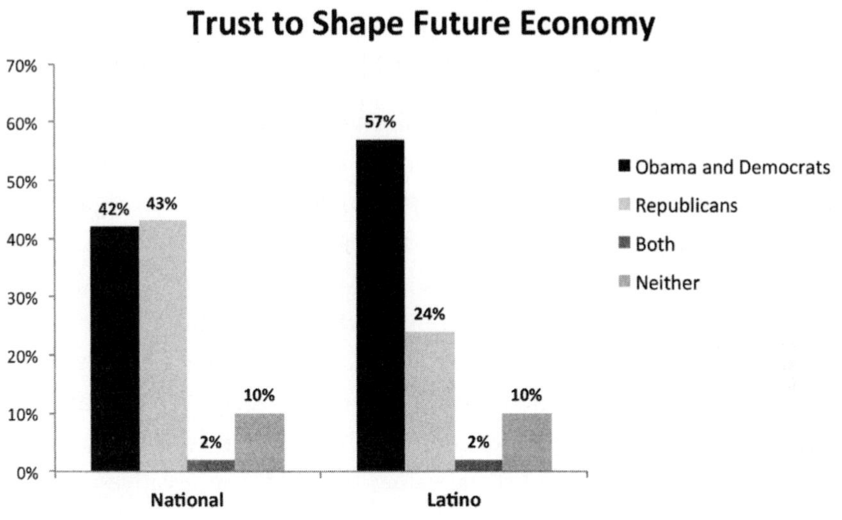

supported raising taxes on the wealthy, compared to only 7% who said the solution is to cut existing programs and 37% who preferred a combination of tax increases and spending cuts. Altogether, 83% of Latino voters supported a deficit reduction plan that includes tax increases on the wealthy to help America balance the budget. This support is consistent with the previous attitudes of Latino voters. In a February 2011 tracking poll, Latino Decisions reported that only 27% of Latino registered voters supported extending the Bush tax cuts for the wealthy, while 64% opposed the tax cuts for the wealthy.[7] Moreover, by about two-to-one, Latinos supported federal investment in infrastructure projects (57%), as opposed to tax reductions (30%), as a way to stimulate and improve the economy.

This general finding was consistent all the way through the November 2012 election. In our Latino Decisions election eve poll, the "cuts only" approach drew just 12% support, while tax increases on the wealthy and corporations attracted 35%, and a combination approach 42%. Again, 77% of all Latino voters who turned out in the November 2012 election favored some form of tax increase, a clear indicator of their preferences regarding how government should act.

IS RELIGIOSITY AN INDICATOR OF CONSERVATISM?

A second possible exception to the idea that Latinos are inherently progressive, as noted by pundits and politicians alike, is in the area of so-called social issues: specifically, the issues of abortion and gay rights. This claim is based in the frequently cited rates of church attendance among Latinos, who are on average more likely to attend church than most other Americans; Latino Catholics in particular are more churchgoing than other Catholics. So, the theory goes, Latinos' religious convictions (coupled, more often than not, with the pundit's unspoken stereotype of Latinos as undereducated and traditionalist rather than worldly) should imply a set of political and social values to which conservatives and Republicans might appeal.

In November 2004, the *New York Times* announced that "moral values [are] cited as a defining issue of the election," and numerous anecdotal claims were made that President Bush benefited from a spate of same-sex marriage initiatives across the country that boosted turnout among churchgoing social conservatives. As part of this supposed "moral values" wave, even Latinos, some claimed, turned out in larger than expected numbers for Bush. For example, the *National Journal* wrote that, "for Bush, the evangelical Latino community proved to be an ideal target constituency, because in pursuing it the GOP could push the hot-button issues of abortion and gay rights in ways that had been powerfully effective among white evangelicals." Examining the 2004 exit polls, Marisa Abrajano, Michael Alvarez, and Jonathan Nagler, after controlling for a host of other well-known factors, found that Latino voters who ranked "moral values" as their top concern—as 18% of Latinos did—were statistically less likely to vote for John Kerry.[8]

Still, if 18% of Latinos said that moral values were their top concern in 2004—a high-water-mark year for the relevance of moral values—82% cited some other issue as their top concern, such as the economy, the war on terror, the war in Iraq, education, or health care. In the 2012 election,

FIGURE 3.9 What Latino Voters Understand Politics to Be About

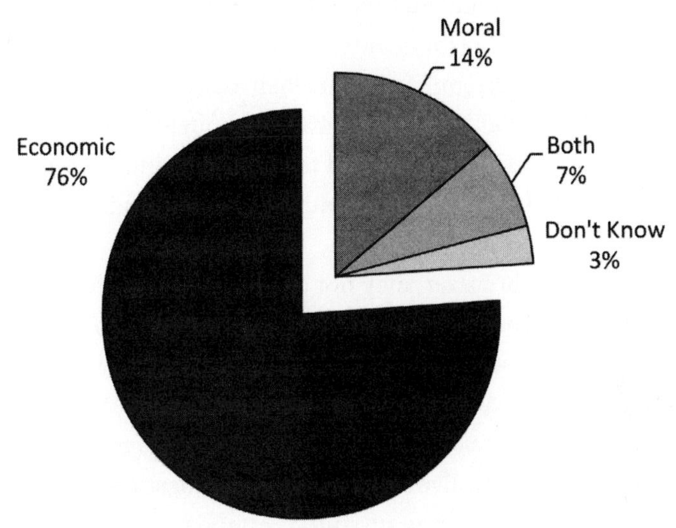

by contrast, despite President Obama's very public stance on both abortion and, more surprisingly, marriage equality for gays and lesbians, he polled almost three-quarters of the Latino vote (71% in the national exit poll, 75% in the Latino Decisions election eve poll). So what can we say about religion and social issues politics among Latinos?

In December 2011, as part of the Latino Decisions–ImpreMedia tracking poll of Latino registered voters, we carried out an extensive study on the topic of religion and moral values among Latinos. The attention that moral values received in past elections, the claims among Republicans that religiosity was the GOP's bridge to the Latino electorate, and the prospect of the first Mormon presidential nominee brought some urgency to the question of whether and how Latinos would bring their religious beliefs to the polls in 2012.

Latino Decisions asked the following question: "Which statement comes closest to your view: 'Politics is more about economic issues, such as jobs, taxes, gas prices, and the minimum wage,' or 'Politics is more about moral issues such as abortion, family values, and same-sex marriage.'" We asked, in other words, what politics was *about* to our Latino respondents. To avoid making the question a leading one, we randomized the order in which respondents heard the two statements. An overwhelming majority of Latino respondents—75% to be exact—said that politics is more about the economic issues in their daily lives than about moral issues such as same-sex marriage (14%). Although another 7% said that politics is about both areas, it is hard to escape the initial conclusion that so-called values issues do not predominate in the minds of Latino registered voters.

This conclusion, however, may not be so obvious. Latinos are indeed a religious group. According to our data, 46% of Latino registered voters attend church every week, while the American National Election Study estimates that just 23% of all Americans were weekly churchgoers in 2008. Further, 60% of Latino voters told us that religion provides "quite a bit" of guidance in their daily lives. Among foreign-born, naturalized citizens, we found an even higher rate of church attendance and religiosity. Yet despite this commitment to religion, a majority of Latino registered voters in December 2011 said that religion would have no impact on their vote in 2012. Even among Latinos who attend church every week, 45% said that it would have no impact on their vote compared to 32% who said that it would have a big impact.

One of the avenues through which religion and moral values often shape or influence politics is the pulpit. Politicians often make direct appeals on Sunday and engage in very public demonstrations of religiosity, and pastors and preachers may reinforce these messages in the following weeks. Ministers have been pivotal on both the right (witness the religious mobilization around anti–gay marriage initiatives) and the left, as best exemplified by the historic role of the black church in African American voter turnout.

Yet Latino registered voters clearly reject this overt connection between religion and politics. When asked if religious leaders should tell their members which candidates to support, 82% said no and just 15% said yes. Even among Latinos who described themselves as born-again Christians, three-quarters did not want their pastors talking about politics.

Perhaps more importantly, when asked if politicians with strong religious beliefs should rely on their beliefs to guide their decisions in

FIGURE 3.10 Religious Leaders Should Tell their Members which Candidates to Support

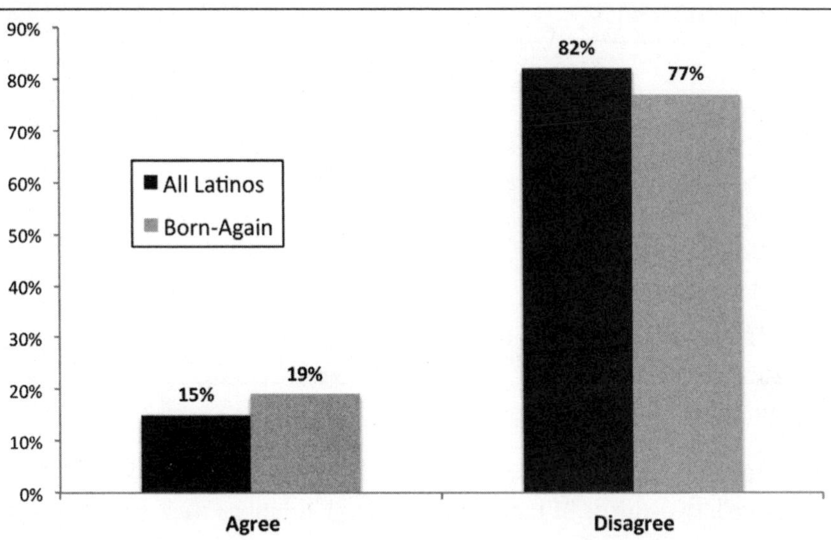

FIGURE 3.11 Politicians with Strong Religious Convictions Should Rely on their Beliefs to Guide their Decisions in Government

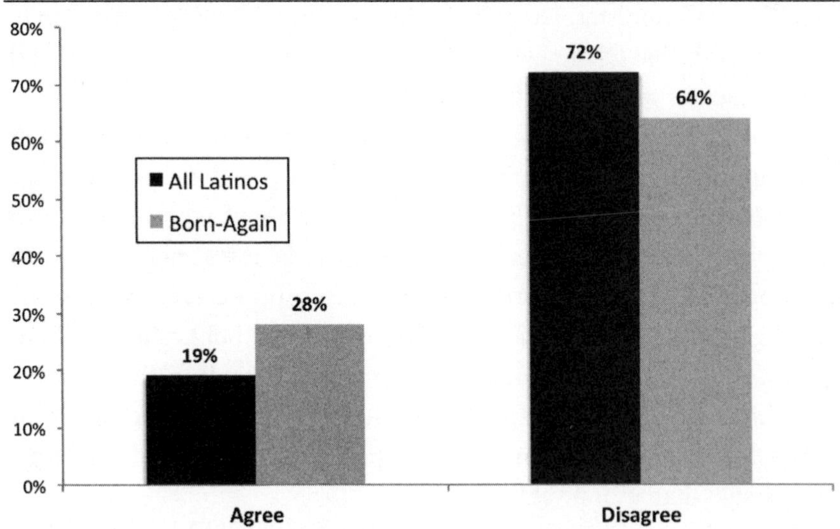

TABLE 3.1 Opinions on Whether Politics Is About Economic Issues or Moral Issues, by Respondent Characteristics

	Economic	*Moral*
US-born	75%	16%
Foreign-born	76	11
Catholic	74	13
Protestant	75	20
Weekly churchgoer	73	13
Born-again	75	14
Religion provides a "great deal" of guidance	75	12

governing, 72% of Latinos said no and 19% said yes. And on this question as well, two-thirds of Latino born-again Christians were still opposed to government officials being guided by religion. This is a stark finding given the overwhelming prevailing norm in US politics regarding politicians and their faith. Recall President Bush, in a debate, answering, "Jesus Christ," when asked which philosopher had most deeply influenced him. Think of the endless handwringing in the 2008 primary season over President Obama's minister, Jeremiah Wright, or the widespread suspicion in some quarters that Obama was secretly a Muslim. Most Latino voters just wish politicians would keep this sort of concern to themselves.

The split between Latino voters who said that politics is more about economic issues such as jobs, taxes, gas prices, and minimum wage (75%) and those who said that politics is more about moral issues such as abortion, family values, and same-sex marriage (14%) holds across all meaningful demographic groups within the Latino electorate. Weekly churchgoers told us by better than five-to-one that politics is not about moral issues. Likewise, around three-quarters of both self-described born-again Christians and those for whom religion provides "a great deal" of personal guidance were convinced that politics is more about economic policy issues than moral values.

Though Latinos are often religious—and demonstrably more so than other Americans—religion plays a fundamentally different role in Latino politics than in the politics of whites and African Americans. The claim that religiosity is an obvious potential source of GOP outreach to Latinos is entirely based on assumption. Though the claim lacks an empirical foundation, it has become, as it were, an article of Republican faith. This is not to say that religion, religious belief, and religious organizations play no role in the political lives of Latinos; clearly there are some relationships.[9] But the model for how religion shapes the political beliefs and actions of American voters is not smoothly transferred across racial and ethnic boundaries.

ABORTION AND LGBT RIGHTS

Of course, to say that religion does not have the same effect on Latino politics as it does on white and African American politics is not to say that so-called values issues are irrelevant to this part of the electorate. It remains entirely plausible that Latino tradition and culture have given rise to wildly different views of abortion and homosexuality than those held by other Americans.

No such distinction exists, however, with respect to LGBT (lesbian, gay, bisexual, and transgender) rights. Latinos are not significantly more conservative on gay rights than their non-Hispanic fellow citizens. In November 2011, a Univision News–Latino Decisions poll found that a plurality of all Latino registered voters (43%) favored same-sex marriage equality and another 17% favored civil union recognition. Less than one-quarter of respondents opposed government recognition of same-sex relationships. More recently, a Pew Study found majority support, 52% versus 34%, for same-sex marriage rights.[10] Indeed, the 2008 American National Election Study showed that Latino support for marriage equality (43.2%) exceeded that of non-Hispanic whites (39.6%); that Latino support for the right of gays to adopt children (53.3%) was marginally higher than among non-Hispanic whites (52.5%); and that Latino support for nondiscrimination protection for gays (71.3%), while slightly lower than among whites (75.5%), was still espoused by a supermajority. None of these findings suggest that Latinos' opinions on gay and lesbian rights deviate significantly from their overall liberalism; nor do they imply an opportunity for Republican outreach.

Abortion is different. Every measure of opinion on reproductive choice does suggest that Latinos are more conservative on this issue than non-Hispanic whites. The difference is less significant, however, than generally assumed. In the 2008 ANES, 39.5% of non-Hispanic whites favored broad abortion rights; the comparable number among Latinos was 33.1%. Similarly, while 46.6% of whites supported choice in instances of rape or incest or when the life of the mother is in danger, the comparable figure for Latinos was 44%. In short, while Latinos appear to be marginally more conservative than whites on the issue of reproductive choice, the difference hardly seems sizable.

Perhaps most damaging to the idea that social conservatism is a bridge from Latinos to a more conservative or Republican identity is the persistent lack of interest in these issues shown by Latino registered voters themselves. Polls of Latino voters that ask respondents to identify the issues most important to them generally find that these voters pay little attention to gay rights and abortion. When Latino Decisions has asked registered Latino voters about the issues that matter most to them when they vote, we have never polled more than 3% for all social issues—abortion, marriage equality, and the like—combined.

Claims and counterclaims regarding Latino policy preferences are built on two stereotypical ideas about Latinos, both incorrect. The first is that Latinos have evolved toward Democratic partisanship by accident, that they are insufficiently informed, and that their policy preferences are inconsistent with their voting behavior. The second idea is that Latinos are so traditionalist and religious that a proper Republican outreach campaign would swing a large number of them into the GOP camp. Neither of these claims is true.

Despite a strong commitment to the norm of self-reliance, Latino registered voters have a generally positive and activist view of government. This position is not unanimously held, by any stretch. But it is fair to say that generally progressive views of government—and orientations toward government—are held by about two-thirds of all Latino voters.

Though churchgoing, Latinos see religion as playing a decidedly different role in politics than do their fellow citizens of other racial and ethnic groups. Latinos do not want ministers involved in politics, do not want politicians relying on religion to shape policy, and generally think that politics should be about bread-and-butter issues rather than so-called morals issues.

These findings do not close off the possibility that there is considerable room for GOP growth among the Latino electorate. There certainly is. George W. Bush's 40% showing in 2004 made it clear that not all Latinos are liberals and that a fair share can be persuaded to come over to the GOP side, especially if the Republican Party removes a couple of policy platforms that are truly toxic to their chances of making gains with Latino voters (the subject of later chapters).

But in the short term there are limits to GOP growth among Latinos, who look to be a center-left constituency for the foreseeable future.

Chapter 4

NOW YOU SEE US, NOW YOU DON'T: THE IMPLICATIONS OF POLITICAL PARTICIPATION LAGGING POPULATION GROWTH

With Sylvia Manzano and Adrian Pantoja

Somewhere between 11.2 million and 12.2 million Latinos voted in the November 2012 election.[1] That we don't know for sure is no surprise; not all states keep records of the race and ethnicity of voters, so our own estimates are derived from those jurisdictions where we do have this information, as well as from analysis of the Current Population Survey (CPS) data, exit polls, voter registration changes by location, and other data.

About half of all the Latinos who could have voted in 2012 did not—that is, among the eligible population, Latino voter turnout is hovering around 50%. According to the 2010 CPS, the voter registration rate is 68.2% (about ten points less than the rate for non-Hispanic whites and African Americans), and the turnout of registered Latino voters is about 70% (again, about ten points less than for others). Of course, this rate fluctuates by election.

A number of groups have performed heroically in registering Latino voters. Early in the Chicano rights period of the 1960s and 1970s, the Southwest Voter Registration Education Project led the way. Since then, other groups, including Mi Familia Vota and Voto Latino, have joined the effort, and multifaceted civil rights organizations, like the National Council of La Raza (NCLR), have participated as well. Even Spanish-language media participates in the widely recognized Ya Es Hora campaign. In addition, many state and local groups have joined in this work.

Registering any group of voters is hard work, and the task is complicated by how rapidly the Latino population and citizenry are growing. By the time 1,000 new voters are registered, there may be 2,000 more waiting. Under-registration leads to under-turnout, the effects of which are easy to identify—Latinos project significantly less political power than their numbers might otherwise suggest—they swing fewer elections, hold fewer seats, and grab the policy attention of fewer elected officials.

Sidney Verba and his colleagues have offered three explanations for why people are driven to participate in politics: they have the resources to participate, they are recruited into politics, or they have some psychological engagement with politics.[2] These reasons for political participation may help us begin to understand why Latino participation in electoral politics is relatively low. Because it requires time, attention, cognitive resources, and money, politics is a luxury that ranks well below more basic needs in the hierarchy of concerns of those with scant resources. Not surprisingly, then, political scientists have long found that those with fewer resources, regardless of race, are less likely to participate—and be influential—in politics. Working-class whites, for example, vote less frequently than well-to-do whites, more highly educated individuals vote more than less educated people, and so on.

The work on minority voters echoes this long-held finding, with a caveat. That is, most work on the political behavior of African Americans and Hispanics repeatedly identifies resource constraints as the principal individual-level factor in undermining minority electoral strength.[3] African Americans have closed the gap primarily to the extent that they have used racial identity as an alternative resource.[4] That is, African Americans overperform relative to their resources, but overall relatively lower incomes and educational achievement levels—the product of generations of discrimination, unequal opportunity, and ongoing manifestations of each—have significantly disadvantaged African Americans and Hispanics in the electoral arena.

Later in this chapter, we discuss the six focus groups conducted by Latino Decisions in Houston, Los Angeles, and Fresno to get some insight into Latino nonparticipation in electoral politics. Participating in these groups were a variety of Latino Americans who either stopped participating in our electoral system or never started at all. For several different reasons, each expressed significant doubts about electoral participation. For example, Rafael, a middle-aged man from Houston,[5] is not registered to vote and, as will soon become evident, is not a fan of the US political system. Anita, a smart and surprisingly informed participant in our study who lives in California, is the daughter of a political family and is registered to vote, but has lost interest in the system. Each illustrates some of the many challenges faced by Latino leaders in mobilizing higher electoral involvement.

We begin by focusing on four factors that we believe are critical to Latino under-registration and lower voter turnout: citizenship and nativity; age; socioeconomic status, including income and education; and mobilization efforts by parties and candidates. We show that those with *resources*—time, information, cognitive skills, and motivation—are more likely to get registered and to vote. Then we turn our attention to the more social and psychological determinants of political participation, including group identity.

MEANS, MOTIVATION, AND OPPORTUNITY—HOW (LIMITED) RESOURCES LIMIT LATINO ELECTORAL PARTICIPATION

The demographic circumstances of Latinos are unique. Noncitizens generally cannot vote,[6] and more than one-third of all Latino adults in the United States are not US citizens (either because they have not met the requirements or because they have chosen not to naturalize, for a variety of possible reasons).

Noncitizenship is certainly a huge and obvious barrier to electoral strength, but even foreign birth among citizens can undermine Latino political strength. Foreign-born citizens—naturalized immigrants—generally come to the United States with only limited familiarity with the US political system, its key players, and US political history. Unlike those attending K–12 school in this country, naturalized citizens begin their engagement with the US political system as adults with almost no background information. Politically active people in the United States are familiar with a host of associations and patterns that are new—if not unknown—to the immigrant. Not knowing, for example, that Social Security is identified with Democrats and tax-cutting with Republicans—to say nothing of the civics-book rules governing our system—makes it much harder for the foreign-born citizen to acquire a party identification, prioritize issues, and choose candidates. The knowledge that most Americans have accumulated over a lifetime of school, news, conversations, and family socialization is knowledge that they can take for granted, but it must be learned wholly new by adult immigrants, for whom the costs of doing so can reduce political participation.

For a long time naturalized citizens were significantly less likely to register and vote than US-born citizens.[7] More recently, the politicization of immigration has motivated a wave of "political" naturalizations and higher voter turnout.[8] But the costs of political participation—the costs of learning an entirely new political system—remain high for adult immigrants.

A second demographic obstacle, one less visible, is the age distribution. Young people generally vote less, and Latinos are very young. Although many Latinos over the age of eighteen are foreign-born, the latest census found that about 93% of those under eighteen are US-born. That means that very young Latinos are heavily represented in the citizen population and will soon enough become eligible to vote. Using Census Bureau population numbers, we estimate that in each month of the year 2014 approximately 73,000 Latino citizens will turn eighteen and enter the eligible electorate.

How much younger are Latinos? As is immediately apparent in Figure 4.1, Latinos are significantly younger than other Americans, with a median age almost eight years younger than African Americans and almost fifteen years younger than non-Hispanic whites. There is little question that this age distribution now works to Latinos' disadvantage—the youth of the United States vote much less frequently than older cohorts. Young

FIGURE 4.1 Median Age by Self-Reported Racial/Ethnic Identity

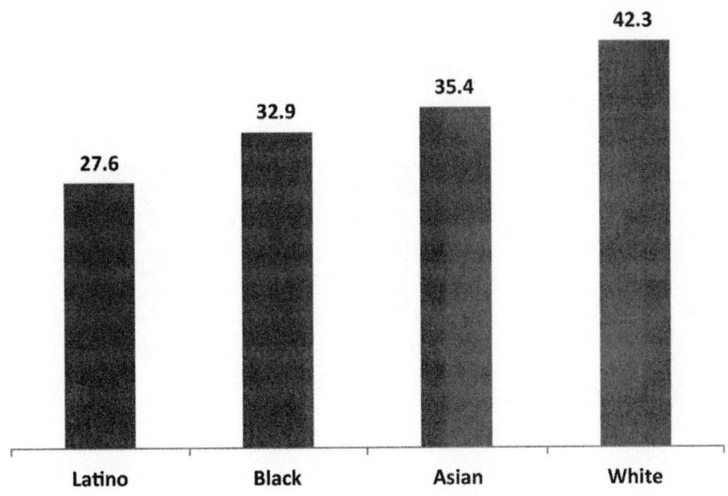

The categories white, black, and Asian exclude those who identify as Hispanic. *Data source:* 2010 US Census Bureau, American Community Survey, 2010.

people are also less connected to their communities, more mobile, less likely to own property, and less likely to have children enrolled in schools. As a consequence, they pay less attention to politics than other Americans, and many issues of governance have lower salience for them. The pace of electoral growth will accelerate significantly, however, as young Latino citizens mature. History suggests that as they begin to raise children and buy homes, to work more and socialize less, they will devote increasing attention to politics and governance.

Age and nativity, of course, are just two of several key demographic characteristics that suppress Latino vote share. A third characteristic is socioeconomic status, by which we mean income and educational levels. As already mentioned, Latino income and education levels are significantly below the national norms. The influence of income and education should not be underestimated. Figure 4.2 illustrates statistical models of voter turnout from Shaun Bowler and Gary Segura, with and without controls for income and education.[9] The darker bars indicate between-group comparisons of racial and ethnic minorities with non-Hispanic whites.

FIGURE 4.2 Minority Turnout Probability Relative to Non-Hispanic Whites, Observed and Estimated, Controlling for Other Factors

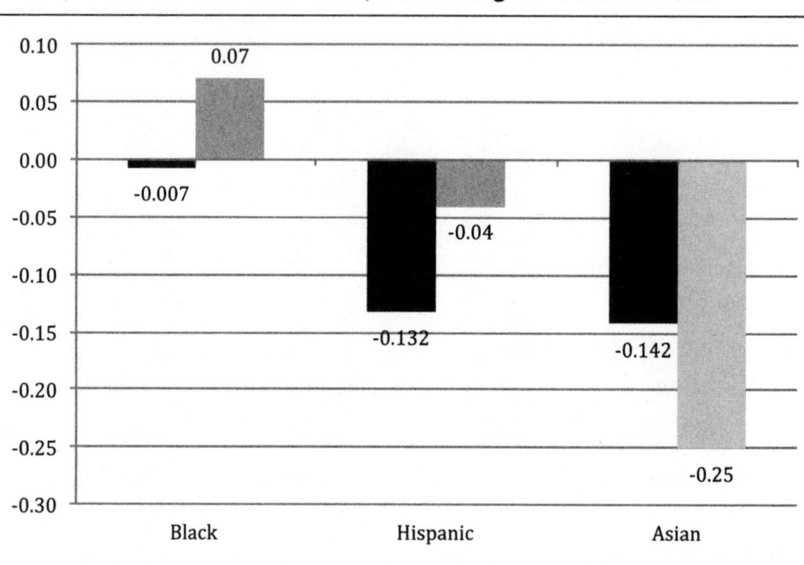

Source: Bowler and Segura (2011), 133. *Data source:* American National Election Study 2008.

African Americans appear to slightly underperform whites when it comes to voting (by 0.7%), while Asian Americans underperform more significantly, at around 14%. Latino citizens are about 13% less likely to vote than non-Hispanic whites.

The lighter bars reestimate those differences by removing the effects of income and education and comparing individuals of approximately the same income and education, letting only race vary. For African Americans, factoring out income and education differences makes an insignificant difference in their turnout compared to whites: their slight disadvantage turns into a 7% advantage. For Latinos, income and education account for nine points of their 13% disadvantage in relation to whites. In both instances, we can conclude that income and education are principal factors in reducing voter turnout for African Americans and Latino Americans. (The disadvantage in turnout reflected in Asian American numbers is made worse when we account for income and education.)

In other words, while Latinos and especially African Americans overperform electorally with respect to their socioeconomic status, Asians dramatically underperform.

Finally, we need to examine mobilization. Do candidates and parties devote relatively less attention to encouraging Latinos to vote, and if so, is this another source of their systematic disadvantage at the polls?

It turns out that Latino citizens are far less likely than similarly situated non-Hispanic whites and others to benefit from mobilization efforts by parties and candidates. Survey data on electoral participation and mobilization make it clear that Latino citizens are less likely to receive turnout messages and other mobilization messages from both parties and candidates. A great deal of the failure of Americans to participate in politics could be laid at the doorstep of the political parties, which have simply failed to try to mobilize voters.[10] Campaign contact can increase turnout by several percentage points, especially if the contact is personal in some way.

Almost 47% of non-Hispanic white citizens surveyed in the 2008 American National Election Studies reported having been telephoned or visited by representatives from the parties. The comparable numbers are 38% for African Americans, 32.3% for Latinos, and 21.2% for Asian Americans (see Figure 4.3). This difference is statistically significant and obviously important. There was an almost fifteen-percentage-point gap in the likelihood that a Latino citizen would be contacted and urged to vote in 2008 compared to non-Hispanic whites.

SOCIAL AND PSYCHOLOGICAL MOTIVATION

An absence of resources can depress political participation, and this is a significant challenge for Latinos. Beyond the usual physical or financial resources, however, some political science research suggests that psychological and social factors can be associated with turnout as well—such as a strong belief that participation is the "right" thing to do, or a sense of group loyalty that includes political action. As we suggested earlier, the electoral participation of Latinos and African Americans may be better than their material resources would suggest. Why would this be?

FIGURE 4.3 Party Mobilization in the 2008 Election

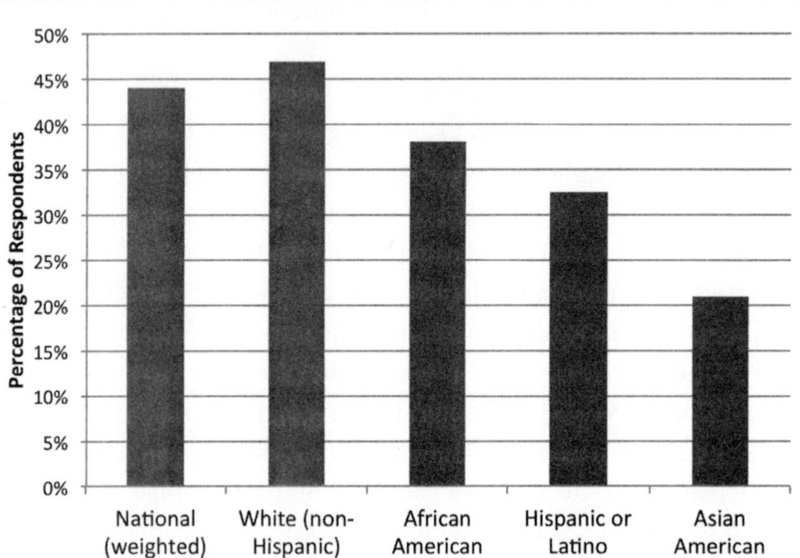

Respondents were asked this question: "As you know, the political parties try to talk to as many people as they can to get them to vote for their candidate. Did anyone from one of the POLITICAL PARTIES call you up or come around and talk to you about the campaign this year?" *Source:* Bowler and Segura (2011), 127. *Data source:* American National Election Study, 2008.

In general, individuals' psychological engagement in electoral politics reflects their socialization to the political system, the level of information they possess, the extent to which they are inculcated with norms of attention and involvement, and the degree to which their career, neighborhood, and social networks impinge on their political engagement. Residential segregation, like foreign birth, reduces opportunities for exposure to both the participatory habits of others and political information that would reduce the costs of participation and increase the perceived benefits. In short, resource deficits can reduce individuals' psychological attachment to voting.

There are other social factors to consider as well, chief among them group identity. Michael Dawson's pioneering work on the critical role of African American solidarity in mobilizing voter participation has since been extended to Latinos and Asian Americans. Identifying with a

FIGURE 4.4 Self-Reported Motivation of Latinos Who Voted, 2012

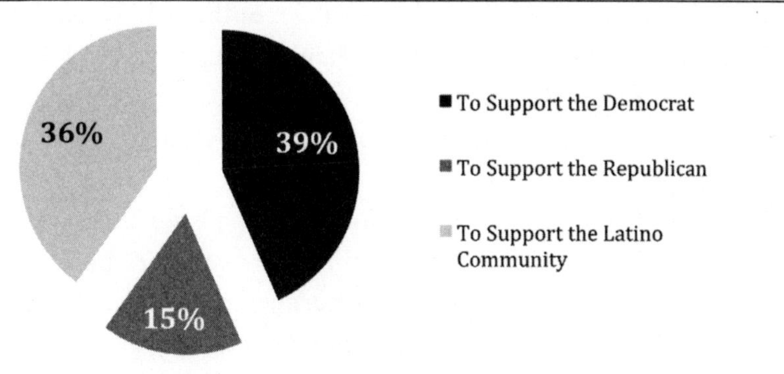

Source: Latino Decisions, election eve poll, 2012.

group—as part of an individual's identification with a community and how that community acts on its own behalf—can be sufficiently mobilizing to motivate the individual to overcome resource deficits and external mobilization and turn out on behalf of the group.

Latino Decisions' polling has repeatedly found evidence of this effect of group identity. In our election eve polls, we have regularly asked Latino registered voters who report voting why they voted in a particular election: did they vote to support the GOP candidate, to support the Democratic candidate, or to support the Latino community? Latinos have frequently identified community support as their reason for voting. In 2012 there were almost as many respondents who identified the Latino community as what brought them to the polls as respondents who identified a desire to vote for a Democratic candidate. Republican candidates as turnout motivators lagged far behind.

One factor to consider that is more psychological than social is whether the citizen is sufficiently empowered to turn out. That is, does the individual Latino citizen feel that turning out to vote will have any effect? Political scientists call this concept "efficacy," and we generally break it down into two components: internal efficacy, or a citizen's feeling that his or her vote has an impact on elections; and external efficacy, or the belief that the outcome of elections can actually change policy. A closely related concept is "alienation": a citizen's feeling that her government does not work on behalf of individuals like her but rather serves the rich, or big business, or some group other than her own. Many citizens have low levels of efficacy and higher levels of alienation; an individual's belief that elections don't matter—or that he or she doesn't matter—clearly reduces political participation.

Though Latinos are overperforming at the polls for their age and socioeconomic status, leaving 11 million or more votes on the table is very detrimental to Latino political empowerment and, by extension, their quality of life. Even as activists and civic engagement organizations try to mobilize more Latinos to participate, register, and vote, a critical question remains: why do Latinos abstain from voting? Are they simply victims of age, lack of education, and low income, or do their attitudes about government and politics partly explain their low turnout?

WHY SOME LATINOS DON'T VOTE

In 2012 Latino Decisions conducted a landmark study of the undermobilized population of Latino citizens eligible to vote. We examined two distinct segments of nonvoting Latinos—those who were successfully registered but failed to turn out, and those who had never registered at all.

We have good reason to believe that these two types of folks differ. Registration is a voluntary act in the United States, and those who choose to take the time to register are different from those who don't. We think of registered voters as a "self-selected" subsample of the population. They are more interested in politics, they pay more attention to it, they see social or civic value in fulfilling their roles as citizens, and they are generally more socially secure. By contrast, people who never register have usually passed up dozens of opportunities to do so—such as when they obtain a driver's license, since most motor vehicle registries now make it easy to register to vote at the same time. Importantly, we should never view nonregistration as a failure to act. Since the advent of "motor-voter" and other regular and frequent opportunities afforded individuals to register to vote, it can no longer be said of most nonregistrants that they never encountered that opportunity. Rather, the nonregistrant is now someone who has repeatedly decided to decline the opportunity to register to vote.

So registered voters are different from the unregistered. But some registered voters participate in elections more frequently than others. This, too, is curious, since nonvoting registered voters have already paid a modest cost to be eligible for the process. Why, after choosing to register, would a citizen subsequently choose not to actually vote?

Admittedly, there is lots of "noise" in the process—random circumstances that can shape both the decision to register and the decision to vote. Some nonregistrants may be hoping to avoid jury duty, and some may not even realize they aren't registered. Among those registering but not voting, work schedules, parenting crises, and even momentary dissatisfaction with the choices in one or more elections might prevent them from voting. But noise notwithstanding, there is clearly a sizable segment of the Latino population (and other Americans as well, of course) who have repeatedly and consciously chosen not to register or, once registered, decided against voting.

Why?

WHAT NONPARTICIPANTS SAY ABOUT ELECTIONS

As mentioned earlier, Latino Decisions conducted six focus groups in Houston, Los Angeles, and Fresno to get some insight into nonparticipation. Across the groups and voter types we found high levels of political alienation and low efficacy. Overall, respondents displayed low levels of internal and external political efficacy, and political trust was low.

When asked why they didn't vote, participants in all groups expressed strong disillusionment with politicians, parties, lobbyists, and the systematic failure of the political system to address issues that mattered to them. Rafael, from Houston, was not registered. When asked how he felt about politics, he had a quick answer. "Frustration . . . the people down here, nothing changes for them. If anything, it is getting worse." David, also from Houston, expressed exceedingly low efficacy. Unlike Rafael, David had been turned off by his direct exposure to politics. "The way the system works, I don't think our vote counts that much. . . . I got really turned off by a lot of things I saw when we were getting involved in the elections."

There was general agreement that politicians and elected officials are primarily interested in their own political gain and have little regard for the concerns and problems that Americans face. Juanita, not currently registered, expressed the sentiment of powerlessness. "My mom always tried to push me to vote, but my vote is not going to make a difference," she said. Rafael specifically cited the corrupting influence of money: "There's too much money in politics." He went on, "Do you think they [Congress] are going to pass a law saying you can't do this [lobbying] anymore? Of course not!"

A second important factor surfaced: respondents had low levels of political information, which was not surprising since the resource of education was in short supply among them. Typically, participants in the political system must have the opportunity, motivation, and ability to gather political information. Our respondents clearly had the opportunity (though some did mention being short on time) and ability to gather information, but lacked the motivation to become politically knowledgeable.

Catalina, an unregistered respondent who lived in California, made it clear to us that she knew how and where to register but had chosen not to. "I've had the [registration] slip every time I go to the DMV to fill out right there, boom. I just don't do it. Well, mostly because I don't pay enough attention, and I don't want to go in here with my eyes closed, filling in dots for people I don't know anything about." Alfredo, in the same focus group of unregistered citizens with Catalina, illustrated how information costs can keep people from being active:

> If I'm going to vote, I want to make an informed decision when I vote. I want my vote to really count and be in my best interest. And that's a lot of work to go there and get to the bottom of these issues, the candidates, the initiatives, and um, I'm kind of lazy right now. I haven't done that . . . it takes a lot of work, you can't listen to the commercials.

A sense of powerlessness coupled with a lack of political knowledge leads many Latinos to feel that elected officials either don't have the power to make a difference or do have the power but are controlled by more powerful external forces. Alfredo voiced his clear belief that government and politics worked to help others, not him. "The government is like, you know, other people that have more power, more money, and control everything. . . . But I mean, elected officials are just puppets."

Finally, the focus groups revealed some structural barriers that made it difficult to find polling places. Coupled with limited time and a lack of comprehensive, nonpartisan information, Latinos seemed to experience substantial impediments to voting. A strong class component came into play here as well—working people work fixed hours, and long lines can severely diminish their participation. Anita, a perky and talkative registered voter from Houston, explained the connection between costs and participation: if online voting were available, she said, a person could vote "in the privacy of your own home, you could really take the time, there's not long lines, it's not late, you're not tired from working all day. Yeah, take your time."

FINDING THOSE MISSING VOTERS

The willingness to vote clearly varied across the three voter types. We thought of a number of focus group members as "leaners"—that is, as people who were already inclined to vote (though not reliably so). Respondents in Los Angeles indicated that political messages from trusted sources could motivate them to participate in politics. The sociodemographic profile of the Los Angeles sample suggested that this focus group was more informed about politics than the other groups. The members of this group were more partisan, and a clear connection between personal economic circumstances and elected officials and parties was suggested by their recall of "better times" under the Clinton administration. Candidate and partisan appeals were likely to resonate with this sample.

Registered Latino voters in Fresno were not as eager to participate in the 2012 election, though most of them could be classified as "persuadable." In both Los Angeles and Fresno, the unregistered we spoke to could best be classified "unreachable." The majority of unregistered voters noted that they planned to "sit out" the election, by which they meant, not that they would ultimately refrain from voting, but that it would take extraordinary efforts to persuade them to vote. Interestingly, some appeared intrigued by the idea of a Latino running for a major political office. A personal or symbolic connection to a candidate or issue could draw these individuals into politics, but any heavy use of political content in a mobilization campaign could turn off this segment.

In Houston, participants in both focus groups expressed a strong willingness to vote, or to consider voting, if they had information about the candidates assuring them that the candidates had well-established records of delivering the outcomes that mattered most to them. Even Rafael, our skeptic, was willing to be persuaded if he could be assured that the quality of the candidates would be better. "If somebody came forward and had a good résumé and background, and showed that they had done some things, then maybe so."

Moreover, the group solidarity among these Latino voters was clear, as was the emergence of a norm of participation. In fact, some of our registered voters who were not voting expressed considerable remorse, recognizing that in not voting they had violated community and family expectations. To Anita, the outspoken registered voter from Houston, not voting felt wrong: "We were out there working those campaigns. . . . I was eight or nine, and I was out there making T-shirts . . . putting up posters, we were very much involved. And that is why I think it's real sad that I feel like it's not worth it anymore. For me not to vote, it's a real sad thing." Anita's sentiments suggest that this sort of voter could be recovered, drawn back into the political system, with the right mobilization and messenger.

By their own account, many of these citizens might have been drawn to the polls if they had personal connections to the electoral process—for example, if their friends and family members voted, or the candidates were coethnics, or they were personally familiar with the candidates. To motivate them, candidates and parties—and even voter mobilization groups—need to focus on rebuilding trust and repairing the relationship between these citizens and the system from which they feel so disconnected. But who are the trusted messengers who will do this work? We return to this question momentarily.

WHAT MAKES (NON) VOTERS (NOT) VOTE?

To examine these populations more systematically, Latino Decisions built on the findings from the six focus groups by conducting a survey of 1,045 Latinos eligible to vote but not engaged in the electorate. The total sample consisted of 443 respondents who were not registered to vote and another 602 respondents who were registered but not voting.

To evaluate respondents in terms of their propensity to vote, we created an index to account for attitudes about government and politics, civic engagement, information about the election, and prior history of participation. In combination, these factors told us whether people had many different attributes that primed them for more or less political engagement. Based on their responses to these items, we categorized respondents into one of three tiers: low, moderate, or high propensity to vote.

Responses to questions about the following subjects were included in this index:

1. How closely are you following the election?
2. Do you know the names of the candidates running for president?
3. Have you heard about or are you familiar with: Mi Familia Vota, Ya Es Hora, NALEO, and NCLR?
4. What is your partisan identification?
5. Would you register if you received a registration card in the mail?
6. "When watching or listening to news, I feel frustrated or angry." (agree-disagree)
7. "I will try to register and vote in this election." (agree-disagree)
8. Reasons for not voting in the 2008 election.
9. Reasons for not registering to vote.

We coded the responses and then used them to create an index that ranged from 0 to 23, with higher values indicating a greater likelihood of participating in politics. Using these scores, we broke all the respondents into three groups.[11]

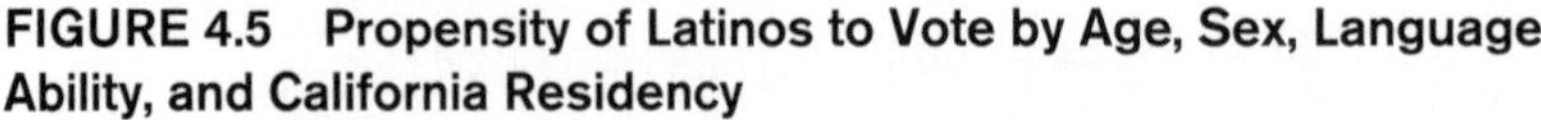

FIGURE 4.5 Propensity of Latinos to Vote by Age, Sex, Language Ability, and California Residency

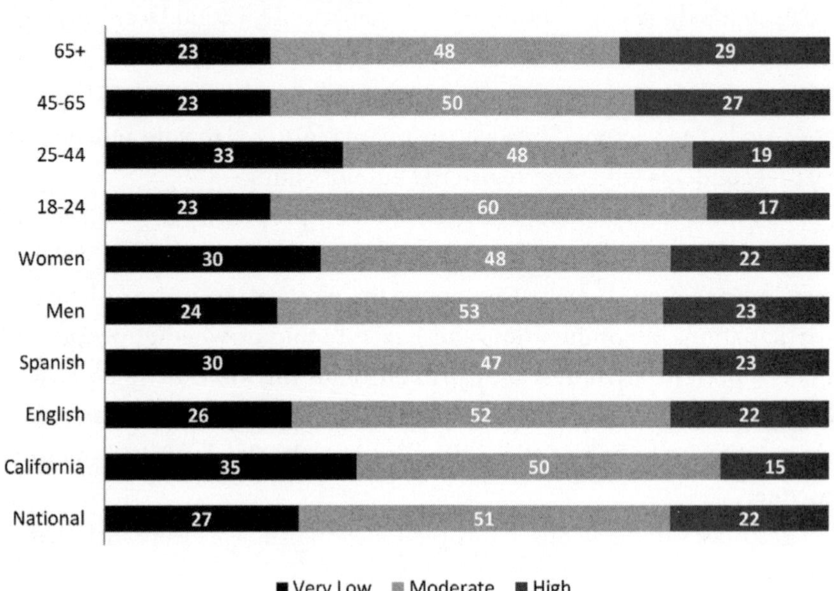

Source: Latino Decisions survey, 2013.

The next two figures illustrate these Latinos' propensity to vote by a series of demographic traits. The moderate-propensity group was the largest for all age, gender, and language ability groups (Figure 4.5). Consistent with all other Americans, the oldest cohort of Latino voters had the largest share of high-probability voters, at 29%. By contrast, young Latinos—those ages eighteen to twenty-four—had the lowest share, only 17%, of high-propensity voters (and the next youngest group didn't do much better). Figure 4.5 clearly illustrates the age resource disadvantage faced by Latinos. Latinos in California appeared to be somewhat less available for mobilization than Latinos nationwide, while there seem to have been similar distributions between men and women and between English and Spanish speakers. This last finding is something of a surprise, since Spanish speakers have greater difficulty accessing political information and are almost certainly foreign-born.

FIGURE 4.6 Propensity of Latinos to Vote, by Registration Status and Demographic Traits

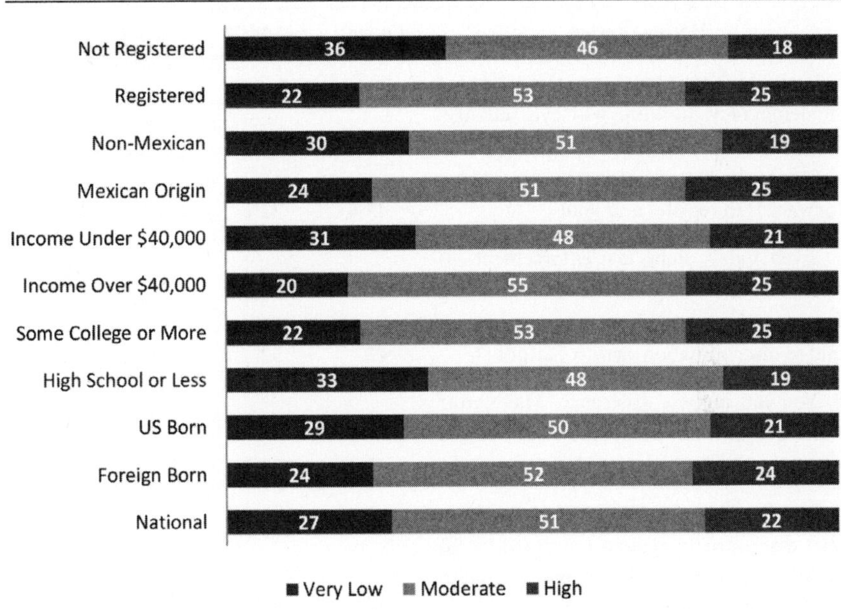

Source: Latino Decisions survey, 2013.

Figure 4.6 shows the nativity, education, income, national origin, and voter registration status of low-, moderate-, and high-propensity voters. Obviously, greater rates of high- and moderate-propensity to vote would be found among registered voters than among those who were no longer registered. Though these nonparticipants had fallen out of the electorate in recent elections, they had paid the costs of registration at some point in their political lives and were more interested in politics than those who had never registered. As we'd expect, more Latinos with higher income and education were in the higher-propensity group. Lower educational attainment is associated with a lower propensity to vote.

Somewhat surprisingly, foreign-born Latinos were more likely to be in the moderate- and high-propensity group relative to their US-born

TABLE 4.1 Percentage of Low-, Moderate-, and High-Propensity Latino Voters to Describe Messages as "Really Convincing"

Message Tested	*Overall*	*Low*	*Medium*	*High*
1. If you don't register to vote and take part in democracy, nothing will ever change. The only way we can change our communities for the better and move our country forward is to register and vote.	45%	32%	45%	61%
2. Even today, some law enforcement officials are harassing and racially profiling Latinos. We must register to vote to put an end to discrimination against Latinos.	42	32	39	64
3. You can make a difference. Make your voice heard in our democracy. We need to register today and vote tomorrow.	42	34	37	62
4. Many states are considering passing laws that discriminate against Latinos, like SB 1070 in Arizona. Only by registering to vote can we change these laws.	41	28	43	50
5. From Mexico to the Middle East, across the world, thousands of people risk their lives to vote and be heard. We can't take it for granted. It's time we register and vote.	40	29	41	48
6. Special interests with lots of money like it when fewer people vote because it's easier for them to influence the actions made by elected officials. The only way to change things is to register to vote.	31	20	33	37
7. Every year critical elections are decided by less than a couple hundred voters. If just a few more people were registered and voted, the entire election outcome could have changed.	29	19	28	45
8. Elected officials determine a lot of what happens for immigration, education, jobs, and the economy. When you register to vote, elected officials listen to you.	20	18	19	28

counterparts. This trend echoes the recent political science research, which finds, first, that naturalized voters in recent years have been more active than naturalized voters in the past, and second, that more time in the United States is associated with declines in Latino efficacy.

PERSUASIVE MESSAGES TO GET LATINOS ONTO THE ROLLS

In our study, we ran a messaging experiment to see which attempt at persuading respondents to vote would be found to be most persuasive. Recall that we were studying the nonparticipating, so our goal was to identify the messages that had the greatest impact.

Table 4.1 reports the messages we tested and the corresponding share of respondents who described each of them as "really convincing." What messages appear to work? The results differ considerably across the three propensity groups we created with our index (low, moderate, high). The difference between the high-propensity group and the others is striking. The majority of the high-propensity group found half of the prompts to be very convincing. Appeals to democracy (messages 1 and 3) and fighting anti-Latino policy (messages 2 and 4) were very powerful motivators for this group. The moderate-propensity group showed some similar trends: their top two messages were also about democracy (message 1) and Latino-targeting policies (message 4).

Curiously, the last message did not resonate much with any segment, more or less validating the expressions of alienation and low efficacy from Rafael, Anita, and others in our focus groups. Few Latino respondents who avoid electoral participation really believe that voting can get the attention of elected officials. With alienation high and efficacy low, that message fails to persuade.

MESSENGERS MATTER

We have spent much of the last several years trying to educate clients and leaders alike on the importance of the messenger. As advertising agencies have long understood, what you are trying to sell determines, in large measure, who is going to be good at selling it: the messenger has to be

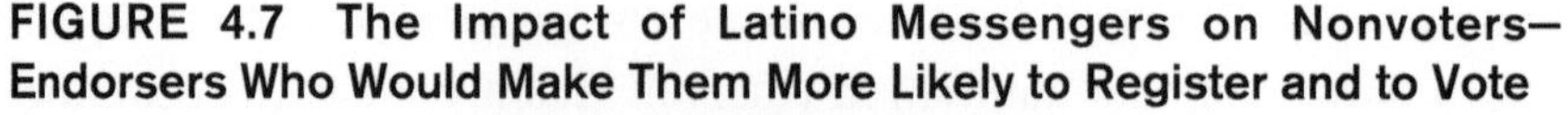

FIGURE 4.7 The Impact of Latino Messengers on Nonvoters—Endorsers Who Would Make Them More Likely to Register and to Vote

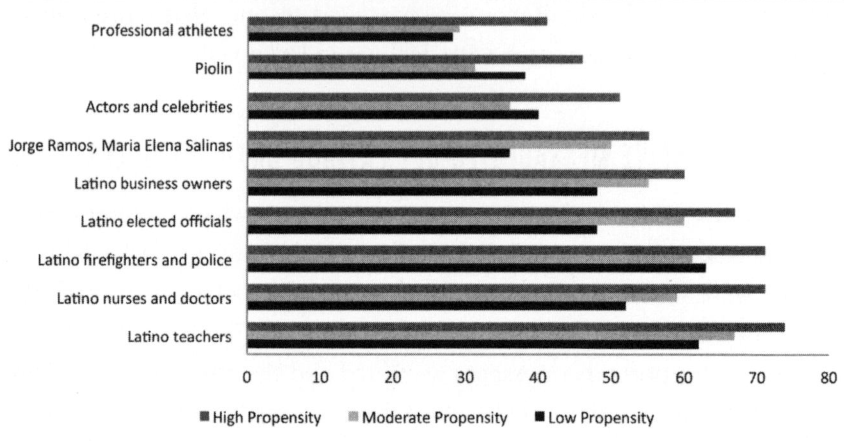

Source: Latino Decisions survey, 2013.

credible and influential and must be someone the target both trusts and sees as worthy of emulation. Civic engagement messages are no different.

Figure 4.7 illustrates the impact that different endorsers would have on the decision of current nonvoters to register or vote. All of the groups agreed that coethnic firefighters, police, doctors, nurses, and teachers as messengers would have a significant influence on them. These community notables, whose leadership is earned through social position and other avenues of trust, consistently demonstrated the greatest persuasive authority in getting nonparticipant Latinos to consider registering and voting. Well over half of low-, moderate-, and high-propensity voters agreed that these Latino endorsers would have a positive impact on their political participation.

By contrast, entertainment figures (actors, athletes, celebrities) did not have much influence, though Univision anchors Jorge Ramos and Maria Elena Salinas remained trusted figures for high- and moderate-propensity groups. Even Piolin, the syndicated radio personality often credited as one of the significant influences on the massive mobilizations during the 2006 immigration marches, does poorly when compared to nurses, teachers, and firefighters. To be clear, this does not mean that these individuals have a negative effect; we have no evidence that they drive people away from the voting booth. Moreover, different people respond to different messages, and mobilization of this hard-to-reach electorate may require a variety of players and pitches. We do, however, clearly find that famous people are less important than trusted community members when mobilizing people to vote. Of course, other factors beyond the boundaries of the Latino community might also have an effect. Figure 4.8 highlights the influence of certain non-Latino individuals on political participation. Family and friends have a consistently strong positive impact for all groups: if asked by a close family member or friend to vote, two-thirds or more said that they would do so, and this finding is consistent with all we know about Latino familial closeness and the importance of family information networks.

Unions are powerful endorsers for high-propensity nonvoters, but not so much for low- and moderate-propensity groups. Organized labor is consistently one of the strongest advocates for Latino civic engagement and immigration reform. This support derives from the fact that the labor movement comprises a growing share of Latinos, a natural consequence of the movement of Latinos into the building trades and the movement of unions into the service sector of the economy. The influence of unions as messengers was greatest among those nonvoters we found to be more readily persuadable.

It is striking, and entirely contrary to popular narrative about Latinos, that priests and ministers rated lowest for moderate- and high-propensity groups. The most informed and engaged nonvoters were less likely to be influenced by the endorsements of religious leaders. This powerful piece of information echoes the earlier observation that Latinos, no matter how religiously observant they are, do not look to their religious leaders for political guidance.

Finally, Figure 4.9 reports the effect of specific family endorsements on voting decisions. The results are essentially what we might expect: mothers, fathers, and spouses or partners had the most positive influence relative to all other family members. It is quite noticeable that the low-propensity voters seemed to be much less moved by family opinions, which were so potent for others in the survey.

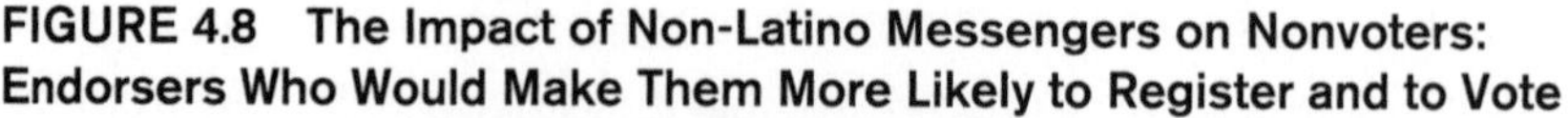

FIGURE 4.8 The Impact of Non-Latino Messengers on Nonvoters: Endorsers Who Would Make Them More Likely to Register and to Vote

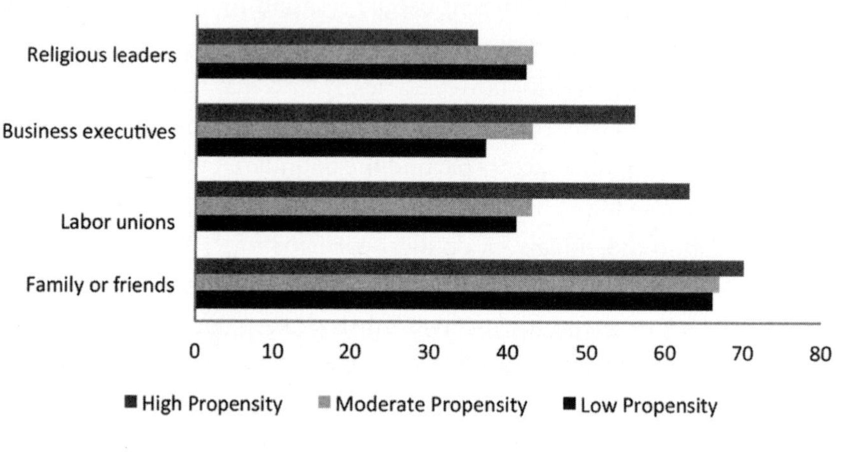

Source: Latino Decisions survey, 2013.

WHAT HAVE WE LEARNED ABOUT THE MISSING LATINO VOTERS?

Eleven million uncast ballots is a huge wasted resource that Latinos can ill afford. Improving voter registration and turnout is the sine qua non of increasing Latino electoral clout.

Some Latino resource disadvantages (age, specifically) will diminish over time, and there are also considerable attitudinal advantages that will keep Latino turnout within striking distance of the goal of parity. The most salient of these advantages is group identity: it is clear that identity concerns drive turnout decisions for as many as one in three Latino voters.

The Latino share of the electorate, though still low, has approximately tripled in the last generation, and it grows with each passing election. Latinos have begun to play a pivotal role in national politics and national elections. We turn next to exactly how, and with what effect, they are taking on this role.

FIGURE 4.9 The Impact of Family Messengers on Nonvoters: Endorsers Who Would Make Them More Likely to Register and to Vote

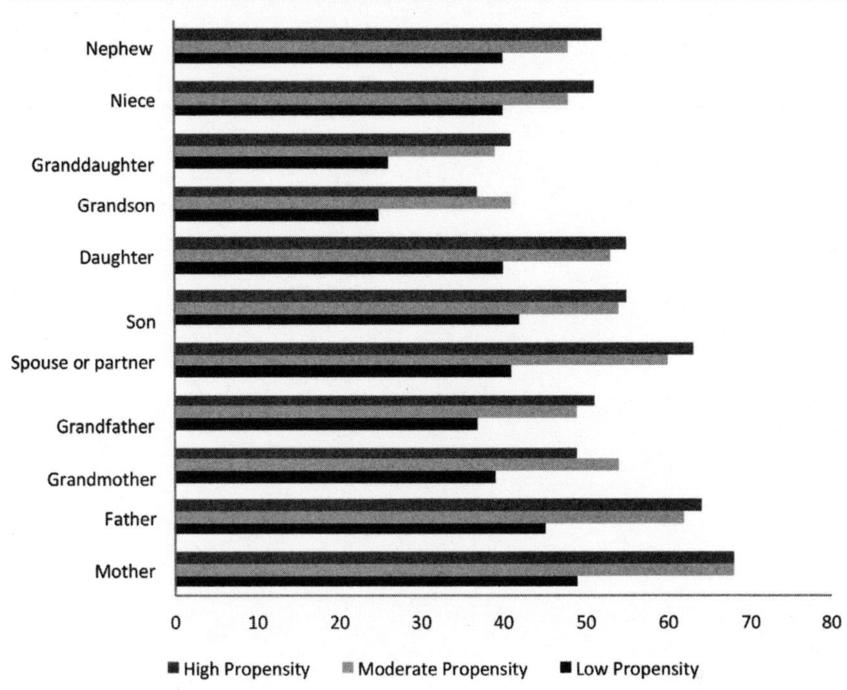

Source: Latino Decisions survey, 2013.

Part II

LATINOS AT THE POLLS, 2008–2012

Chapter 5

THE 2008 DEMOCRATIC PRIMARY

With Sylvia Manzano, Gabriel Sanchez, and Ali Valenzuela

Latino voters received unprecedented attention from candidates and media in the 2008 presidential election. During the primaries and general election, campaign staff and political observers repeatedly noted that electoral competitiveness and outcomes hinged on the Latino vote in many states. Frequently referred to as Hillary Clinton's "Latino firewall" in the primary season, Latinos came through for Clinton: she won the Latino vote by two-to-one margins in nearly every state. It was a defining moment in Latino American politics as Latinos became decisive.

Before 2008, Latinos had had few meaningful opportunities to shape or participate in primary elections. Competitive primaries typically occur early in the primary season, because states that hold their contests early have higher turnout rates and greater influence in determining the party nominees.[1] The states that hold the first primaries and caucuses are also among the most homogenous in the country: in 2008, 93% of Iowa's and New Hampshire's eligible electorate were non-Hispanic white voters.[2] Primary candidates quickly abandon their presidential campaigns after a front-runner has been established.[3] Once this happens, voters have little incentive to participate as primaries become noncompetitive and even

TABLE 5.1 States with a Significant Latino Population in 2008

State	*Primary Date*	*Latino CVAP*[a]	*Democratic Primary Electorate Latino*
Nevada	January 19	10.2%	15%
Florida	January 29	12.6	11
Arizona	February 5	17.9	18
California	February 5	21.4	30
New Jersey	February 5	8.5	12
New Mexico	February 5	37.4	35
New York	February 5	10.5	10
Colorado	February 5	11.6	16
Illinois	February 5	7.0	10
Texas	March 4	24.3	32
Puerto Rico	June 3	100.0	100

Source: US Census Bureau, Current Population Survey, November 2008; CNN primary exit polls, 2008.
a. CVAP = Voting-Age Population by Citizenship and Race

perfunctory exercises. With America's Latino electorate geographically concentrated in a handful of states (nearly half of all Latino voters reside in California and Texas alone), the opportunity for Latino voters to participate in primaries of actual consequence or to influence the nomination outcome is especially sensitive to the party-established schedule that dictates when each state holds its primary.

The Democratic Party changed the 2008 primary schedule, in part to address the lack of Latino representation in the early primary states. That institutional change, coupled with the enduringly competitive contest between Hillary Clinton and Barack Obama, made it possible for the Latino electorate to claim a new and powerful role in choosing the Democratic Party's presidential nominee. Because so many heavily Latino states held primaries on or before February 5, 2008, Clinton and Obama developed Latino outreach strategies early in the primary season and deployed those resources throughout their campaigns—a first in American politics. Clinton's Latino effort was more advanced than Obama's, but both camps signaled their seriousness by including high-profile Latino campaign staffers and consultants, actively seeking endorsements from Latino elected officials and public figures, investing in Spanish and English ads targeted at Latino audiences, and establishing field offices in locales to maximize Latino outreach.[4]

In the three traditional early primary states, Iowa, New Hampshire, and South Carolina, Latino voters accounted for less than 1% of the statewide electorates. But Latino voters comprised more than 10% of the electorate in New Mexico (35%), California (30%), Arizona (18%), Colorado (16%), Nevada (15%), New Jersey (12%), Florida (11%), Illinois (10%), and New York (10%).[5] Conventional wisdom held that Texas, with its March primary date, would be "too late to matter," but instead, the state played a pivotal role in keeping Hillary Clinton's campaign alive when she narrowly won. One-third of the electorate was Latino.[6]

THE POLITICAL CONTEXT OF PRIMARIES

The factors that influence vote choice in presidential primaries and caucuses are fairly well established. Perceived viability, candidate quality, and candidate strength are of the utmost importance. Voters want to support a candidate who has a realistic chance to win the nomination and the general election.[7] Candidates with deep pockets tend to win early, creating momentum that funnels more contributions.[8] Hillary Clinton entered the race with significant advantages on these points. Many political professionals considered her nomination inevitable, and her capacity to fund-raise was unmatched by any other Democrat at that time.[9]

Voter preferences are also shaped by issues and ideology. These distinctions can be more difficult for voters to make in primary elections than in general elections.[10] In the Clinton and Obama contest, policy and ideological differences were not especially sharp. Both favored immigration reform that included a pathway to citizenship, health care reform, and withdrawal from Iraq. There was no party-defining issue on which the two held opposite views (as we saw, for example, in the 2012 Republican primary when Governor Rick Perry of Texas voiced support for in-state tuition rates for undocumented immigrants). Beyond these traditional factors, targeted mobilization has proven especially effective with

Latino voters, who tend to respond positively to coethnic and bilingual outreach.[11] Clinton held a clear advantage in this area.

PRO-CLINTON = ANTI-OBAMA?

During the bruising 2008 Democratic contest, a narrative emerged asserting that racial prejudice among Latino voters accounted for their strong support for Hillary Clinton. Journalists produced many articles echoing the notion that racism kept Latinos from voting for Obama.[12] Clinton campaign insiders perpetuated the claim too. Soon after Clinton's victory in the New Hampshire primary, Sergio Bendixen, who conducted Hispanic polling for the Clinton campaign, told *The New Yorker,* "The Hispanic voter, and I want to say this carefully, has not shown a lot of willingness or affinity to support black candidates." Even in late June, when the contest was all but over, Clinton's campaign chairman, Terry McAuliffe, told reporters that Obama had a problem with the Latino community and could not close out the votes needed with this key constituency.[13]

Bendixen and McAuliffe were not alone. Following Hillary Clinton's impressive performance with Latino voters on Super Tuesday, conservative commentator Raoul Contreras wrote in the *Los Angeles Times,* "When truly given a choice, Latinos will not vote for a black candidate."[14] From this beginning, the story was spun into a broader discussion of black-brown political tension and even became the subject of press conferences by academics.

The political dynamics between African Americans and Latinos have been the subject of extensive academic research. Social science research and election results show that African Americans and Latinos share similar issue preferences and broad ideological positions, owing to their similar socioeconomic standing.[15] Sometimes this commonality can yield real or perceived competition for scarce economic and political resources, such as public-sector jobs or even elective office.[16] Others have found that, in the South and in politically competitive contexts, Latinos can hold negative racial stereotypes about blacks, perceive greater commonality with whites than with blacks, and see their own political gains in zero-sum terms.[17]

There is an important caveat to these studies: research focused on mass opinion among Latinos that does not account for political context or leadership can lead to erroneous conclusions. Generalizations overestimate the scope of Latino antipathy and underestimate Latino willingness to vote for black candidates, even in the face of numerous election results to the contrary.[18] Studies on Latino racial resentment typically examine the presence or magnitude of negative attitudes (antipathy measures are the dependent variables), but they spend less time considering whether those opinions are reflected in Latino voting behavior.

The claim, then, that Hillary Clinton's support was somehow evidence of Latino unwillingness to support African American candidates was wrong on its face. Latino voters have demonstrated strong support for African American candidates in the past, across a variety of circumstances. Black and Latino leaders, activist groups, and voters frequently bridge attitudinal divides in state and local elections. Harold Washington, David Dinkins, Wellington Webb, and Ron Kirk were all elected mayor of a major American city with Latino vote shares from 70% to 80%. More recently, African American mayors have won a majority of the Latino vote in elections against white women: in Cleveland's 2005 mayoral contest, Frank Jackson won an estimated 65% of the Latino vote, defeating Jane Campbell. In Inglewood, California, Roosevelt Dorn won more than 70% of the Latino vote to defeat Judy Dunlap. Congresswoman Maxine Waters has regularly won over 80% of the Latino vote, sometimes even running against Latino opponents. Waters herself stated in a National Public Radio interview that "somebody said that Latinos wouldn't vote for a black. They vote for me all the time. There are any number of instances where our districts are majority Latino . . . and they vote over and over [for blacks]."

Among the African American candidates who have enjoyed the support of Latinos is none other than Barack Obama himself. Prior to running for the presidency, Obama had a solid record of success with Latino voters in Chicago and Illinois. In his unsuccessful bid for Congress in 2000, Obama won more Latino votes than African American votes when he ran against incumbent Bobby Rush in the Democratic primary. In 2004, when Obama ran for the US Senate, more Latinos voted for him than for his Latino challenger, Gerry Chico, in the Democratic primary. A few months later, Obama went on to win 84% of the Latino vote in the general election. These three statistics were regularly ignored in news stories that reported on Obama's alleged "Latino problem." The claim that Latinos would not vote for Obama was easily refuted: it had no basis in reality.

The theory of racial animosity among Latino voters was thoroughly examined in an analysis of racial attitudes and voting behavior among Latinos and non-Hispanic whites in the 2008 primary and general elections.[19] We will turn our attention to those findings in the next chapter when we consider the historic Obama-McCain race. In the election in which the first African American nominee appeared on the presidential ballot, would antiblack prejudice significantly shape Latino voting attitudes? As far as the primary went, the claim had little empirical basis and was not a significant factor in the Clinton-Obama drama.

LATINO SUPPORT FOR HILLARY CLINTON AND BARACK OBAMA, 2007–2010

From the outset, Hillary Clinton enjoyed substantial support from all corners of the Democratic base. Throughout 2007 and well into the 2008 primaries, her nomination was repeatedly described as inevitable. It is not surprising that Clinton scored repeated two-to-one vote margins or better among Latinos in nearly every state. As she continued to win large majorities of the Latino vote throughout the primary season, political observers and professionals reported these results as validation of Obama's "Latino problem," one steeped in racist attitudes in the Latino community. But Clinton's victories were the product of an established relationship with Latino voters, an effective Latino strategy, and her overall strengths as a candidate who had dominated the news just months before. Looking at changes in Latino voter opinions over time, it is evident that Obama's problems were lack of name recognition and a very strong competitor—not Latino racism directed at him.

Close examination of the trends from 2007 to 2010 provides a more complete picture of Latino opinions about the candidates and the factors contributing to their vote choices.[20] The campaign for the Democratic nomination began in early 2007, Hillary Clinton made it official in January, and Obama announced the following month. Over the course of that year the share of Latinos with no opinion of Obama actually increased, from 35% to 43%. Among foreign-born Latinos, that figure was especially high: nearly 60% had no opinion of Obama in 2007. This is important to note in light of claims that singled out foreign-born Latino voters as especially driven by racial resentment to vote against Obama.

Obama's unfavorable ratings were quite consistent from 2007 to 2010. From when he was a relatively unknown political figure to the middle of his first term, Obama's negative ratings remained at 20% of Latino registered voters. This is virtually the same share of the Latino electorate that also regularly identifies as Republican. When the primary campaign charged ahead in 2008 and dominated the news, the share of Latinos with no opinion about Obama dropped off sharply, and Obama's favorability ratings rose from a mere 41.3% in August 2007 to 66.2% in February 2008. These strong positive trends took shape despite the fact that Obama continued to lose the Latino vote to Clinton by wide margins in state after state.

Hillary Clinton's favorability trends are remarkably different from Obama's. From the start of her campaign in March 2007 until the middle of 2008, Clinton rated 80% or better among foreign-born Latinos. Across the entire Latino electorate, fewer than 10% had no opinion of her, and her unfavorable share was nearly the same as Obama's. During the entire period when Obama kept losing the Latino vote to Clinton, his unfavorable ratings were no worse than hers. By the time Clinton conceded and officially exited the race in June 2008, Obama's favorability ratings had risen to levels nearly as high as Clinton's.

As Obama became better known, his positive rating with Latinos also increased. He won 70% of the Latino vote in the general election, and his approval rating with this constituency peaked at 81% in April 2009, after 100 days in office. If Latino votes for Clinton had been racially motivated against Obama, then the share reporting no opinion of Obama would have eventually fallen into the unfavorable category. In reality, the opposite occurred: the share of Latino voters with no opinion about Obama steadily decreased as the campaign season grew older, and Obama's positive ratings increased.

BUILDING AND SUSTAINING THE LATINO FIREWALL

As the primary season progressed both Clinton and Obama poured tens of millions of dollars into Latino-specific outreach and mobilization efforts.[21] Clinton's Latino-targeted campaign emphasized her long-standing ties with the community. English and Spanish ads referred to her as *nuestra amiga* ("our friend"), suggesting an almost personal relationship of long endurance.[22] In front of Latino audiences, she cited her personal history working on voter registration in Mexican American neighborhoods and highlighted her familiarity with Hispanic culture.[23] During the primary she picked up endorsements from more state and local Latino elected officials than any other candidate in either party.

The Clinton campaign had an especially focused Latino strategy.[24] Her campaign began with a Latino woman, Patti Solis Doyle, serving as campaign manager. A Latino specialist pollster was brought onto the team too. Early on, Clinton locked up endorsements from influential Latino elected officials and political figures, then deployed them to mobilize voters. Former Los Angles mayor Antonio Villaraigosa served as a campaign cochair, making many appearances on Clinton's behalf. Former HUD secretary and San Antonio mayor Henry Cisneros appeared in campaign ads and at events across the country. Labor leader Dolores Huerta personally endorsed Clinton in 2007, then delivered the endorsement of her union, the 26,000-member United Farm Workers of America, in 2008.

Obama's Hispanic effort was far less sophisticated. There were few Latino elected officials at any level of government who had not already endorsed Clinton. Obama had few direct lines to the Latino local officials who could have been crucial to tapping into grassroots allies. Congressman Luis Gutiérrez (D-IL), one of the few Latino elected officials to endorse Obama early in the campaign, criticized the Obama campaign's Latino effort as "insufficient, poor, and ineffective." With amigos like that, it is no wonder that Obama had difficulty dispelling the notion that he had a "Latino problem."

TABLE 5.2 Candidate Favorability—Latino Voters in the 2008 Primary in Nevada, California, and Texas

	Nevada (N = 400)		*California (N = 600)*		*Texas (N = 500)*		*Overall (N = 1,500)*	
	Clinton	*Obama*	*Clinton*	*Obama*	*Clinton*	*Obama*	*Clinton*	*Obama*
Very favorable	46%	16%	50%	12%	49%	28%	48%	19%
Somewhat favorable	30	27	28	29	27	38	28	31
Total favorable	76	43	78	41	76	66	76	50
Somewhat unfavorable	5	8	6	9	8	11	6	9
Very unfavorable	10	6	7	6	9	10	9	7
Total unfavorable	15	14	13	15	17	21	15	16
No opinion	7	12	7	14	7	9	7	12
Never heard of	2	32	2	30	0	3	1	22
Total don't know	9	44	9	44	7	12	8	34

Source: Latino Decisions primary surveys, 2007, 2008.

Because there are fewer substantive differences in primaries, the candidates' personal qualities become more decisive factors. In this respect, Clinton held a tremendous advantage because of her familiarity to Latinos. She was well known and well liked. Throughout the campaign her team made sure to incorporate a Latino strategy. Never assuming that Clinton's so-called Latino firewall would endure, her campaign actively worked to register, motivate, and mobilize Latino voters at every opportunity.

LATINO VOTERS IN THE 2008 DEMOCRATIC PRIMARY

One way to establish that votes were pro-Clinton rather than anti-Obama is to look more closely at favorability ratings and vote choices specifically among Democratic primary voters. Latino Decisions surveyed Latino Democratic primary voters in California, Nevada, and Texas prior to their state party election; the survey data from these three states allow us to consider the factors that shaped Latino voter opinion during the primary contest.

In most cases favorability ratings are highly correlated with vote choice.[25] In this particular contest, however, Latino voters had a positive view of both candidates, even though they consistently voted for Clinton at much higher rates. Obama was rated favorably by 50% of the sample Latino primary electorate, but only 13% said that they would cast their primary ballot for him. In a California exit poll conducted by Loyola Marymount University, 93% of Latinos said that the country was ready to elect a black president, even as Clinton won nearly 70% of the California Latino vote.[26]

It is important to account for the factors that explain why Clinton performed so well with this ever-growing constituency; it is not enough to establish that race was not a factor in Latino voter decisions. Our quantitative data analysis of Latino Democratic primary voters and qualitative evaluation of the Clinton and Obama campaigns provide a theoretically consistent explanation for her success with Latino voters: Clinton's strong performance among Latino voters was rooted in her extraordinary name recognition within the Democratic electorate and effective Latino outreach effort.

We turn first to the survey data collected in three states at different points in the primary season.[27] These data show that name recognition and ethnic cues were predictive of both favorability evaluations and vote

TABLE 5.3 Primary Vote Choice among Latinos in Three States

Candidates	*Nevada*	*California*	*Texas*	*Combined*
Hillary Clinton	58%	64%	60%	61%
Barack Obama	7	9	22	13
Undecided or other	35	27	18	26

Source: Latino Decisions primary surveys, 2007, 2008.

choice. As Table 5.2 reports, 76% of all Latino Democratic primary voters had a favorable impression of Clinton, and 48% had a *very* favorable view. The majority of Latinos, 50%, also had favorable views of Barack Obama, though his "very favorable" number was only 19%. His newcomer status worked against him—rather high proportions of Latino primary voters had never heard of him just weeks before their state election. California's and Nevada's Democratic Latino electorates knew little about Obama: 44% either had never heard of him or had formulated no opinion of him. In mid- to late 2007, when the candidates were heavily focused on intraparty debates, Obama was nowhere near being able to fill arenas and stadiums. Once his campaign became a national phenomenon, however, Latino voters learned more about him and his "never heard of" number dropped off substantially. By late February, when the contest had reached a fever pitch, both Clinton and Obama were commanding audiences that numbered in the thousands several times a day on the campaign trail. At that point, only 3% of Latinos in the Texas Democratic electorate were unfamiliar with Obama, and 66% had a favorable view of him.

Obama's increasing popularity did not come at Clinton's expense. Her standing with Latinos never wavered: the fact that three out of four Latino primary voters liked Hillary Clinton gave her an incredible advantage no matter how much time passed on the campaign trail. Table 5.3 reports Latino primary voter preferences in the three states surveyed. Early in the campaign and later in the season, Clinton maintained her commanding share of the vote: 58% in Nevada, 64% in California, and 60% in Texas.[28] Obama's favorability ratings outpaced his vote share throughout the primary season. Even though his favorability ratings within the Latino community had increased by over twenty points over the course of a few months, his vote share with Texas Latinos was a mere 22%. Obama performed best among voters who were following the election closely: he picked up only 6% of the vote among those not following the election, but his share more than doubled to 15% among those closely following the race. Obviously, an unknown candidate is at a significant disadvantage in relation to a well-known, well-liked candidate.

ISSUES AND ETHNIC TIES

To assess what motivated Latino support for Clinton and Obama, we tested several favorability and vote choice models. We found that policy issues mattered differently for Latino voters than we might have expected; we also found that ethnic cues were especially important in shoring up Clinton's base support. Neither immigration nor health care had a statistical relationship with favorability or vote choice, and her nuanced support for the Iraq War was actually a winning issue for Clinton. Obama had supported the states in issuing driver's licenses for undocumented immigrants, and Clinton had been associated with health care issues since her efforts during her husband's administration.[29] Still, the fact that these issues did not matter, but ethnicity did, makes sense for a couple of reasons. Both candidates advocated large-scale overhauls of the health care system and supported immigration reform with a pathway to citizenship; their plans differed only in the details. Clinton's team, however, developed a strategy with the specific goal of appealing to Latino voters via ethnic appeals.

Only one issue, the Iraq War, registered as a significant factor in candidate support: Latino Democratic primary voters who thought the Iraq War had not been worth fighting were significantly more likely to support Clinton over Obama. This may be somewhat surprising considering that Obama had consistently opposed the war, while Clinton agreed with the initial decision to send troops to Iraq and only later became a critic of the war. It is likely that her evolving position was not a political liability because it closely tracked the national temperament on this issue. Like most Americans, Latinos supported the war the first two years after the United States invaded Iraq. As the years went by support waned among the general public as well as among elected officials.[30]

By all demographic indicators, including income, education, age, gender, language preference, and nativity, Hillary Clinton outperformed Barack Obama in the 2008 Democratic primary on favorability and vote choice. She ran especially strong with Latinas and working-class voters earning $40,000 to $60,000 a year. Despite having a foreign-born father, Obama did not capitalize on this potential connection with Latino voters: naturalized citizens were more likely to side with Clinton. Obama's best showing, though it lagged far behind Clinton, was with college-educated Latinos who were closely following the election.

The two candidates had very different Latino outreach campaigns. Latino voters told us that they were more likely to vote for candidates who had been endorsed by coethnic leaders and that they placed a high value on their own ethnic identity. So it is not surprising that these same voters overwhelmingly cast their ballots for Clinton, who made these direct appeals. Fifty-six percent of Latinos with no interest in ethnic endorsements supported Clinton, but her support jumped to 67% among those who responded positively to the coethnic political cues—an increase of eleven percentage points.

For Obama the opposite was true: he *lost* traction among those who placed a high value on Latino campaign outreach. Only 10% of those who responded positively to coethnic outreach said that they would vote for him, compared to 13% of those who did not respond to such appeals. This pattern fits with the reality on the ground: Clinton had many more state and local Latino officials vouching for her in campaign events and ads than Obama did. Among prominent Latino elected officials in the lead-up to the primaries, only Congressman Gutiérrez from Obama's home of Chicago, as mentioned earlier, was an early endorser of Obama in his primary fight for the nomination.

LESSONS LEARNED

Latino voters made up a large share of the Democratic primary electorate in several states in the long 2008 nomination contest. The factors that shaped Latino turnout, opinions, and vote choices were quite varied. Voter participation surged owing to institutional forces—specifically, a nominee had not been determined when primaries were being held in the states with the largest Latino electorates, making the Latino primary vote of greater political importance than it had been in years past.

The racialized narrative about Latino support for Hillary Clinton spread by pundits, journalists, and campaign insiders was nonsense in the extreme. Clinton enjoyed tremendous name recognition, a litany of prized endorsements, and the halo of approval from her husband's two terms, whereas a sizable percentage of Latinos had never heard of Barack Obama. The fact that Obama's vote share remained low despite his strong approval ratings says less about him and more about Clinton's political strengths with Latino voters. Once he was nominated, Latino support for Obama reached levels consistent with—and even superior to—Latino support for past Democratic nominees.

Chapter 6

NOVEMBER 2008: THE LATINO VOTE IN OBAMA'S GENERAL ELECTION LANDSLIDE

With Loren Collingwood, Sylvia Manzano, and Ali Valenzuela

History will record that on the day Barack Obama was elected to the presidency, he received overwhelming support from the Latino electorate.* On election night, the exit polls reported that Latinos had comprised approximately 9% of the voter turnout and that Barack Obama had received two-thirds (67%) of their ballots. Some estimates were even higher.

Did that matter?

How Latinos voted is not in dispute, but the two bigger questions regarding the 2008 election are these. First, why the enthusiasm for Obama? George W. Bush had managed to get somewhere north of 40% of the Latino vote just four years earlier. John McCain was a longtime and noted champion of immigration reform, and as a consequence the

*An earlier version of part of this chapter appeared as "Measuring Latino Political Influence in National Elections" by Matt Barreto, Loren Collingwood, and Sylvia Manzano, *Political Research Quarterly* 63, no. 4 (2010).

issue of immigration played almost no role in the general election of 2008. On the basis of recent history and the specific policy positions of the two nominees on the key Latino issue, there was no reason to have assumed that Obama would do so well. Second, was the Latino vote influential in the election? Since the Latino margin was smaller than the total vote margin—Obama's victory in 2008 was broad, deep, and overwhelming in the Electoral College—the simplest calculation was that Latinos had no effect on the outcome.

In this chapter, we address both of these questions and offer a theory for evaluating group influence in presidential elections.

WHY DID LATINOS SUPPORT OBAMA IN 2008?

Did Latinos vote for Barack Obama just because of the pattern of minorities supporting the Democratic Party? Was it that Latinos, compared to whites, have lower household income and that such working-class voters are more likely to support the Democratic Party? Or are other factors also at play? We certainly need to examine the divides in the Latino community that we identified in Chapter 2—naturalized versus native, the differences between national-origin groups—to see whether they had any effect. We need to examine the possibility that characteristics specific to Latinos as a political group played a role. Finally, what can we say about race and the 2008 election specifically with respect to how racial sentiments may or may not have shaped the views of whites and Hispanics toward Obama? This is a topic we began to explore in the last chapter.

We think the story of the 2008 election among Latinos—that is, understanding which Latinos supported President Obama and why—requires us to focus on five key factors. First, there were two issues that weighed heavily for Latinos—the economy and the Iraq War. Both tilted heavily against the incumbent party and its nominee. Second, Latinos got significantly more Democratic in the wake of two failed attempts at immigration reform in 2006 and 2007. Despite McCain's bona fides on the issue, Latinos were more likely to vote Democrat across every category of partisan identification. Third, some Latino-specific characteristics had a significant effect on vote choice in 2008, including national-origin differences, generation, and nativity. Fourth, we show that the growing strength of Latino group identity and pan-ethnic consciousness contributed to the Democratic vote. Finally, we consider again the highly charged claims regarding Latino citizens' propensity (or lack thereof) to vote for black candidates, first articulated by the Clinton campaign's Latino pollster, Sergio Bendixen.[1]

THE 2008 ISSUE ENVIRONMENT FOR LATINOS: IRAQ AND THE ECONOMY

Latinos generally have a very favorable opinion of the military.[2] Historically, the military has served as one venue for Latinos to increase their educational and job opportunities and assimilate in this country.[3] As the United States went to war with Iraq in 2003, Latino involvement in the conflict was high, and soon it became evident that Latinos were disproportionately suffering war deaths.

There were extensive casualties in the first year of the war among Latino soldiers, many of whom were serving in lower-level infantry positions.[4] *USA Today* reported that, while Latinos were just 10.5% of the military at that time, they made up 17% of US combat forces (higher than their share of the population) and over 11% of those who were killed in action.[5] The salience of the war was raised among Latino voters because military recruiters focused more on Latino youth, many of whom chose military service as a path to citizenship or to escape poor educational and employment opportunities in the civilian sector.

Even early in the war, Latino attitudes had soured on Iraq, and the Pew Hispanic Center reported that Latinos had a more negative view than other Americans.[6] As it became clearer to the American public that there were no weapons of mass destruction (WMD) in Iraq, many in the Latino community began to question why so many Latino soldiers had been put at risk in the conflict. In 2004, Senator John Kerry tapped into the frustration with the Iraq War and made this a major campaign issue. Indeed, published research on the 2004, election found that Latinos with family members in military service were more likely to support Kerry, contrary to a national trend of support for President George W. Bush among

FIGURE 6.1 The Latino Vote in 2004, by Opinion on Latino Military Service

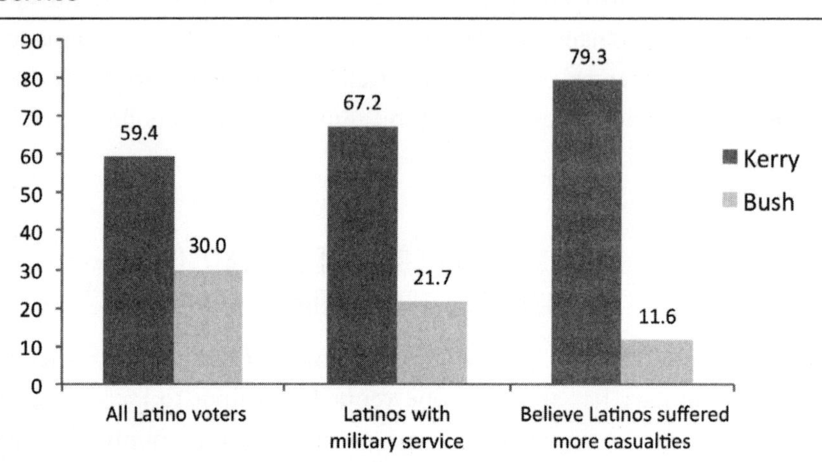

military families.[7] Further, those Latinos who believed that Latinos were being disproportionately affected by war casualties were the most likely to cast a vote for Kerry in 2004.

Iraq continued as a major issue for Latinos and non-Latinos alike in the 2006 midterm elections. By then, many Americans believed that President Bush had misled the public and provided misinformation about the administration's true motives for the war. The number of American casualties in Iraq had hit 3,000 in 2006, and Latinos continued to be disproportionately affected. As they had done in 2004, Latino voters in 2006 identified opposition to the Iraq War as one of the major issues in their vote choice. According to a poll by the Latino Policy Coalition in September 2006, 64% of Latino voters said that a candidate's position on the Iraq War was "very important" in how they would vote, while 56% said that Bush's handling of Iraq had made them more likely to vote Democratic in the 2006 midterms. In fact, by April 2007 another Latino Policy Coalition Survey found that 46% of Latino registered voters had a close friend or family member serving in Iraq or Afghanistan, and that two-thirds of all Latino voters felt that the Iraq War had been a mistake.

Because Hillary Clinton had voted to authorize US force in Iraq in 2003, Barack Obama decided early on to make his opposition to the Iraq War a major campaign issue in 2008. He anticipated that this would create a clear division between him and Clinton and help him with more liberal voters, who were growing increasingly frustrated and upset over the billions of dollars in expenditures on the war and the thousands of US war casualties. Because of his consistent opposition to Iraq and the inconsistency of John McCain—who sought to criticize President Bush at times while also supporting stronger military involvement—Obama leaned into the Iraq War issue in 2008, and this may have helped position him with Latinos. Even a year out from the election, Pew reported that two-thirds of all Latinos wanted the United States to withdraw its forces.[8]

In the months prior to the 2008 election, Latino Decisions polled in the four battleground states of Colorado, Florida, Nevada, and New Mexico. In those four states (all of which would switch from the GOP to the Democratic side that November), opposition to the Iraq War was palpable. In Florida, 61% of Latino registered voters said that the war was not worth fighting, while in the other three states that number ranged from 74.7% to 78.1%. In terms of policy preference, 76.4% in Florida favored either beginning troop reductions or immediately withdrawing. In the other three states, that number was over 80%.

According to a Latino Decisions poll in November 2008, Latino attitudes on Iraq were directly related to their vote choice in 2008. For example, among those who felt that the current policy in Iraq was working and should be continued, 74% said that they cast a ballot for John McCain. In contrast, those who said that they favored an immediate withdrawal of US forces voted 83% in support of Barack Obama. Of course, the overwhelming preponderance of Latino voters favored withdrawal and so voted for Obama. Not only was the Iraq War a mobilizing issue for Latinos in 2008, but it may have even eclipsed other policy issues like immigration and health care in delivering votes to Obama. For example, Obama won an estimated 73% among Latinos who agreed that it was very important for Congress and the president to pass immigration reform in 2009, and 77% of Latinos who supported a shift to universal health insurance voted for Obama in 2008—both of those figures being

FIGURE 6.2 The Latino Vote in 2008, by Preferred Policy Position on Iraq

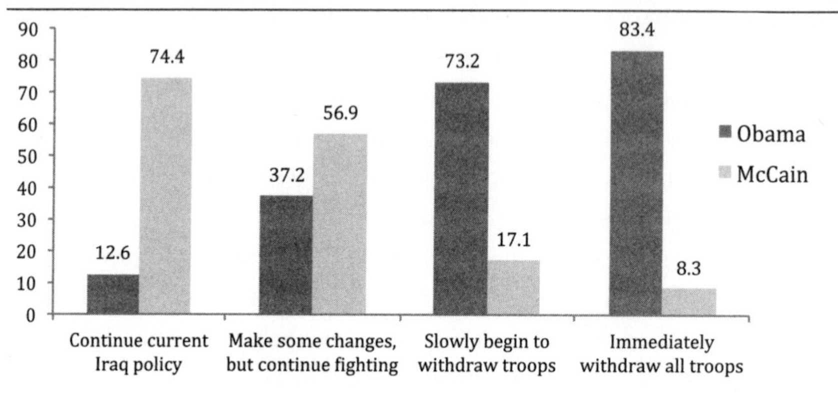

below the 83% of the vote Obama won among Latinos who favored an immediate withdrawal from Iraq.[9]

The salience of the Iraq conflict and the intensity with which its costs were felt and visited upon Latino voters surely had an effect in the 2008 election. Because then-Senator Obama made opposition to the war a cornerstone of his campaign, he was able to draw a particularly stark difference between himself and his opponent. Senator McCain was an outspoken supporter of the war, both at its inception and during the election, and was generally regarded as a "hawk" on military matters, not entirely surprising given his own life history and military career.

The economic catastrophe of the fall of 2008 was a similarly focusing issue, though one hardly unique to Latinos. Nevertheless, as discussed in earlier chapters, Latinos are particularly vulnerable to the fluctuations of economic cycles; like other low-income people, they have a narrow margin for weathering tough times.

Senator McCain was never credible on the economy issue, particularly after pronouncing in Jacksonville, Florida, on the morning of September 15 (repeating a claim from a month earlier) that "the fundamentals of our economy are strong." Lehman Brothers filed for Chapter 11 bankruptcy protection just hours later. The Dow Jones Industrial Average lost 504 points that day.

The electoral impact can be seen directly in the movement of states from the GOP to the Democratic column in 2008. When Latino Decisions conducted polls just six weeks out from the election in the four key battleground states (Nevada, New Mexico, Colorado, and Florida, all four of which cast their electoral votes for Bush in 2004), the results in three of those states showed an overwhelming preference for Senator Obama among Latino voters, ranging from 67% to 71%. Only in Florida was the contest within the margin of error at that time. Latino voters in that state gave us an earful on the economy, which was their top priority. More than one-third reported having had trouble paying their mortgage in the past year.[10] By December 2008, just a month after the election and just three months since the crisis had begun, Pew found that nearly 10% of Latino homeowners had missed a mortgage payment, and more than one-third (36%) were worried about being foreclosed.[11]

Even if McCain had been personally credible on economic issues, the incumbent administration is generally blamed for economic struggles, and the Bush administration ineptitude in handling the crisis proved to be an obstacle that McCain could not overcome with Latino voters (or, indeed, with the American public at large). The issue environment, both domestically and internationally, made the 2008 election a steep climb for the McCain campaign. As history shows, it was too much to overcome.

PARTISAN EFFECTS ON THE LATINO VOTE IN 2008

Party identification is a powerful predictor of vote choice for all Americans, and Latinos are no exception. The effects are not necessarily consistent, however, across elections and groups. Zoltan Hajnal and Taeku Lee have found that foreign-born Americans frequently have weaker party attachments and are more likely to identify with "none of the above" in terms of political parties.[12] Moreover, Latino Decisions has repeatedly found that a clear majority of Latinos—52% in a 2013 poll—have voted Republican at least once in their life, a significant share of the group given recent outcomes at the presidential and congressional levels.

In the data from the 2008 American National Election Study, party identification had a similar impact for whites and Latinos; however, the size of the effects and the degree of certainty surrounding our estimates reveal striking differences. The top graph of page 101, Figure 6.3, illustrates the predicted probability that a non-Hispanic white citizen voted for John McCain. As whites move along a seven-point party identification scale, a very predictable vote outcome emerges, with very few exceptions. The shaded band illustrates the confidence interval—effectively, how much uncertainty there is around each estimate based on the number of respondents at each level of partisanship who did *not* end up near the predicted probability. As is apparent, the estimates are very good. Party is a strong and accurate predictor of votes among white voters, controlling for other factors.

We should note, however, that the graph does not start at the origin. That is, for the strongest Democrats the probability of voting for McCain is just under 0.2. That means that, in these data, the model predicts that just under 20% of white strong Democrats will vote for McCain. Our model predicts significant defection among white Democrats. At the opposite end, nearly all white strong Republicans are predicted to vote for McCain.

Now examine Figure 6.4, the predicted probability that Latinos will vote for McCain. There are two important differences here compared to the graph for non-Hispanic whites. Although there is an upward slope, the distribution is shifted. Among strong Democrats, our model predicts virtually no McCain votes. That is, strong Latino Democrats are more reliably likely to vote for Obama than strong white Democrats, all other things being equal. At the opposite end, the McCain vote still trails partisan identification. Even among self-identified strong Latino Republicans, only about 80% are expected to vote for McCain, leaving a residual 20% support for Obama. Strong Latino Republicans, then, were significantly less reliable in supporting their party's nominee in 2008, John McCain.

The uncertainty in the Latino graph is increasingly large and unstable as we move from strong Democrats to strong Republicans. In practice, the model predicts a wider and wider distribution of the likelihood of voting for McCain at each level—so much so that a Latino weak Republican (point 6) has between a 36% and 100% chance of voting Republican. For whites at the same point (weak Republican), the probability of voting Republican is between 83% and 91%.

The takeaway is twofold. First, white Republicans and Latino Democrats were more reliable voters in 2008 than their opposite counterparts.

FIGURES 6.3 AND 6.4 The Relationship between Party Identification and Vote Choice, 2008

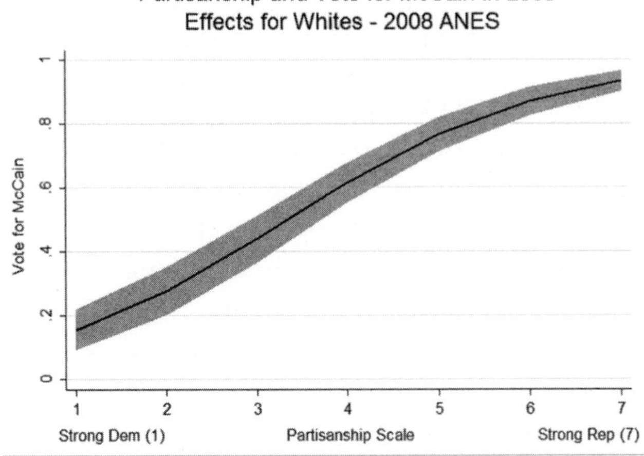

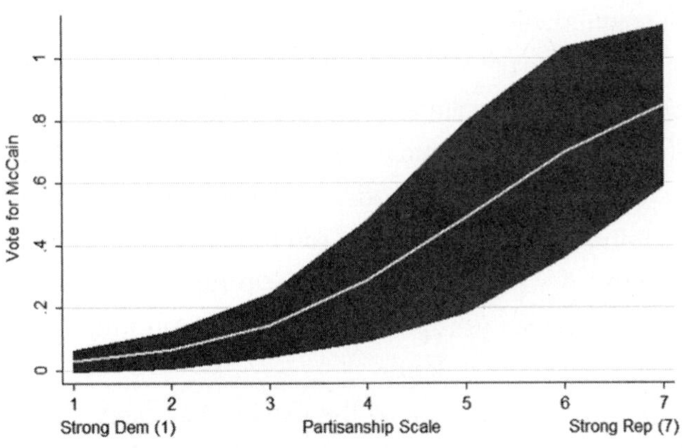

The Latino distribution was shifted toward Obama at every level of partisanship. The issues of the economy and Iraq combined with two years of bruising immigration battles that led to no legislation to move Latinos across the political spectrum away from Senator McCain and toward Senator Obama. And second, for Latino Republicans, partisanship was a weak effect and a terribly inefficient predictor of vote. Lots of Latino

Republicans voted for McCain, of course—indeed, most of them did—but many of them did not.

SPECIFIC LATINO CHARACTERISTICS AND THEIR EFFECTS

National-Origin Differences To begin our discussion of the effects of specific Latino characteristics on the 2008 election, we consider country of ancestry. Cubans demonstrated the highest Republican vote share in previous research, but other national-origin groups showed some variation in 2008.[13] Latinos of Mexican and Puerto Rican origin were statistically more likely to vote for Obama, while Latinos of South American origin were less likely to vote for Obama; a majority of South American Latinos still did vote for Obama, but their rates were noticeably lower than those of voters of Mexican or Puerto Rican ancestry.

Cuban Americans, on the other hand, demonstrated majority support for McCain. Cuban Americans have historically differed from other Latino groups on ideological and policy matters, largely as a consequence of Fidel Castro's takeover of the island and the influx of large numbers of Cubans seeking political asylum in the United States. These refugees came with significant resources—which was one reason why they chose to flee the island—and received substantial assistance from the United States. GOP anticommunism and a residual resentment of the Kennedy administration combined with this history to help form the Cuban American identity as a Republican group. Cubans also face no immigration hurdle once they reach the US mainland.

Cuban interest groups, such as the Cuban American National Foundation, have worked hard to preserve this identity. But younger Cuban Americans are increasingly thinking and acting more like other Latino populations, and the eventual deaths of Fidel and Raul Castro may further erode the GOP identification of this group.

Generation and Nativity A second key factor in ethnic-specific literature is generation status—most importantly, whether the subject is foreign-born or a US-born citizen. Immigration and naturalization, particularly for Mexicans but also for Dominicans and other Central and South Americans, is an exhausting and educative process that requires significant contact with the federal bureaucracy. Those seeking US citizenship through naturalization must merge their political socialization in the home country with their new experiences in the United States, and the difficult life circumstances faced by migrants on both sides of the border often come into play. Thus, we expected that generation—and in particular, status as a foreign-born citizen—would significantly affect the likelihood that Latinos would vote for Obama.

In the end, first-generation immigrants were the most likely to vote for Obama in 2008; there was a small but statistically significant increase in the probability of voting for McCain among second-, third-, and fourth-generation US-born Latinos. Again, we find that, across generations, a majority of Latinos voted for Obama, but there was a stair-step pattern to their voting: with each successive generation, McCain increased his vote share. The relatively older Cuban population may have had some impact on this outcome.

LATINO GROUP IDENTITY, SOLIDARITY, AND VOTE CHOICE

The literature on African Americans has posited an important effect of group consciousness or identity on both the formation of political preferences and the likelihood of acting on them.[14] Michael Dawson's concept of "linked fate" is the perception on the part of African Americans that their individual experiences are likely to be closely tied to those of others in their group. For instance, an individual who perceives that all African Americans are doing better and believes that she will thus do better too is exhibiting a sense of linked fate. Dawson goes on to identify the "black utility heuristic," meaning essentially that, because of their sense of linked fate, many African American voters make judgments about candidates and policies based on what they believe is good for the group overall.

Do Latinos have such a sense of group solidarity? And if they do, is it associated with their voting choices? An expanded ANES in 2008 afforded us a chance to directly test this possibility among Latinos. Pan-ethnic solidarity, as a political resource, is a more problematic notion for Latinos than it is for African Americans precisely because of the national-origin and generational variations we discussed earlier. It is not immediately clear that Mexicans, Salvadorans, Guatemalans, Dominicans, and Cubans should necessarily perceive one another as common members of a single group.[15] Latinos have some characteristics that tend toward commonality, including the Spanish language and their Roman Catholic tradition, history of Spanish colonialism, and increasingly overlapping media and entertainment worlds. On the other hand, their unique national origins, their unique racial histories, and their different experiences in the United States might undermine any sense that the group of all Latinos is (or should be) a unified political actor.[16]

The scholars who conducted the Latino National Political Survey (LNPS) in 1989 saw only limited evidence of pan-ethnic consciousness, a result suggesting that pan-ethnic identification was very unlikely to be much of a political resource. More recent work, however, has documented a substantial increase in pan-ethnic identification.[17] Moreover, there is growing evidence that expressions of pan-ethnic political commonality and linked fate are associated with increases in a variety of "desirable" political activities, including knowledge, sophistication, and propensity to register, to vote, and to engage in civic association.[18] Curiously, pan-ethnic identification is also associated with more positive assessments of associations between Latino interests and the interests of African Americans. By extension, then, we expected that stronger Latino pan-ethnic solidarity would be associated with votes for Obama.

And that in fact turned out to be the case. Based on our model estimates, moving from the lowest to the highest levels of self-reported group identity decreased the probability of a Latino citizen's vote for McCain and increased the likelihood—by over 13%—that that citizen's vote would go to Obama. Those Latinos who more strongly expressed a sense of commonality and linked fate with other Latinos were significantly more supportive of Barack Obama's candidacy. Solidarity among Latinos has a political effect.

RACIAL ATTITUDES AND THE 2008 LATINO VOTE

Finally, we examine once again the highly charged claims that Latino citizens are ambivalent about voting for black candidates, as articulated by the Clinton campaign's Latino pollster Sergio Bendixen. John McCain was unique among 2008 Republican candidates: his extensive contact with Latino community leaders and the perception of him as a Latino advocate on immigration made a GOP vote in his case (let alone a simple abstention) easier to swallow. If racial sentiment was strong, negative, and politically relevant for Latinos, that should have been borne out in the 2008 data.

Even if the trope of black-brown conflict does not seem to hold water, Latinos are not free of prejudice or discriminatory views toward African Americans. The racial histories of Latin American societies are varied and complex, and there is a literature suggesting that Latino views of African Americans are reminiscent of white views.[19] So the claim that racial attitudes might dampen Latino support for Obama was not actually that far removed from similar claims about white voters.

Comparisons between Hispanics and non-Hispanic whites on three different measures of racial sentiment are reported in Table 6.1. The first is a simply battery of stereotypes capturing old-fashioned, negative beliefs about African Americans. We use the comparison of the evaluations of blacks and whites on the lazy-to-hardworking scale and on the intelligent-to-unintelligent scale.[20] The second measure is a four-item index we call "racial resentment": designed to measure antiblack attitudes, this index uses ambiguously worded items that racially motivated respondents can respond to truthfully without fear of identifying themselves as prejudiced. Two of the items are sympathetic to African Americans, and two of the items are critical.[21] The third measure is the affect misattribution procedure (AMP), which estimates the unconscious presence of racial sentiment in a respondent's judgments.[22]

Latinos' mean responses on stereotype measures, the AMP, and the negatively valenced items in the racial resentment index are statistically indistinguishable from those expressed by non-Hispanic whites—that is, there is no meaningful difference in how the two groups score on average. The only distinctions are on the positively valenced items in the racial resentment index: Latinos are less likely than whites to reject these sympathetic statements, and this difference alone drives the difference we find in the overall index. Overall, it is fair to say that while Latino views may be slightly more generous toward their black fellow citizens, Latino beliefs about African Americans look a lot like white beliefs.

TABLE 6.1 Comparing Measures of Antiblack Affect or Racial Sentiments between White and Latino Respondents, 2008

	Latino	*White*	*Significance F-test*	*N Unweighted (white + Hispanic)*
Racial resentment	9.27	10.31	9.77	1,439
(range: 0 to 16)	(3.38)	(3.74)	p = 0.0018	
Positively valenced RR	3.91	4.87	23.26	1,451
(range: 0 to 8)	(2.17)	(2.21)	p = 0.0000	
Negatively valenced RR	5.35	5.44	0.23	1,443
(range: 0 to 8)	(2.12)	(2.08)	p = 0.6313	
Stereotype	0.82	0.79	0.13	1,464
(range: -2 to +2)	(1.09)	(0.97)	p = 0.7205	
AMP difference	0.16	0.17	0.20	1,325
(-1 to +1)	(0.31)	(0.31)	p = 0.7487	

Source: American National Election Study, 2008.
Note: RR = racial resentment; AMP = affect misattribution procedure.

The big question, however, was this: would Latinos vote based on racial attitudes in the same way that white voters did? Latinos may in fact hold stereotypic views of African Americans similar to those held by whites, but we expected that the effect of these views on their voting would be smaller or absent altogether. Research on Latino voter preferences has repeatedly shown an electorate that is more sophisticated than widely believed and that Latinos vote consistently with their issue preferences (on school vouchers, abortion, gun control, and other matters), are less swayed by symbolism than previously believed, and are not significantly affected by "social" appeals like anti-abortion and anti-gay policy positions.[23] However, did Latinos' racial sentiments cloud their judgment in 2008?

The results of our analysis clearly demonstrate that no black-brown divide existed in 2008. In other words, racial resentment, or animus, while not altogether absent among Latinos, did not play a meaningful role in shaping their preferences in the 2008 election. Among whites, antiblack attitudes were a significant predictor of voting against Obama,

FIGURE 6.5 Marginal Effects of Racial Resentment on Probability of Voting For Barack Obama in 2008, Latinos and Non-Hispanic Whites

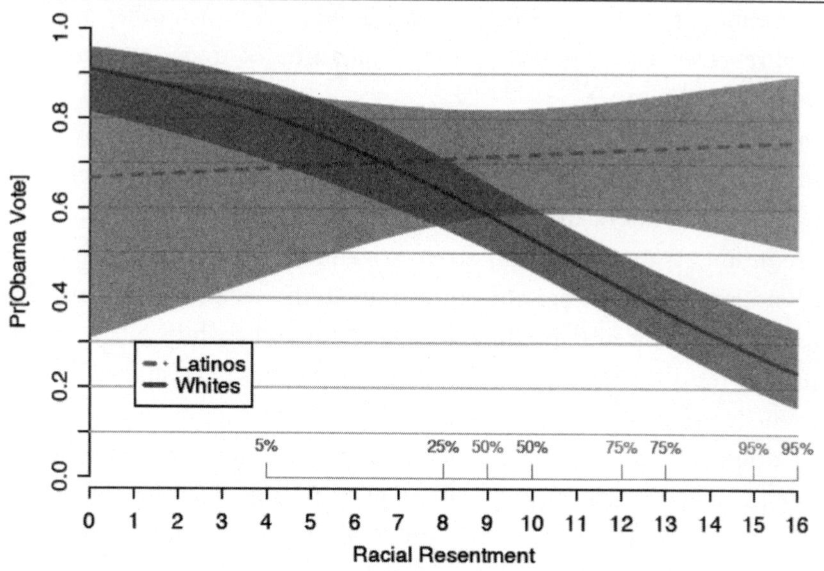

Source: Based on statistical estimations by Gary Segura and Ali Valenzuela.

so antiblack attitudes in this group signaled a decrease in the probability that they would vote for Obama that was quite robust. Just 25% of whites holding the most negative views on the racial resentment scale voted for Obama, compared with 90% among the least resentful. Yet for Latinos this variable appears to have carried no particular political salience—that is, it was not statistically significant in their vote choices with a black candidate running for president. This relationship is best depicted in the graph of predicted probabilities found in Figure 6.5. Although the slope is positive, it is not statistically significant, and in fact the confidence bounds widen noticeably around those with conservative racial beliefs.

We also addressed the topic of group relations and racial attitudes between Latinos and blacks by including a variable about antiblack attitudes to see whether this contributed to voting against Obama among Latinos, and also among whites. Unsurprisingly, Latinos who agreed that African Americans and Latinos have political and economic issues in common were significantly more likely to vote for Obama. Coupled with our earlier finding that Latinos with a high sense of shared linked fate were also more likely to support Obama, the data give us strong reason to reject the idea that Latinos and African Americans are at odds with each other over political representation, or that Latino racial attitudes are so extreme as to prevent a coalition.

There can be little doubt that racial sentiments continue to play a role in American elections, and 2008 was no exception. Despite the election of an African American president, the evidence remains strong that racial sentiments remain an important covariate of party attachment and, beyond, predicted support or opposition to the Obama candidacy and even strength of views on him. Obama's share of the white vote was considerably less than half, diminished vis-à-vis Kerry's in several states, and extremely small in a number of deep-south states.

Curiously, and in contrast to claims by pundits and scholars alike, the evidence suggests that racial thinking played a significantly weaker role in the voting decisions of Latinos in 2008 than in the voting decisions of whites. When weighed against other factors, racial sentiments do not appear to have entered into Latinos' evaluation of the Obama candidacy.

SO LATINOS SUPPORTED OBAMA—TO WHAT EFFECT?

Despite constituting the largest minority group in the United States, Latinos typically receive only superficial attention from candidates and the media when it comes to presidential politics. The peculiarities of the Electoral College, a state-level winner-take-all system, has led Latino politics research to focus on explaining Latinos' negligible influence on the outcomes of presidential elections. The political climate changed in 2008 when mainstream media outlets and campaigns, not just advocacy groups, began repeatedly to describe Latinos as the single most important voting bloc in presidential elections. For example, Arturo Vargas, head of the prominent National Association of Latino Elected and Appointed Officials (NALEO), bluntly proclaimed in a 2007 op-ed, "Latino voters will decide the 2008 election. The Latino vote is positioned as the power punch that may deliver the knockout blow in 2008."

The noted Latino politics expert Rodolfo de la Garza of Columbia University vehemently countered this narrative and related media hype, however, by arguing that "the Latino vote is completely irrelevant. The myth was created by Latino leaders who wanted to convince politicians nationally about how important Latinos were."[24] Latino voters were heavily concentrated in uncompetitive states such as California, Texas, and New York, de la Garza pointed out, and too small in number to matter in contested states.[25] These diametrically opposed interpretations from recognized experts would leave observers and scholars puzzled in 2008.

The truth is that it is difficult in presidential elections, if not impossible, for any single group of voters to claim a unique influence in determining the outcome. Despite this difficulty, interest groups, advocates, the media, and scholars spend considerable time debating afterwards whether one group or another tipped the scales. In 2000 it was argued at length that votes for the independent candidate Ralph Nader "cost" Vice President Al Gore the election and that "soccer moms" ensured a Bush victory.[26] In 2004 it was repeatedly said that his gains among Latinos influenced Bush's reelection and that evangelical "values" voters turned out in great numbers to ban marriage for same-sex couples and secure Bush's second term.[27] During the 2008 presidential contest, it was the turn of the Latino vote, which received more hype than ever. Latinos' strong preference for Hillary Clinton during the Democratic primary fed speculation that Latinos could make or break the election. The Associated Press reported—and others agreed—that low Latino support for Obama could doom him in key states, whereas large gains in the Latino vote could lead to a Democratic victory in Republican-leaning states such as Florida, Nevada, and Colorado.

On the one hand, it is true that the Latino electorate cannot meet the empirical threshold necessary to back up claims that they single-handedly *determined* Obama's victory. The fact that Obama defeated John McCain by 365 to 173 in the Electoral College doesn't suggest that it was a close contest. And in any event, the "did the [fill in the blank] group cast the deciding vote?" question is shortsighted—very few segments of the electorate could meet such a daunting standard of influence. Moreover, there is more than one way to measure group influence in an election. Post-election tallies are informative, but they can be too narrow an interpretation of "influence." All this being the case, and despite Obama's significant margin of victory, we argue that Latino voters were still quite influential throughout the campaign, from the drawn-out primary to Tuesday, November 4, 2008.

We use the 2008 election here as a basis for a new framework to evaluate Latino influence beyond vote tallies. We have identified three dimensions to use in measuring Latino influence in electoral politics:

1. *Demographics:* Measured as coethnic group size and growth rate in the state
2. *Electoral volatility:* Specifically, changes in registration rates, partisan preference, or turnout compared to prior contests
3. *Mobilization:* Measured as the media coverage and resources devoted to courting Latino votes

Using these three broad categories, we assess a wide array of publicly available data to create an overall index of Latino influence in each of the fifty states. This approach moves beyond the zero-sum definitions of political clout that neglect these consequential realms of influence.

A newly mobilized or fast-growing electorate can alter the issue agendas of campaigns and debates, cause campaigns to divert resources from other groups, make formerly safe states competitive and competitive states safe, reshape the platforms on which nominees run, and even alter the electoral behavior of *other* groups in society.

In the 2008 presidential contest, fourteen states were clearly identified as swing states that would determine the election outcome, leaving thirty-six states, because of their lopsided partisan leanings, in the "unimportant" category. On election day 2008, 120 million votes were cast, and of those, 40 million came from the fourteen battleground states—accounting for 33% of all votes. So it should come as no surprise that a majority of all voters—white, black, Latino, Asian—reside in noncompetitive states.

Our analysis shows that Latinos were very influential in seven swing states: Florida, Nevada, New Mexico, Colorado, Virginia, North Carolina, and Indiana. Further, we find evidence of extensive Latino mobilization, though it led to a lesser overall impact, in Arizona, Ohio, California, Texas, Missouri, and Minnesota, foreshadowing a greater degree of influence in these six states in 2012 and beyond.

Just four years earlier, Republican president George W. Bush had won close to 40% of the Latino vote overall, as well as winning the Latino-heavy states of New Mexico, Colorado, Nevada, and Florida. For Obama to win in 2008, some or all of those states had to swing, and the Latino vote was vital.

CAN "GROUPS" REALLY INFLUENCE PRESIDENTIAL ELECTIONS?

Ordinarily, the unique structure of presidential elections, from primaries to the general election, diminishes mass influence on electoral outcomes. Most voters reside in noncompetitive general election states, and the fact that very few minorities reside in early primary states limits their ability to influence the early stages of presidential politics. But 2008 was different: Latino influence was palpable well before the first contest of the primary season took place. In 2004 and 2008, George W. Bush received a well-publicized, slightly higher-than-average share of the Latino vote.[28] The actual change in the Latino preference for Republicans was quite small substantively: Bush's receipt of about 7% more of the vote than usual from 8% of the electorate made a difference of just 0.56% in November 2004. But in an era of close presidential elections, half a percent was enough to motivate the Democratic Party to alter the primary calendar to include a Latino-influence state early in the season. Nevada was the third state to host a Democratic nominating contest. Including this Western state with a growing Latino electorate early in the process was a strategic decision. The party wanted to shore up Latino support, which they feared was softening, and enable Latinos to have more influence in determining the party nominee. These changes to the primary election calendar were the catalyst for a larger Latino influence in the general election as many competitive Democratic contests continued to highlight the Latino vote as a key demographic.[29] When the general election campaign season arrived, the record turnout in the primaries, in addition to their experience with

Latino electorates in their home states, made both the Obama and McCain camps keenly aware of the Latino vote.

It is a truism that turnout peaks when elections are decided by a small margin.[30] It stands to reason, then, that the political environment should be evaluated *prior* to election day so as to identify the factors that will contribute to creating the perception of a competitive race. States can be characterized as competitive when certain conditions apply, foremost among them being: pre-election polls indicating a very close race; media reports framing the closeness of the contest as important to the outcome; and candidates spending millions on advertisements and voter outreach in the state. When these conditions hold in a state, its voters are influential because the political environment is competitive. Such conditions are set well before a single ballot is cast.

Once the votes are tallied, however, even seemingly competitive contests may yield lopsided margins, for a variety of reasons. One party may have made a stronger outreach effort, for example, or conducted a superior get-out-the-vote drive. So even if the election result appears noncompetitive, the state may continue to be important during the actual campaign because of the significant resources and attention invested there.

That is why simple post-election tallies miss the real impact that a group has on election outcomes during the weeks and months of the campaign. Nevada exemplified this impact in 2008. Exactly two weeks before the election, the Politico/Insider Advantage poll put Nevada at 47% Obama, 47% McCain, and 6% undecided. The campaigns spent $13 million on television advertising alone in the state, which was inundated with television and radio ads, candidate appearances and events, and voter outreach efforts.[31] Ultimately, Obama won Nevada by twelve points, with an estimated 76% vote from Latinos, up from 60% for Kerry in 2004. This is Latino influence, whichever way we want to count it.

Voter traits and trends, of course, are standard measures of influence, but there is more to deciding whether a given group is influencing the political landscape. Voters, the media, and campaigns tell each other how close a race has become. Campaigns rely heavily on polling and are especially attuned to short-term, recent trends in turnout, partisanship, margins of victory, voter registration, and demographic composition. Using this information, they decide where to spend money and how best to get the vote out. National and regional media communicate to both voters and campaigns the closeness of the race and the importance of particular issues and groups of voters. When voters see these reports on how close the election is, the increasing attention and excitement has been shown to affect turnout.[32]

In this vein, news stories that highlight the importance of the Latino vote convey to campaign staffs and the broader electorate the importance of Latinos in creating statewide competitiveness and winning coalitions. Online media provided another unique contribution to assessing and publicizing campaign competitiveness in 2008. Three sites—FiveThirtyEight.com, Pollster.com, and RealClearPolitics.com—developed a national following for their regularly updated (at weekly and daily intervals), empirically derived predictions of state-by-state election outcomes, and FiveThirtyEight.com's Nate Silver even became a star eventually. National, state, and local news outlets regularly sourced the "RCP average" and the "538 prediction," based on the survey and poll results that were posted and analyzed by both websites, as authoritative measures of national and state-level campaign competitiveness in the weeks leading up to election day.

Of course, voters are also influenced by direct mobilization: television, print and radio advertising, mailers, phone calls, and online mobilization efforts signal to voters that their state is in play.[33] Latino voters are no exception, though as we pointed out in Chapter 4, they are less likely than other groups to be the target of outreach, particularly from parties and candidates. A spate of recent research points to the effectiveness of targeted campaign appeals to Latinos.[34]

The Obama campaign brought peer-level innovation to online mobilization and incorporated this technology into unique Latino outreach strategies already in place.[35] As anyone who ever contacted the 2008 Obama campaign knows, it revolutionized the use of electronic communication and social media for political purposes. The campaign website facilitated extensive contact in two directions: (1) directly from the campaign to voters, and (2) voter to voter. Those who provided contact information to the campaign regularly received text messages and emails encouraging their participation (as voters, contributors, or volunteers) in the primary and general elections, which were consistently described as "tight races" and "tough battles." Individuals were also encouraged to self-identify with multiple online peer groups (for example, "Latinos for Obama," "Ohioans for Obama," or "Obama-mamas"), each of which had its own Web-based organizational arm. Every one of these organizations conducted outreach activities aimed exclusively at its particular affinity group in key states.

As we discussed earlier, it is often easier to get Latinos mobilized by resorting to friends and family rather than spokespeople, famous or otherwise. For average Latino voters—many of whom are never contacted at all by candidates or parties—making it easier for them to interact repeatedly with influential familiars and to be contacted by them was an important and potentially pivotal strategy shift.

SÍ SE PUEDE? MEASURES OF LATINO INFLUENCE IN 2008

In the aftermath of Obama's victory, many efforts were made to assess the relevance of the Latino vote. Using nothing more than post-election tallies to evaluate whether the Latino vote caused a state to be won or lost, analysts found the Latino influence to be weak. In addition, Obama had won many states by a wider margin than expected, and that made it difficult to find the math proving that Latinos cast the deciding ballots. In our own assessment, we find strong and consistent evidence across our three key areas—group size, electoral patterns, and mobilization—that Latinos in key states did influence the 2008 election. Further, our data may foreshadow which states will merit the attention of pundits down the road as the Latino influence grows in new regions and new states (two strong candidates being Montana and Georgia).

The traditional post-hoc election result tally is one of the measures of influence cited by de la Garza and DeSipio in their quadrennial analysis of the Latino vote in presidential elections, though they (correctly) dismiss it as too unrealistic.[36] Latinos may have influenced the 2008 election if the margin they provided for the winner was larger than the overall margin of victory. In other words, if no Latino had voted, would Obama have won?

TABLE 6.2 Did Latino Votes Provide the Margin of Victory in the 2008 Election?

	Latino Vote			*Real Election Vote Counts*			*Latino Votes Cast*		
	BO	*JM*	*%*	*BO*	*JM*	*Margin*	*BO*	*JM*	*Latino Margin*
North Carolina	72	25	3	2,142,651	2,128,474	**14,177**	92,256	32,033	**60,223**
Indiana	77	23	4	1,374,039	1,345,648	**28,391**	83,766	25,021	**58,745**
New Mexico	69	30	41	472,422	346,832	**125,590**	231,767	100,768	**130,999**
Nevada	76	22	15	533,736	412,827	120,909	107,908	31,237	76,672
Florida	57	42	14	4,282,074	4,045,624	236,450	664,550	489,669	174,882
Colorado	61	38	13	1,288,576	1,073,589	214,987	187,320	116,691	70,629
Ohio[a]	72	25	4	2,933,388	2,674,491	258,897	161,507	56,079	105,428
Virginia	65	34	5	1,959,532	1,725,005	234,527	119,747	62,637	57,110
New Jersey	78	21	9	2,215,422	1,613,207	602,215	268,770	72,361	196,409
Pennsylvania	72	28	4	3,276,363	2,655,885	620,478	170,849	66,441	104,408
Michigan	64	33	3	2,872,579	2,048,639	823,940	94,487	48,720	45,767
California	74	23	18	8,274,473	5,011,781	3,262,692	1,769,729	550,051	1,219,678

Note: BO = Barack Obama and JM = John McCain. Electoral outcomes are from statement of vote in each state. Latino estimates are based on exit poll estimates multiplied by total votes cast.

a. Because the North Carolina and Ohio state polls are not available, the national average from the Latino Decisions poll has been substituted for each.

Looking at Table 6.2, we find three instances in which the overall state victory margin for Obama was smaller than the vote margin provided to him by Latinos alone. By this crude measure, it is possible to argue that Latinos directly influenced the election results in North Carolina, Indiana, and New Mexico.

However, this measure dismisses the influence that Latinos probably had in other states, such as Nevada, Florida, and Colorado, where the overall victory margin was too great for Latinos alone to have provided it. This type of analysis is problematic for several reasons. First, it offers no leverage in predictive research questions about the conditions prior to election day and about the states that will matter because it is based solely on tallies of election results. Second, it ignores the states where there may have been Latino influence during the campaign through outreach, advertising, or mobilization but the election results do not back this up. Third, this analysis may artificially categorize a state as an "influence" state just because the overall margin was razor-thin there. As we have noted, it is more than possible for a state to be perceived as a close contest but to be deemed noncompetitive after the votes are counted.

Group Size and Growth

A prerequisite for a group to have influence is that it meets a minimum group size and, preferably, it should be cohesive or mobilized. If the presidential election in Maine or North Dakota is very close, it is impossible for Latinos to influence the outcome because their group size is too small in those states and it's not growing rapidly. Thus, a simple starting point for any analysis of a minority group's influence is to assess the share of all registered voters that it represents. Data from the 2006 Current Population Survey, which provide the best estimate for Latino percentages among registered voters for all fifty states, show a range from a low of 0.1% in Maine to a high of 30.4% in New Mexico. In particular, it would be very difficult to ever witness Latino influence in a statewide election in a state that is less than 2% Latino among registered voters. According to the CPS data, twenty-five states were 2% or less Latino among citizens registered to vote in 2006. The patterns depicted in Figure 6.6 are predictable and consistent with Latino population figures that are now well

FIGURE 6.6 Percentage Latino among Registered Voters, 2006

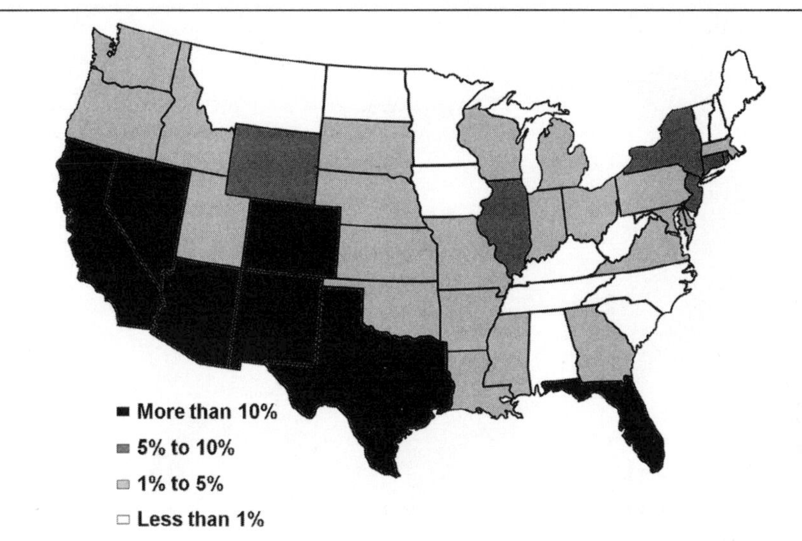

known. States in the Southwest and the Mountain West have significant Latino registered-voter populations, as do Florida and some states in the Northeast.

In addition to group size, the growth rate among registered voters is particularly important as a gauge of influence. Figure 6.7 reports the change in the Latino-to-white voter registration share over an eight-year period, 1998 to 2006. This estimate gives us a sense of the absolute gains in Latino voter presence vis-à-vis the largest group in the state (whites). The states depicted in lighter shading reported little to no change in the Latino-to-white comparison. That is, if Latinos were 10% of all registered voters in 1998, they still made up about 10% of registered voters in 2006. In contrast, the states depicted in darker shades experienced accelerated Latino registration growth. For example, in 1998 the Nevada electorate was 86% white and 5% Latino; by 2006 that had changed to 75% white and 10% Latino, resulting in an eleven-point difference for whites and a positive five-point change for Latinos and yielding a net increase for Latinos of +16. Other states, such as Wyoming, Missouri, Ohio, Maryland, and Massachusetts also witnessed a net increase in registered Latino voters of over 7%. These sizable shifts in ethnic composition within the electorate are remarkable because they occurred in less than a decade.

FIGURE 6.7 The Growth in Latino Registration Relative to White Registration, 1998–2006

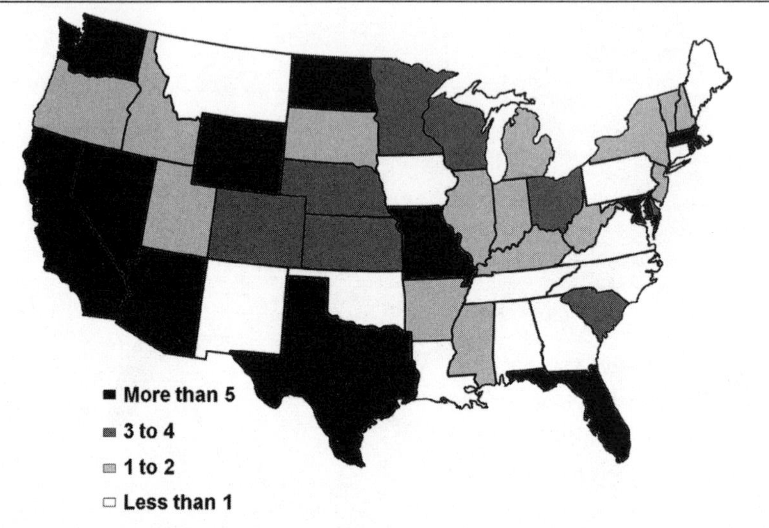

Of course, we would expect Latinos to exert some influence where they are a sizable share of the population. They may also have influence in states where they are relatively small in number but are becoming a rapidly increasing share of the electorate, signaling the demography of the future voting public. Growth measures alone may miss the influence of Latino voters in places where there is a large and relatively stable share of Latinos in the electorate. New Mexico is a case in point: the growth in the Latino percentage of the population between 1998 and 2006 is unremarkable, but nonetheless nearly one voter in three in New Mexico is Latino, and the state has a long history of electing Latinos to office, including the US Senate and the governor's office. Indeed, the last two governors of New Mexico have been Latino—former Democratic governor Bill Richardson and the current governor, Susana Martinez, a Republican. So it is the combination of population size and growth rate that more realistically captures a group's opportunity for influence in a state election.

Electoral Patterns and Volatility

For a group to demonstrate electoral influence, election-specific factors are of obvious importance. Here we focus on two: the degree of voting

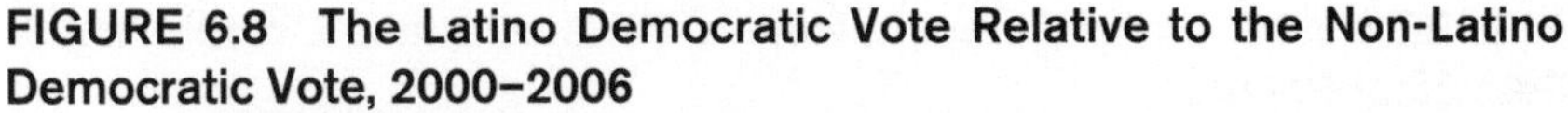

FIGURE 6.8 The Latino Democratic Vote Relative to the Non-Latino Democratic Vote, 2000–2006

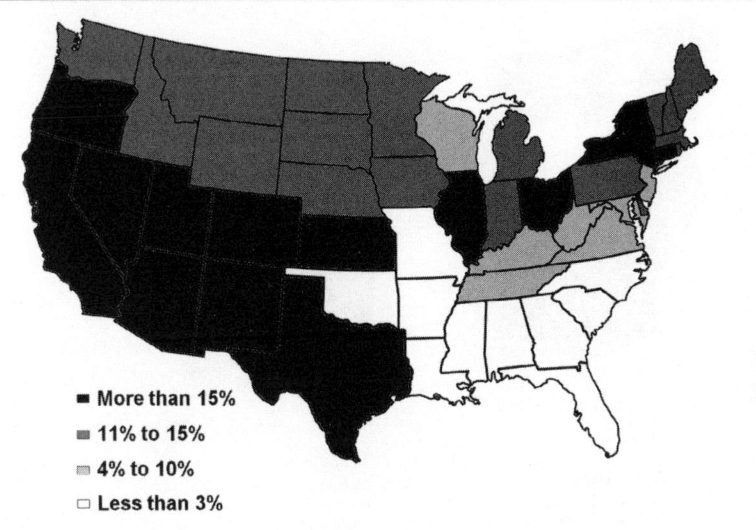

cohesiveness among Latinos, and the degree of expected competitiveness of the state election.

Voting cohesiveness is measured as the average Democratic vote among Latinos from 2000 to 2006 minus the average Democratic vote among non-Latinos. For Latinos to have influenced a state's election, they ought to have demonstrated somewhat different voting patterns than non-Latinos in the state. Using the National Election Pool (NEP) state polls for the 2000, 2002, 2004, and 2006 elections, we created a measure for average Democratic vote for Latinos and non-Latinos by state. Figure 6.8 shows the Latino Democratic vote differential for all states. States shaded dark are those where Latinos vote much more consistently Democratic than do non-Latinos in the state, while states shaded lighter are those where Latinos and non-Latinos demonstrate very similar partisan vote preferences. Latinos tend to vote more Democratic than non-Latinos do throughout the United States, and this is most pronounced in the Southwest and Mountain West, where four states—Texas, Arizona, Colorado, and Utah—have a Latino population that is about twenty points more Democratic. There is a notable pattern of Democratic vote cohesion among Latinos throughout the entire West.

FIGURE 6.9 Average Competitiveness Level by State, October 2008: Real Clear Politics

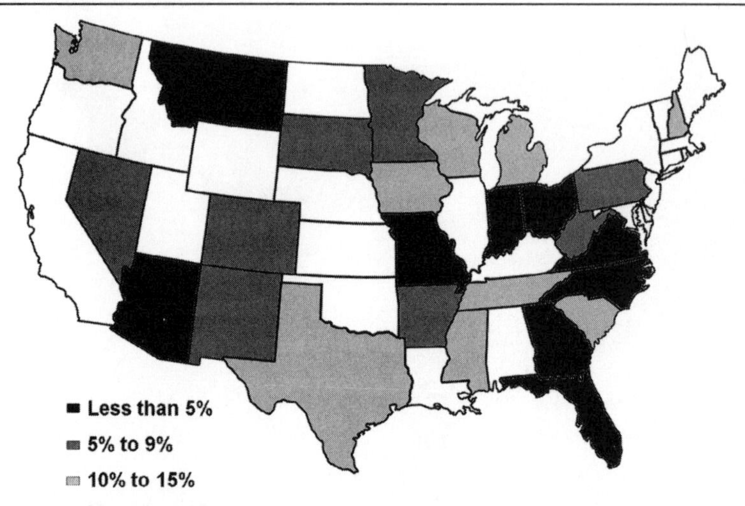

The second important piece of electoral information is the expected competitiveness in the state election. This is one of the most important indicators of group influence. Without a doubt, it is much more difficult—though not impossible—to influence an election in a state that is completely uncompetitive. Although it is worth pointing out that some states, like California, are uncompetitive largely *because* Latinos are influential.

However, the traditional measure of looking to post-election results is not a complete guide to competitiveness. A group has influence, not after the election, but during the active campaign, most likely in the last thirty days. We took the average poll rating one month before the election from Real Clear Politics' state poll average in 2008.

The map in Figure 6.9 is familiar to most readers: it shows the anticipated closeness of the 2008 presidential election in each state. The most darkly shaded states were those with very close pre-election poll averages, while the very lightly shaded states were not expected to be close at all. Coupled with the data reported in Figure 6.8, it is possible to sort out the states with more or less Latino influence. For example, a state like Ohio was expected to be very competitive, and it had a Latino electorate that voted considerably more Democratic.

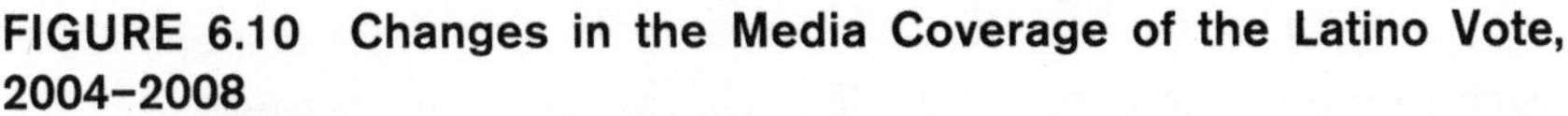

FIGURE 6.10 Changes in the Media Coverage of the Latino Vote, 2004–2008

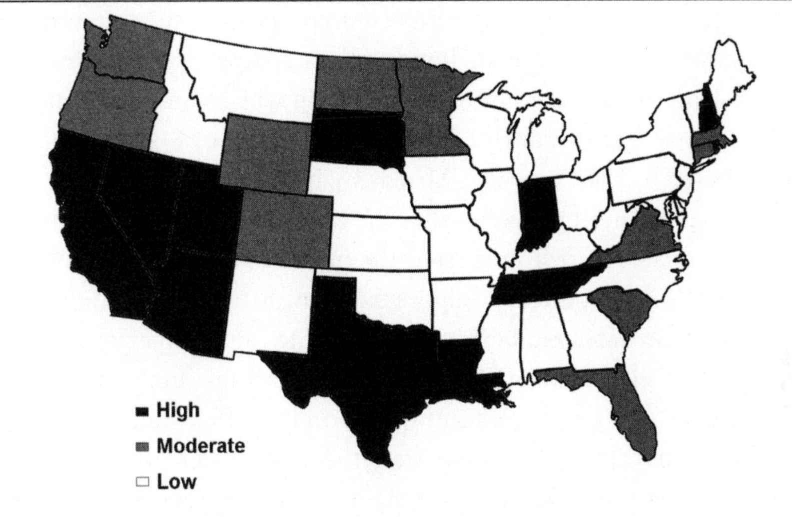

As we add in additional factors, such as those collected in Figures 6.6 and 6.7, the overall influence story begins to take shape. We turn next to the last piece of this puzzle: the components of mobilization.

MOBILIZATION AND RESOURCES

The final set of criteria that we believe to be important is how a campaign engages—or fails to engage—the Latino community. The campaign itself must have taken note of Latinos as a potential influence group. That is, as the candidate campaigns and the media covers the campaign, both must have paid attention to the Latino vote as a crucial bloc. We assess this by measuring three factors: the change in media coverage of the Latino vote; the campaign ad buys targeting Latinos; and the campaign's ethnic mobilization. Using Lexis-Nexis content data on the Latino vote and the 2004 and 2008 presidential elections, we amassed data on both the rate of news stories on the Latino vote and the change in this rate from 2004. These data are normalized and combined in Figure 6.10. The darker states are those where media coverage of Latino voters increased; as the map shows, almost every state saw a steady increase in the coverage of the Latino vote during the presidential campaign.

Spanish-language television ads are an easily collectable proxy for outreach to the Latino community. TV ads are important because they are costly; the decision to spend finite resources on the Latino community would have emerged from an important campaign calculus. However, Spanish-language ads are not the only way in which campaigns targeted Latino voters. Unfortunately, data on the content of English-language ads, collected by the Campaign Media Analysis Group (CMAG) project, are not available until two years after the election. In contrast, Spanish ad data are available in real time from the public disclosures on campaign spending. We do not include a figure on Spanish TV ad expenditures because only four states ran both Obama and McCain campaign ads: Florida, Nevada, Colorado, and New Mexico. The fact that none of the other states had such ads puts significant weight on these four states.

In addition to TV ad spending, we gathered data on Latino group mobilization by the presidential campaigns. Although data were available only from the Obama campaign, they were very rich. Again, for each state we collected the number of members of Latinos for Obama groups, and also the amount of money raised by these groups, both normalized over the state's total Latino registered voter population. In Figure 6.11, we map the Obama campaign's Latino mobilization. Before we can accept or dismiss the claim that Latinos had influence in a particular state, we should assess the degree to which they were mobilized. For example, Figure 6.11 shows that Latino mobilization by the Obama campaign in 2008 was fairly strong in Virginia, North Carolina, Indiana, and Nevada. It also shows that Latinos in Missouri and Arizona were less likely to be mobilized by the Obama campaign; Obama narrowly lost these two states, but might have won them had his campaign engaged in stronger Latino mobilization. Latino activity was brisk in noncompetitive states like Illinois, New York, and Texas. The online participation and monetary contributions of Latinos in these states especially matter to the political elites and fund-raisers, irrespective of the electoral competitiveness of their state.

We can depict Latino influence by combining all of these data points into a single model. Drawing on these three categories, we include group size and growth, electoral volatility, and mobilization to explain Latino

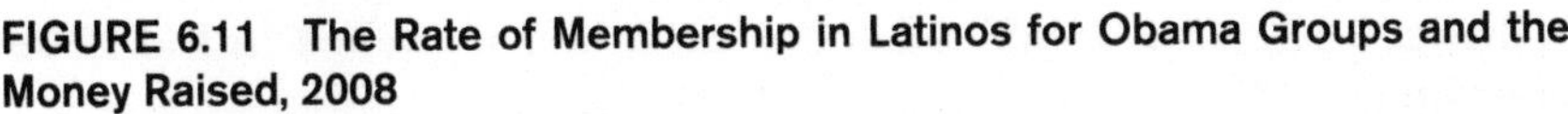

FIGURE 6.11 The Rate of Membership in Latinos for Obama Groups and the Money Raised, 2008

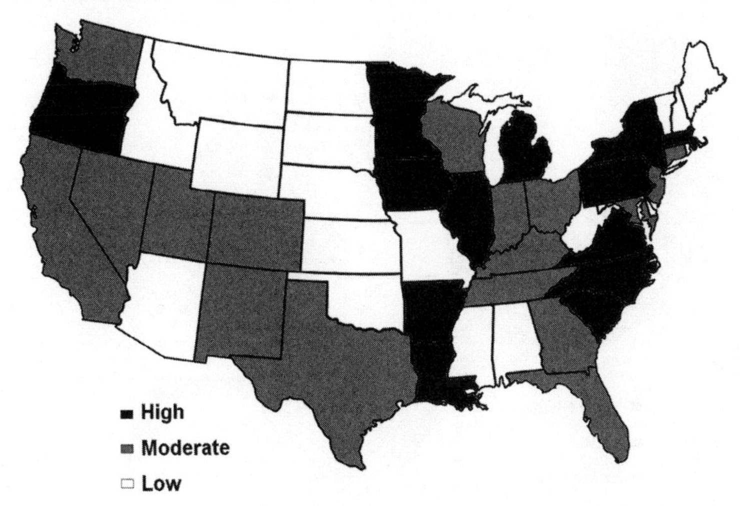

influence in the 2008 election. The final Latino influence map (Figure 6.12) combines all prior metrics. The darker states had higher Latino influence composite scores, while states that are white had practically no Latino influence. Theoretically, a state with the absolute strongest Latino political influence meets the following conditions: it has a large Latino population, rapid growth in Latino voter registration, record increased rates of partisan cohesiveness compared to non-Latinos, a competitive electoral environment, media focus on the Latino vote, and extensive campaign outreach to and mobilization of Latinos. Anecdotally, the darkest states on the map seemed to have had the greatest Latino influence: Florida, Nevada, Colorado, and New Mexico. Texas and Arizona also score high because on a number of metrics they demonstrated considerable Latino influence; however, they did lack a key element in 2008, namely, competitiveness and/or campaign outreach. The states shaded gray matched our expectations: Virginia, Indiana, and Ohio all demonstrated high Latino influence in 2008. Missouri, Minnesota, California, and Washington were also Latino-influence states, but they did not score consistently high across all dimensions.

FIGURE 6.12 The Combined Index of Latino Influence in the 2008 Election

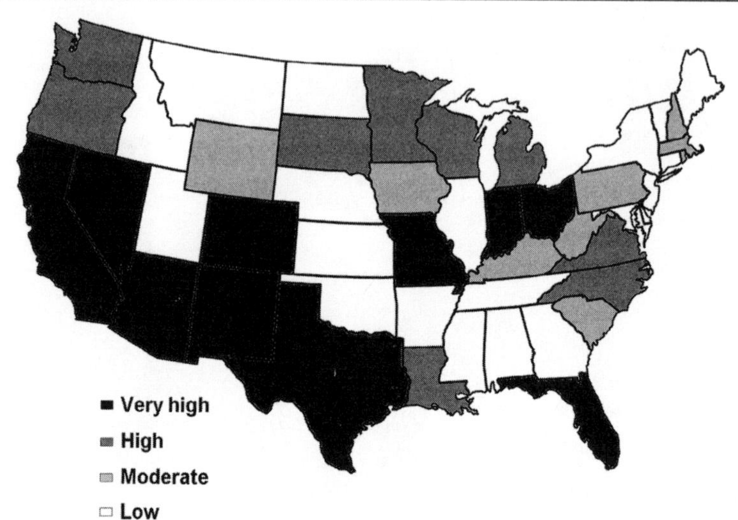

Source: Map created by the authors based on Index of Latino Influence.

FINAL ANALYSIS: THE INFLUENCE OF LATINOS ON THE 2008 ELECTION

Our findings indicate that both the Vargas and de la Garza claims about Latino voter influence in 2008, mentioned at the outset of this chapter, are overstated. The Latino vote did not deliver the power punch in what became a landslide victory for Obama, but Latinos were far from irrelevant. Latino influence was greatest in Nevada and Florida, two of the most hyped battleground states; both flipped from Republican to Democrat from 2004 to 2008.

No matter what metric we use, our analyses demonstrate that Latinos, like any other group, have an influence that is not absolute but rather tempered by a combination of factors. Latinos alone cannot be credited for the Obama victory—or for the two prior Bush wins for that matter. At the same time, discounting the entire Latino electorate as categorically irrelevant to the outcome in 2008 is a misguided generality that overlooks a measureable influence that was critical to constructing a winning coalition in specific states.

Thinking about political influence in broad terms allows us to understand more about racial and ethnic dynamics at the mass and elite levels, and it highlights the relevant trends that address substantive questions regarding the role of Latinos in presidential politics. Importantly, the approach we outline and demonstrate here can be applied in different types of elections and to other segments of the electorate. This framework attends to factors that are theoretically relevant to an increasingly diverse electorate and will be useful over the long term as the racial and ethnic politics research develops.

As we look back on the 2008 election, we now have a clearer vision of whether and where Latinos had an effect. The Iraq War and the economic meltdown of 2008 dominated the issue agenda, and Latinos had little interest in what John McCain had to sell on those two issues, despite his long-standing support for immigration reform. Though the two-party vote among Latinos varied by a number of key factors, including national origin and generation, it is clear that most Latinos—and nearly all Latinos with a strong attachment to Latino pan-ethnic identity—voted for Barack Obama. Indeed, the attraction to Obama was so powerful that Latino Democrats demonstrated lockstep unity while many Latino Republicans strayed away from the fold to vote for the Illinois senator.

Dozens of academic research studies have been published on the sole topic of racial attitudes and voting in 2008. Some political science journals have devoted entire symposia issues to this issue, and their papers have empirically proven that racial attitudes had a noticeable effect in 2008. Efforts to isolate a racial effect among Latinos, however, have yielded little evidence of Latino reluctance to vote for black candidates. Beyond the high level of Latino support for Obama in November 2008, any variation in expressions of racial resentment appears to have been unrelated to voter choice—in clear contradistinction to the findings for non-Hispanic whites.

Obama began his presidency with strong enthusiasm from the Latino electorate. Could he keep it?

Chapter 7

WHAT THE GOP VICTORY IN 2010 HAS TO SAY ABOUT LATINO POLITICAL POWER

The story of the 2010 midterm election was dominated by the Tea Party, the Affordable Care Act (ACA), and the sweeping Republican victory that emerged. The GOP took control of the House of Representatives and numerous state legislatures and gubernatorial offices in a variety of states, including Michigan, Wisconsin, Ohio, Florida, and Pennsylvania, as well as in heavily Latino states like New Mexico and Nevada. On the face of it, the 2010 election would appear to refute our central claim—that given the current distribution of policy and party preferences and the issue agenda of the GOP, Latino population growth is moving the country relentlessly toward the Democrats and their candidates. The results from 2010 compared to those from 2006 would appear to make this claim for Latino electoral influence specious on its face. Political observers would be quick to suggest that Latino voters didn't make a difference in 2010.

They'd be wrong.

First, in 2010 the issue of immigration and the GOP attempts to legislate against immigrants rose to become a primary yardstick—if not *the* primary yardstick—whereby Latinos judged the GOP. The passage of SB

1070 set into motion the immigration dynamic that defines the Latino-GOP relationship to this day. (We cover this relationship in much greater detail in Chapters 9 and 10.)

Second, the results of the 2010 election, rather than refuting our claims regarding demography, illustrate its increasing importance. The 2010 election varied little from elections before or since in how the electorate responded to the parties. The GOP was able to drive up its share of the vote among whites, while the standard decline in turnout by left-leaning voters, seen in all midterm elections, made that white vote share more determinative.

Finally, Latino voters and the issue of immigration were of pivotal importance in saving the Senate for the Democrats and in other significant elections. In short, 2010 would have been a lot worse for the Democrats without the Latino effect, from the reelection of Senate Majority Leader Harry Reid of Nevada to the election of Governor Jerry Brown in California.

Rather than demonstrating the residual weakness of the Latino voting bloc (and by extension, our argument), the 2010 results laid the groundwork for Latinos' historic contributions in 2012—and the immigration debate in the 113th Congress.

THE WARM-UP

Before we examine 2010 up close and begin to tell the immigration story—which will be an almost constant subtext for the remainder of the book—we must ask an obvious question: why was immigration almost wholly missing from the story of 2008? The answer is easy: the two major-party candidates (and Obama's primary rival Hillary Clinton) all held basically the same views on immigration.

More specifically, however, the complete absence of immigration from the 2008 general election was a cross-aisle conspiracy of silence, if you will. John McCain's support of comprehensive immigration reform in the US Senate in 2007 very nearly derailed his entire presidential campaign. By midsummer in 2007, McCain's fund-raising was dried up and he was laying off staff. Anti-immigrant rhetoric was ramping up strongly in the GOP at that time, and McCain, long a champion of immigration reform, was on the wrong side within his own party. By the time he made it through to the general election, he had no incentive to raise immigration as an issue.

Why didn't Obama raise it, then, if the issue had the potential to create such mischief for his opponent? Then-senator Obama believed that immigration was a losing issue for Democrats, and this position was an article of faith among his advisers, Jim Messina, David Plouffe, and David Axelrod. They saw lots of negatives and little upside in engaging in an immigration debate. Though Obama did address immigration during the campaign when asked about it, immigration was not a focus of his message, and it played little role in his public outreach. Immigration was the great unspoken issue in the 2008 general election.

Midterm elections are different from general elections: they are won on party core constituents, not on the part-time voters and ticket-splitters—those with less interest in the political system, weak attachment to either party, and low levels of information—who occasionally turn up for presidential elections but almost never for midterms. The midterm demobilization of the president's electoral coalition is almost an American tradition.

As the Democrats looked ahead to the 2010 election, they realized that on almost every key issue the president had forsaken a core constituency, either through inaction or in the process of trying to attract and retain moderate and independent voters. Gay and lesbian activists had organized a boycott of fund-raising by the Democratic National Committee (DNC) and Organizing For Action (OFA) because of the president's inaction on LGBT legislative priorities. Organized labor had worked tirelessly for the Obama candidacy in hopes of achieving a more pro-labor regime, including card-check union organizing elections. What they got for their efforts was a tax on union-quality health care plans. Financial reform advocates were still waiting for the first perp-walk of Wall Street charlatans (who continued to receive taxpayer-subsidized bonuses over little or no White House objection). Civil libertarians got no torture trials or indictments for transgressions of the previous administration associated with the wars in Iraq and Afghanistan and the "war on terror" (and none ever appeared), and the prison at Guantánamo remained open. The Democratic base was, to say the least, restless in 2010.

For Latinos, the promise of immigration reform—signaled during the campaign for action during the administration's first year, then before the midterm election—was as yet unfulfilled. Instead, stepped-up enforcement by the border patrol, including sweeps and raids that targeted working mothers and fathers rather than employers and criminals, were justified with the claim that this was the price of buy-in by those on the right for comprehensive immigration reform. In 2014, as we write this, the same logic is in place.

The collective effect of this rightward drift and frequent inaction by the Obama administration was a shocking enthusiasm gap between Democrats and Republicans, which was documented widely in the blogosphere and elsewhere. Latinos were no exception. When Latino Decisions attempted to estimate this effect among Latinos in a March 2010 poll, we found Latino enthusiasm for voting in an upcoming election at an all-time low.

In 2006, when Republicans held the White House, the Senate, and the House and immigration marches mobilized millions of Latinos around the country, interest in the midterm elections was at record levels (Figure 7.1). Four years later, many Latino voters saw no urgent need to turn out. In an April 2006 Latino Policy Coalition survey (which we helped write), 77% of Latino registered voters stated that they were certain to vote, a measure of enthusiasm that grew by September 2006 to 89% who were determined to vote. By that November, about 60% actually voted. In 2008 enthusiasm was higher, but that's generally true in presidential election years.

Compare those numbers to March 2010, when just 49% of Latino registered voters said that they were very enthusiastic about voting. Since 60% of Latinos turned out in 2006, when their self-reported enthusiasm was 77%, what would that spell for 2010 if the starting point for enthusiasm was only 49%?

The low enthusiasm for voting mirrored the low levels of excitement about both the Democratic and Republican Parties. When party members were asked how their excitement for their party had changed since January 2009, neither party had close to majority excitement (see Figure 7.2).

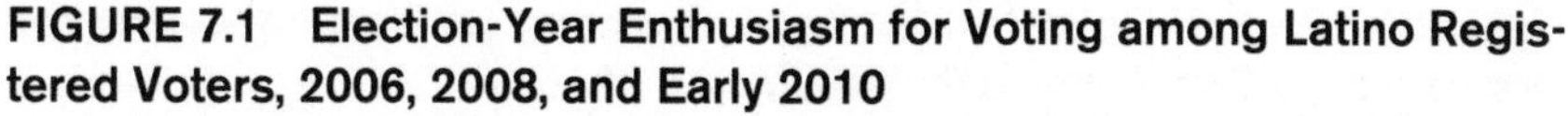

FIGURE 7.1 Election-Year Enthusiasm for Voting among Latino Registered Voters, 2006, 2008, and Early 2010

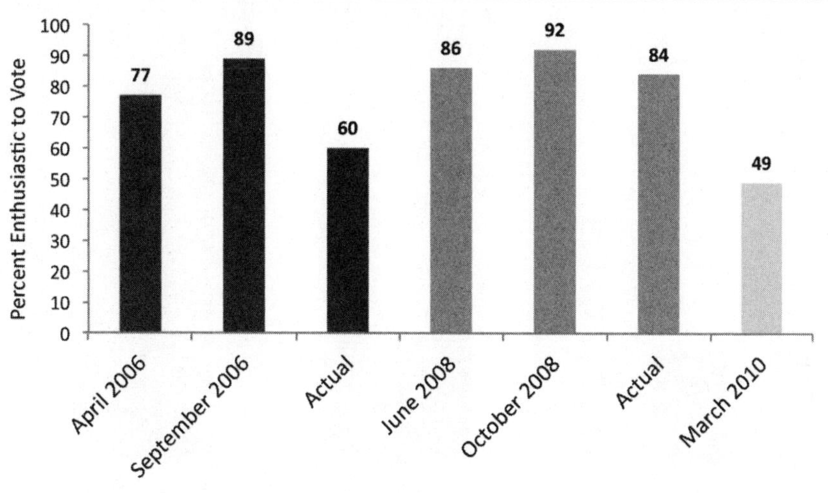

Republicans in Congress, who made little attempt to reach out to Latinos, continued to suffer a credibility gap—18% of Latinos were more excited about the GOP, compared to 62% who were less excited and 20% who registered no change. Since Latinos nationwide generally reported a GOP partisan identity between 16% and 20%, that excitement number in 2010 should be read as reflecting core partisanship, but the high number for "less excited" suggests that there had been some hardening of Latino attitudes against the GOP, even by 2010.

For Democrats, however, the numbers weren't much better: 38% of Democratic Latinos were more excited about the party, 40% were less excited, and for 22% there was no change. This significant variation from normal partisan patterns was strongly suggestive of the disappointment level felt by many Latino voters leading up to the 2010 midterms. Perhaps some of the decline in enthusiasm was inevitable—no administration can live up to all voters' expectations at the time of election. But there were no excuses for the Democrats: from 2008 to 2010, they controlled all three elected branches of national government. Knowing who was in power,

FIGURE 7.2 Self-Reported Excitement among Latino Registered Voters about the Two Political Parties, March 2010

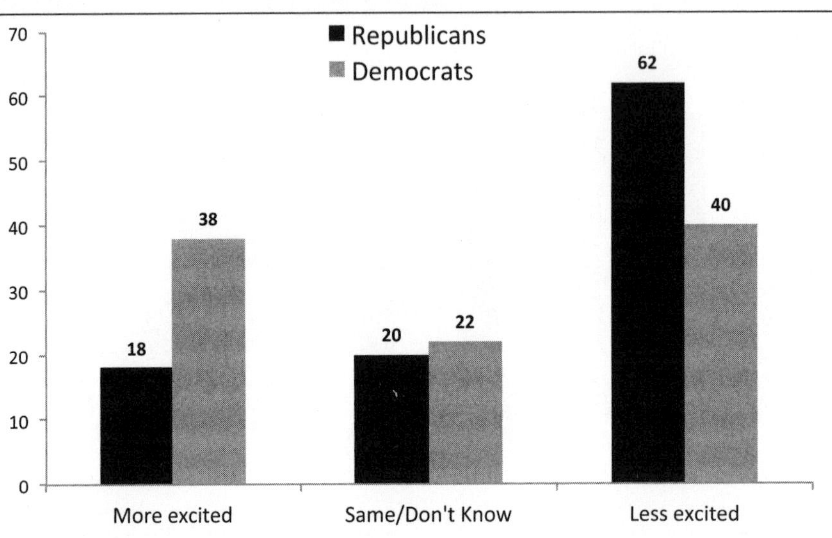

Latinos knew where to channel their disappointment—so the Democrats' numbers were net negative.

In March 2010, then, Latino excitement about Democrats and enthusiasm for the 2010 midterm elections was lower than when Obama was elected, and lower than it was for the 2006 midterms. With the stage set for significant declines in Latino turnout, it was an open question, early in that year, whether any event or policy action could restore Latino energy and support for the Democrats.

SB 1070, THE DREAM ACT, AND IMMIGRATION IN 2010

As it has done for a generation, and as it did for Democrats in 2006, the saving moment came over immigration. Republican anti-immigrant rhetoric and policy actions served to poison their brand with Latino registered voters.

On April 23, 2010, Jan Brewer, the elected Republican secretary of state in Arizona who had succeeded to the governorship of that state upon the appointment of Democratic governor Janet Napolitano as secretary of

Homeland Security, signed Senate Bill 1070 into law. Dubbed the "papers please" law, the statute included a series of restrictions and penalties on undocumented persons, as well as changes to how law enforcement officials would interact with persons "suspected" of being undocumented. The sweeping elements of the law were subject to multiple legal challenges and widespread opposition by immigrant and Latino advocates.

Latino Decisions polled Arizona's Latino registered voters just seven days later, on April 30. That poll was the first—and, for some time, the only—poll of Latino citizens regarding their views of the law.

Opposition to the law was widespread and intergenerational. Arizona Latinos whose grandparents were born in the United States—that is, fourth-generation or more—were opposed to the law by more than a two-to-one margin. Among the generations who had arrived in the United States more recently, opposition was even higher. The reason was clear—the vast majority of Latino voters in Arizona believed that ethnicity (racial profiling) would be the mechanism of enforcement. Any Latino citizen and/or legal resident of the United States could conceivably be stopped and asked for identification that would prove that their presence in the United States was legal. Imagine being a fourth-generation US citizen but being legally required to carry your documents with you at all times!

Whether targeted against immigrants or not, SB 1070 imposed a burden on all Latinos through its racial mechanism of enforcement. Over three-quarters of our Latino registered voter respondents believed that the law was explicitly racial and would never have been adopted if most immigrants were white.

The partisan effects of the passage of SB 1070 were immediate. In the minds of the Latino electorate in Arizona, the GOP was overwhelmingly to blame for its passage, which was accurate in terms of the legislative votes in the Arizona legislature. Among Latino voters, 59% held the GOP responsible, compared with just 2% who believed that the Democrats were to blame. However, we'd be remiss if we failed to point out that one-third of Arizona voters (33%) blamed both parties. This, too, had a basis in the legislative record, as several Democrats either voted for the legislation or were conveniently absent for the roll call.

FIGURE 7.3 Latino Registered Voters' Beliefs Regarding Whether SB 1070 Was Passed Because of the Racial Composition of the Immigrant Population, Arizona, April 2010

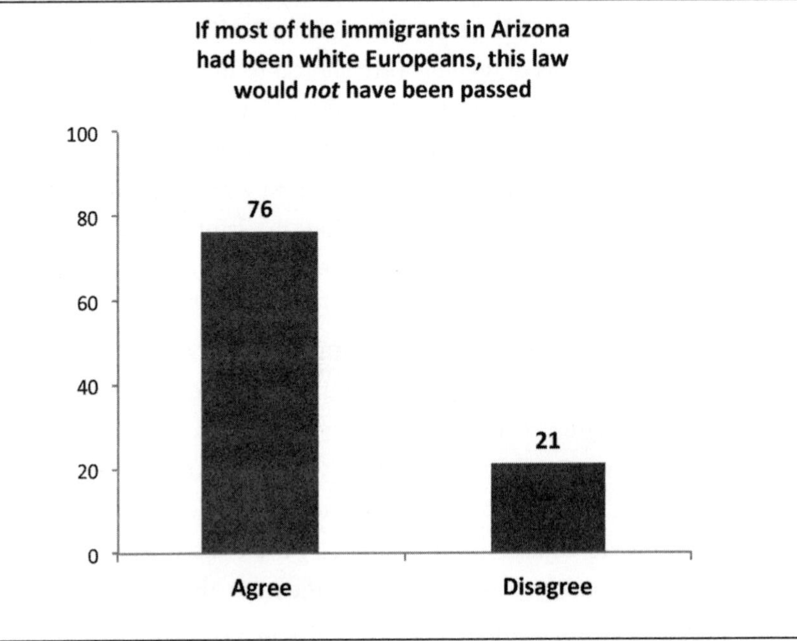

The second major event on the issue of immigration occurred in September. The administration's actions had continued to dampen Latino enthusiasm for participating in elections and supporting Democratic candidates, even after Obama's Department of Justice filed suit to block some of the provisions of SB 1070. The turnaround came in September less than six weeks in advance of the midterm election. On September 21, 2010, Senate Majority Leader Harry Reid, himself facing an uphill path to reelection, brought forward a cloture vote on the DREAM Act, an immigration policy proposal, originally authored by Republicans, that would grant legal status to some undocumented persons who had been brought across the border (or had overstayed their visas) under the supervision of parents or guardians and hence had no culpability in their undocumented immigration status. If such individuals were attending college or volunteering for the military, they would receive legal status. The cloture vote

FIGURE 7.4 Latino Voters' Perceptions of Democratic and Republican Actions on Immigration Reform, August–September 2010

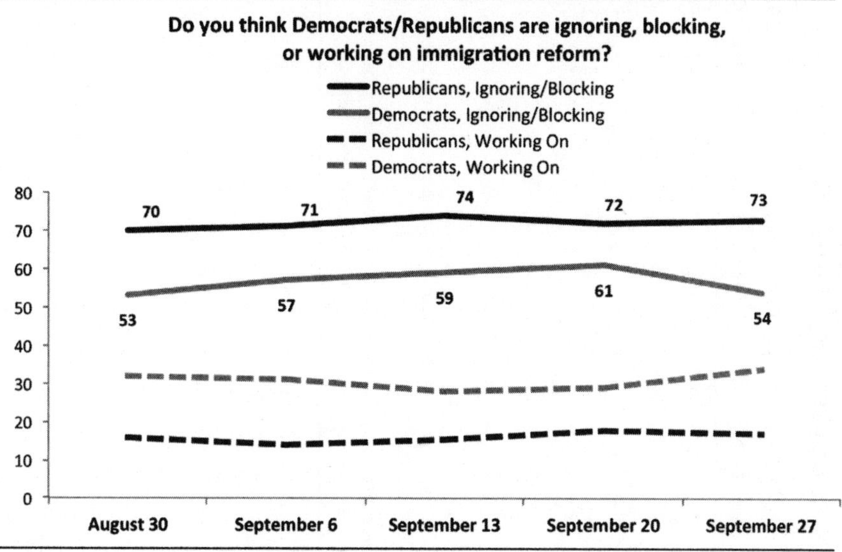

fell three votes shy, 56–43 (with Senator Reid switching his vote to the minority at the last moment for procedural reasons). Of the forty-two sincere "no" votes, forty-one were cast by the Republican minority.

When Harry Reid brought the DREAM Act to the floor, Latino Decisions was in the midst of a weekly tracking poll. The data from the poll showed that 77.5% of Latino registered voters supported the DREAM Act amendment, versus just 11.5% who opposed it.

At the same time, the Democrats saw a favorable turn in perceptions that they were working on immigration reform. In the week prior to the vote, our data indicated that 61.1% of Latinos felt that Democrats were either ignoring or blocking immigration reform; that number dropped to 53.8% during the week of the vote. Likewise, the percentage who thought that Democrats were actively working on passing reform went up from 25.7% to 30.8% in one week. This trend, which continued for the remainder of the 2010 electoral season, is illustrated in Figure 7.4.

As a result of the DREAM Act cloture vote, Republicans continued to suffer reputation decline among Latino voters. Just three weeks earlier, our tracking poll reported that 63.2% of Latino registered voters were

TABLE 7.1 The National Popular Vote Share in NEP Exit Polls, by Race and Ethnicity, 2004–2012

	2004			2006			2008			2010			2012		
	Share	*R*	*D*	*Share*	*R*	*D*	*Share*	*R*	*D*	*Share*	*R*	*D*	*Share*	*R*	*D*
Whites (non-Hispanic)	77	58	41	79	51	47	74	55	43	78	60	37	72	59	39
African Americans	11	11	88	10	10	89	13	4	95	10	9	90	13	6	93
Asian Americans	2	44	56	2	37	62	2	35	62	1	40	56	3	26	73
Latinos or Hispanics	8	44[a]	53	8	30	69	9	31	67	8	34	64	10	27	71
Others	2	40	54	2	42	55	3	31	66	2	43	53	2	38	58
Total		51	48		45	53		46	53		52	45		48	50

Source: NEP exit polls, as tabulated by CNN.

Note: Numbers are percentages. The rows do not report votes for third parties and hence may total less than 100. The columns may not add to 100 owing to rounding error.

a. Owing to the particular characteristics of the NEP Latino sample in 2004, and as we have documented elsewhere, Latino Decisions, like most other observers, is deeply skeptical of this number. A better estimate of the Latino vote percentage for Republicans in 2004 is approximately 40%. See Barreto et al. (2005).

"less excited" about the GOP—in the wake of the vote, 71.3% were saying that they were "less excited" about the GOP compared to a year earlier. Just weeks before the 2010 election, the GOP brand was heading in the wrong direction among Latino registered voters.

THE 2010 RESULTS IN CONTEXT

So, with the passage of SB 1070 in Arizona and the Senate's consideration—and ultimate rejection—of the DREAM Act, how did Latino voters end up voting in 2010? Despite the description of that election as a dramatic GOP victory, the underlying dynamics of the election were very similar to elections before and since. That is, like all American elections, the local elections were won on the margins.

Table 7.1 illustrates the vote by group as reported in the National Election Pool (NEP) exit polls over the last decade of elections. In 2010 the GOP did marginally better among all groups than it did in 2006, largely owing to changes in the composition of the electorate: midterm elections turn out fewer voters of lower income and lower levels of education, resulting in a significant drop in minority turnout. In 2010 non-Hispanic whites constituted 78% of the electorate, compared with 74% two years earlier and 72% two years later. More importantly, those who tend to fall off in midterm years are disproportionately Democratic voters.

In 2010 a substantial majority of whites voted Republican, as they have in every election since 1964. For all other racial and ethnic groups, even with the decline in turnout disproportionately affecting Democratic voters, majorities voted Democratic.

HOW THE WEST WAS WON, 2010 EDITION

Despite the fact that the year started with significant disappointments and frustration with the Obama administration, the passage of SB 1070 by the Arizona GOP and Republican Senate unity in blocking the DREAM Act were sufficient to restore Latino enthusiasm for electoral participation. Latinos were approximately 8% of the electorate in 2010, the same as in 2006 when nationwide immigration marches generated substantial electoral enthusiasm. And though their support for Democrats was diminished compared with 2008—by 3%, the smallest decline in any demographic—in exit polls Democrats still outpolled Republicans among Latinos by nearly two to one. And that was in the exit polls that, as we have argued elsewhere, significantly underestimated the Latino Democratic vote.[1] The Latino Decisions estimate, based on our 2010 election eve poll, was a 76% Democratic vote share in the two-party House vote.

So, despite national political trends and earlier disappointments, Latinos voted heavily Democratic in 2010, either two to one or three to one. But did they make a difference?

In four elections—the gubernatorial elections in California and Colorado and the senatorial elections in Nevada and Colorado—Latinos made a critical difference to the outcome, either in terms of actual votes cast on election day or in how the race took shape rhetorically, and usually in both ways.

This is not to say that Latinos did not matter elsewhere. In Illinois, Pat Quinn's election as governor was a squeaker—he prevailed by 0.3%. Solid Latino turnout and an approximate 83% vote share for Quinn among Latinos contributed a net margin of 4.2%, which was far larger than his actual win. (Latinos were not enough to save Alexi Giannoulias, who lost his Senate race to Republican Mark Kirk). Also, Kamala Harris's election as attorney general of California would not have been possible without an extremely strong Latino vote.

The Colorado Gubernatorial Race John Hickenlooper was elected governor of Colorado in 2010 with only 51.01% of the vote in a three-way race with GOP nominee Dan Maes and Congressman Tom Tancredo, who ran on the "Constitution Party" ticket. Tancredo, a former GOP member of Congress, has made anti-immigrant politics a hallmark of his political career, and it remains the raison d'être for his career. He bolted from the GOP in that cycle, ostensibly because he believed that neither primary candidate had the political strength to win the general election. Though Hickenlooper received more than 50% of the vote, including a net 6.3% from the state's Latino electorate, the division of conservative forces no doubt played a significant role in his victory. Nevertheless, the third-party candidacy of the nation's most outspoken opponent of undocumented immigrants, coupled with the Latino vote share, signaled a critical role for Latinos in the state's politics.

The California Gubernatorial Race The race to replace California's termed-out governor, Arnold Schwarzenegger, was unusual, to say the least. The Democratic nominee was previous two-term Democratic governor Jerry Brown, who had returned to political life to serve as mayor of Oakland and as attorney general before running for his old office. The state's partisan evolution since the 1990s made this an uphill race for any Republican, despite the fact that Brown had shown increasing reluctance to fund-raise, campaign, and the like.[2] The conventional wisdom was that the only GOP candidate who stood a chance would be someone like Schwarzenegger—a socially moderate, fiscally cautious candidate with little or no connection to the state party establishment.

Say, someone like Meg Whitman.

At the time, Whitman was the former CEO of eBay and widely respected in corporate and Silicon Valley circles. She had a history of public-spirited action, but not as an elected official. Her business acumen looked to be an ideal selling point in a state that was suffering (at that time) serious fiscal problems. Finally, and most importantly, she had a huge bankroll and a willingness to spend a bunch of it on the election.

In the end, Meg Whitman spent over $140 million of her own money in addition to a sizable sum raised elsewhere. And she lost by 1.3 million votes, 53.8% to 40.9%. How such an attractive candidate could lose by such a large margin deserves explanation. Moreover, Whitman lost to someone with almost no campaign infrastructure and no Spanish-language website.[3] Despite the absence of a Spanish-language website, Latinos turned out in droves for Jerry Brown. Latino Decisions' 2010 election eve poll estimated that Brown received 86% of the Latino vote, which, at 18% of the electorate, meant that Latinos contributed a net 13.1% of Brown's overall total.

Without Latinos, the race would have been a virtual tie.

There were four reasons for the Latino enthusiasm for Brown. First, several independent expenditure groups ran a sophisticated messaging campaign designed to mobilize support for Brown, even though he had little campaign infrastructure to reinforce the message. Despite the campaign's paltry efforts, there were Latino-targeted ads in English and Spanish running in most of the state's media markets, as well as large-scale direct mail and get-out-the-vote phone campaigns.

Second, Meg Whitman got caught using different campaign messages with different audiences. Specifically, while running ads in Spanish saying that she had no interest in Arizona-style anti-immigrant legislation, she was giving interviews to conservative talk-radio and telling a somewhat different story. This was particularly true during the primary, when Whitman was working to put away more conservative primary rivals by touting her opposition to in-state tuition and other state benefits for the undocumented. The juxtaposition of these clearly mixed messages was called out by the Brown campaign and its surrogates as *dos caras,* or "two-faced." The label stuck.

Third, any credibility that Whitman had on immigration was further eroded when she appointed Pete Wilson, the former Republican governor and architect of the Prop 187 anti-immigration initiative, as a co-chair of her election campaign. Though this came sixteen years after the passage of the dreaded initiative—one credited with reshaping California politics[4]—a huge share of Latino voters in the state held strongly negative associations with Pete Wilson. Figure 7.5 illustrates attitudes about Wilson among Latino voters. Even among eighteen- to thirty-year-old voters, who were between the ages of two and fourteen when Prop 187 was passed, 86% were somewhat or very concerned that Whitman had tapped Wilson.

Finally, the salience of the immigration issue was raised, not lowered, over the course of the campaign by the revelation that Whitman had an undocumented person performing domestic labor in her home. Exacerbating the situation, Whitman had fired this person in June 2009, on the eve of her campaign for governor. In the minds of the voters, Whitman was wrong twice. Her credibility on immigration was undermined by her alleged knowledge of having an undocumented worker in her employ. And her treatment of that employee was similarly found to be both hard-hearted and self-serving.

FIGURE 7.5 California Latino Voters' Perceptions of Former Governor Pete Wilson, September–October 2010

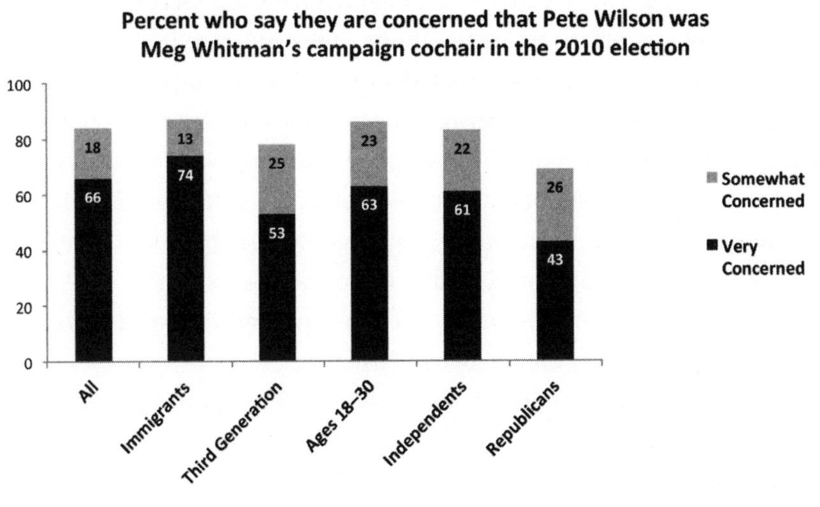

The Colorado Senate Race Like the gubernatorial race, the Colorado Senate race featured at least one candidate identified with the ideological, or "Tea Party," wing of the Republican Party. Ken Buck, the GOP nominee in Colorado, held forcefully articulated views on immigration and immigrants. He made his name in state politics as the district attorney of Weld County, a role in which he masterminded what was then the largest immigration raid in US history—a 2006 raid of a beef processing plant in Greeley. A profile in *The Nation* described his interest in the immigration issue as "obsessed."[5] During the course of the campaign, he accused incumbent senator Michael Bennet of favoring "amnesty."

But Colorado's electorate was 17% Latino in 2010 (and almost 20% today). Using our 2010 election eve poll, Latino Decisions estimated that Senator Bennet received 81% of the Latino vote, meaning that Latinos contributed a net 6.2% to Bennet's total on election day. Since the statewide margin was only 1.7% of the vote, a more even distribution of Latino votes would have meant an easy win for Buck. Senator Bennet owes his seat to Latino voters.

The Nevada Senate Race Harry Reid is pivotal to our story in two very important ways. First, as the Senate majority leader, it was he who brought the DREAM Act to a vote in September 2010. Second, as an incumbent seeking reelection, he faced one of the most explicitly racialized campaigns of the year, run by his challenger, Sharron Angle.

Angle, a former Republican member of the state legislature, ran an insurgent campaign against the presumed nominee, Sue Lowden, a former local TV news celebrity, and two others. Angle defeated Lowden by around fourteen percentage points, in some measure because Democrats and their allies had targeted Lowden (who they perceived as the bigger threat) with ads during the primary campaign, and in part as a consequence of the Tea Party emergence in 2010.

Angle is, to put it mildly, erratic in public. She's prone to gaffes and appears to have fringe beliefs regarding 9/11, the Department of Education, Muslims, the United Nations, and other bêtes noires. But none of her views attracted as much attention as her views on immigration, which became the centerpiece of her advertising campaign.

In a widely decried ad—a version of which other GOP nominees ran in other states—Senator Reid's support for the inclusion of undocumented persons in several federal benefits programs was illustrated with images of apparent gang members who Reid would help go to college, frightened and frustrated (white) Americans, and a classroom full of (white) American children who would apparently be prevented from speaking English if Reid was reelected.

To be sure, Reid was aided by substantial voter registration efforts in Nevada between the 2008 and 2010 elections by organizations like Mi Familia Vota and the Hispanic Institute, among others. But there is no question that Angle's specifically racial ads had a significant effect on Latino mobilization and vote choice.

Almost every major poll predicted an Angle victory. But on election day, Reid defeated Angle by almost six percentage points. A Latino Decisions election eve poll estimated that 90% of Latino voters chose Harry Reid (a number we have since validated with precinct-level analysis). Without Latinos, or with an even distribution of Latino votes, Reid would have lost and Angle would have won.

FIGURE 7.6 Latino Voter Attitudes on the Importance of the Immigration Issue to their Vote Choices, Election Eve 2010

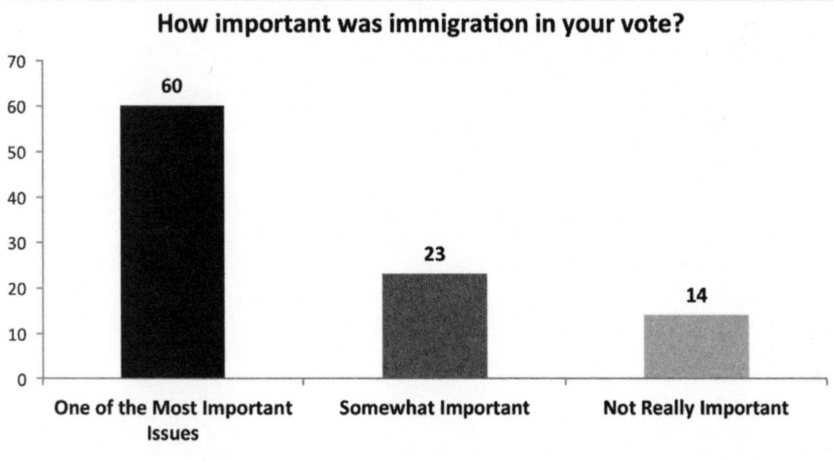

Although overall the 2010 midterms were a pretty thorough defeat for Democrats, in numerous elections in 2010, and particularly in elections in the West, Latinos showed that they are a critical element in the Democratic coalition—without them, Democrats lose elections. Immigration was front and center in the minds of the voters we interviewed. As we report in Figure 7.6, 60% of Latino voters said that immigration was "very" important to their choice to vote and their choice of candidate, while another 23% said that it was "somewhat" important. Immigration politics affects the vote choices and mobilization of Latinos across national-origin groups and generations, and it has become even more important to Latinos as some states have tried to regulate immigration in harsh and racially suspect ways.

Chapter 8

A "DECISIVE VOTING BLOC" IN 2012

With Loren Collingwood, Justin Gross, and Francisco Pedraza

In 2012 the Latino vote made history.* For the first time ever, Latinos accounted for one in ten votes cast nationwide in the presidential election, and Obama recorded the highest ever vote total for any presidential candidate among Latinos, at 75%.[1] Also for the first time ever, the Latino vote directly accounted for the margin of victory—simply put, without Latino votes, Obama would have lost the election to Romney (at least in the popular vote). Indeed, the day after the election dozens of newspaper headlines proclaimed 2012 the "Latino tide" and lamented the GOP's undeniable "Latino problem." As Eliseo Foley wrote on the Huffington Post site, "The margins are likely bigger than ever before, and bad news for the GOP. . . . 'Republicans are going to have to have a real serious conversation with themselves,' said Eliseo Medina, an immigration reform advocate and secretary-treasurer of the Service Employees International Union. 'They need to repair their relationship with our community. . . . They can wave goodbye to us if they don't get right with Latinos.'"[2]

*An earlier version of part of this chapter appeared online and is forthcoming in print as Loren Collingwood, Matt Barreto, and Sergio I. Garcia-Rios, "Revisiting Latino Voting: Cross-Racial Mobilization in the 2012 Election," *Political Research Quarterly* (2014).

TABLE 8.1 Latino Contribution to National and State Margins for Obama, 2012

	National	*Arizona*	*California*	*Colorado*	*Florida*	*Massa-chusetts*	*North Carolina*	*New Mexico*	*Nevada*	*Ohio*	*Texas*	*Virginia*
Latino vote for Obama	75	79	78	87	58	89	72	77	80	82	70	66
Latino vote for Romney	23	20	20	10	40	9	27	21	17	17	29	31
% Latino in 2012 among all voters	10.4%	20.2%	27.3%	14.1%	17.4%	6.9%	3.9%	39.7%	16.7%	2.2%	26.6%	3.3%
Net contribution to Obama	5.4	11.9	15.8	10.9	3.1	5.5	1.8	22.2	10.5	1.4	10.9	1.2
Final vote margin	2.8	-10.1	20.6	4.7	0.9	12.0	-2.2	9.9	6.6	1.9	-15.8	3.0
"Growth in Latino vote, 2000–2010"	52%	72%	67%	30%	66%	98%	117%	21%	117%	47%	38%	76%

However, the performance of Latino voters in 2012 had not been guaranteed. Early in 2012, many journalists, campaign consultants, and scholars had questioned whether Obama would be able to win over Latinos. Would the struggling economy and the lack of progress on immigration reform result in millions of disaffected Latino voters?

It was not until the summer of 2012 that Obama solidified his image as a champion of immigrant rights, and at the same time Romney solidified his own image as out of touch with working-class families and, even worse, as anti-immigrant. From the summer to the fall, Obama stuck to a script of extensive, ethnic-based outreach to Latinos while Romney, in hopes of winning more conservative white votes, continued to oppose popular policies like the DREAM Act. The result, of course, was the worst showing ever for a Republican candidate among Latino voters.

Among Latino voters, Barack Obama outpaced Mitt Romney by a margin of 75% to 23% in the 2012 election—the highest rate of support ever among Latinos for any Democratic presidential candidate.[3] While turnout declined nationally from 2008 to 2012 (by 2%), among Latinos there was a 28% increase in votes cast in 2012 (from 9.7 million to 12.5 million), and Obama further increased his vote share among Latinos in 2012 compared to 2008.[4]

However, this outcome was not a foregone conclusion: many theories circulated after 2009 suggesting that the Latino vote might be underwhelming in 2012.[5] Given the high rate of Latino unemployment and the record number of immigrant deportations during Obama's first administration, why did he do so well?[6] Latinos' historic party identification with the Democratic Party was strong evidence that Obama would win a majority of Latino votes.[7] The other indicators, however, such as age, resources, and connections to politics, pointed toward lower turnout and less enthusiastic support for Obama.[8] As late as September 2012, a common headline in the popular press was something along the lines of "Latinos' Enthusiasm Gap Worries Dems," and there was widespread concern that the Latino vote seemed to be "fading."[9]

In the end, post-election media accounts of the 2012 Latino vote suggested that Obama performed so well among Latino voters precisely because of their unique demographic characteristics: Latino voters are younger than average voters (younger voters tend to vote Democratic), they have lower-than-average incomes (historically, poorer voters side with Democrats), and, perhaps as a result, they tend to identify as Democrats.[10] Others have suggested that Obama did so well among Latinos because he supported the DREAM Act and initiated an executive order (DACA, or Deferred Action for Childhood Arrivals) that authorized immigration officials to practice "prosecutorial discretion" toward undocumented Latino youth.[11] Finally, some activist organizations have also suggested that Romney's move to the right on immigration had a negative impact on his campaign among the Latino electorate.[12]

This chapter puts these accounts to the test. The 2012 Latino vote may be explained in large part by traditional vote-choice models, which include items such as partisanship, political ideology, gender, age, religion, presidential approval, views on the economy, and most important issues. These models have "worked" for fifty years, from *The American Voter* by Angus Campbell and his colleagues (1960) to *The American Voter Revisited* by Michael Lewis-Beck and his team of researchers more recently (2008).[13] As we detailed the 2008 election in Chapter 6, however, we demonstrated that traditional models of voting don't work quite as well for understanding Latino voting patterns. Further, as the electorate continues to diversify, scholars need to begin to ask how vote-choice models can be improved to better explain minority vote choice.

As it was in 2008, a critical part of the story in 2012 was Latino group solidarity, this time better stimulated by the extensive debate over immigration in the GOP primaries and through the general election season. When minority voters turned out at rates higher than anticipated by most seasoned election experts, scholars, following on the theorizing of Michael Dawson, attributed this to the strength of group identification and a common belief in a shared political destiny—what Dawson calls "linked fate."[14] His argument is that group identity shapes and structures political behavior by serving as an organizing principle for engaging the various issues at stake in the political system—in short, it is an "ideology." While white voters may put a premium on sociotropic evaluations of the economy—how good the economy is for people in general, not just for themselves individually—the candidate who can best tap into minority voters'

TABLE 8.2 The Importance of Immigration and the Economy to Latinos in 2012

	Economic Issues		*Immigration Issues*	
	Latino Decisions	Gallup	Latino Decisions	Gallup
January	57%	66%	45%	3%
August	53	65	51	4
September	58	72	40	4
October	54	72	39	2
November	52	64	37	3

Source: For the Latino Decisions tracking poll, respondents were asked, "What are the most important issues facing the Hispanic community that you think Congress and the President should address?" For the Gallup weekly poll, respondents were asked, "What is the most important problem facing the nation?"

shared identity and improve those voters' perception that the candidate is "on their side" should do best.

Indeed, existing research suggests that ethnic identification, ethnic attachment, and ethnic appeals may be an especially salient feature of minority politics.[15] Even when the candidate is of a different race, scholars have shown, certain appeals may work to tap into voters' sense of shared identity. In what is coined "messenger politics," some researchers have found, for instance, that using Latino campaign volunteers in mobilization efforts can improve GOP prospects at the national level.[16] Both Ricardo Ramírez and Melissa Michelson find similar evidence that Latino voters are more susceptible to coethnic get-out-the-vote drives.[17] So a new lens is needed to understand not just minority politics but all of American politics in the twenty-first century.

THE ECONOMY AND IMMIGRATION, 2008–2012

In the wake of the Great Recession that began in December 2007, numerous reports detailed the disproportionate impact of the economic downturn on Latinos.[18] By the end of 2008, only one year into the recession, one in ten Latino homeowners reported that they had missed a mortgage payment or been unable to make a full payment.[19] Compounding the problems created by unemployment and home-ownership insecurity, by

2009 Latinos had sustained greater asset losses relative to both whites and blacks.[20] By 2011 Hispanics registered record levels of poverty in general, and especially among children.[21]

For these reasons and others, from 2011 through 2012 the economy was consistently the most important issue identified in our surveys by Latino respondents, and this remained true right up to the election (see Table 8.2). What is most interesting about that data point, however, is how misleading it turned out to be. Decision-makers in both campaigns thought that Latinos' concern about the economy meant that the immigration issue had faded for them; in fact, it remained a foundational issue for many Latino voters.

Concurrent with these economic patterns were major immigration enforcement efforts that were having a negative impact on Latino communities across the country. Chief among these efforts were the US Immigration and Customs Enforcement (ICE) memorandums of agreement and "Secure Communities" programs, which marked an unprecedented shift in immigration enforcement from preventing entrance at the US-Mexico border to focusing heavily on enforcement and expulsion within the interior of the United States.[22]

The fact that comprehensive immigration reform did not even make it onto the president's active agenda during the first two years of his administration was widely viewed as a broken promise. By early 2011, against the backdrop of this record enforcement and the failure of the Senate to invoke cloture on the DREAM Act in September 2010, the Latino community was deeply unhappy. Though the Obama campaign repeatedly claimed that it was the economy that would cement Latinos to his cause, his campaign staff understood that they had a public relations problem. Even as the administration repeatedly claimed to have no choice but to aggressively enforce the law, the activist community just as repeatedly demanded some form of action to lessen the devastating impact of deportations, then approaching 1.2 million.

In May 2010, Obama traveled to the border to deliver a speech on immigration reform in El Paso, Texas. The White House billed this event as a reboot of the immigration reform push, and it was coupled with several high-profile and well-covered meetings on the issue, but Latino voters were not buying it. In a June 2011 poll of Latino registered voters by Latino Decisions, 51% felt that the president was getting "serious about immigration reform," but another 41% felt that he was "saying what Hispanics want to hear because the election is approaching." He received 67% of the Latino vote when he was elected in 2008, but now only 49% were committed to voting for his reelection. The president simply didn't enjoy the trust he once had with the Latino electorate, at least not on this issue.

Perhaps most importantly, this poll showed that huge majorities of Latino voters supported the president taking action alone to slow the deportations, and almost three-quarters (74%) said that they favored the administration halting deportations of anyone who hadn't committed a crime and was married to a US citizen. Support was similar for protecting other groups of undocumented persons.

The administration's repeated claims that they could do nothing administratively to provide relief from the deportation crisis were similarly rejected. At the 2011 convention of the National Council of La Raza, a speech by the president became an occasion for direct confrontation. When the president took the podium, DREAMers rose in the audience wearing T-shirts that said OBAMA DEPORTS DREAMERS. When the president again said that he was powerless to act, the crowd rose to their feet and began chanting, "Yes you can," a bitter recycling of the president's 2008 campaign slogan—which itself was, ironically, the English-language translation of the slogan of the Chicano and farmworkers' movements of the 1960s, *Sí se puede.*

This more or less constant barrage of bad news with potentially significant political impact finally moved the administration. On August 18, 2011, the administration issued what has come to be referred to as the "prosecutorial discretion" directive. Based on a memo dated June 17—when the president was insisting that he had no room to act—the directive instructed the Department of Homeland Security (DHS) and ICE officials to use more discretion in selecting cases for deportation. The memo was further refined on August 23, particularly in relation to parents and other caregivers.

Most immigration advocates would say that this memo and the subsequent interpretations and administrative instructions had little practical effect, and indeed, by late May 2012 the Latino community was still deeply disaffected. The administration took constant heat from Univision anchor Jorge Ramos and others in Latino media. Ramos asked the president directly why he had deported so many immigrants who had families, even children, in the United States. Even Congressman Luis Gutiérrez, the first prominent Latino politician to endorse Obama back in 2007, publicly questioned whether Latinos should give their votes to Obama in early 2012. And Latino enthusiasm remained very low. In February, Latino Decisions found that the "certain to vote for Obama" share of the Latino electorate had dropped further, to 43%.

As they had done in July 2011, the DREAMers stepped into action. After quietly and not so quietly threatening to take action against the Obama campaign, two DREAM-eligible young people staged a sit-down hunger strike at the Obama campaign office in Denver. They ended their strike on June 13, but not without the National Immigrant Youth Alliance (NIYA) announcing plans to stage civil disobedience protest actions at Obama and Democratic offices across the country. They hoped the visual of minority youth being hauled away from Democratic offices would move the president to act—a stark change from the images of energetic and enthusiastic young people and college students supporting the 2008 Obama campaign.

And as he had done in 2011, Obama acted. On June 15, 2012, two days after the end of the hunger strike and the same week as NIYA's announcement, the Obama administration announced DACA—Deferred Action for Childhood Arrivals. Within existing legal constraints, the president issued a directive that prevented the deportation of youth who would otherwise have been eligible to stay if the DREAM Act had passed.

This action was a double win for the Obama campaign. First, there was huge Latino support for the decision, and it was immediately reflected in polling numbers for Obama. Within days of the announcement, Latino Decisions—which, serendipitously, was in the field with a poll right as the policy was announced—found an increase in support for the president and in enthusiasm for the election.

Second, since the DACA directive announced by the president was an administrative order issued by an executive agency, Romney had to decide whether, if elected president, he would allow it to continue or halt it. When asked, Romney eventually stated that his administration would not participate in the deferred action policy and instead would ask Congress to take up a permanent solution to immigration issues, a position reiterated by the Romney campaign in the last week of October.

During the GOP primaries, every candidate except Texas governor Rick Perry clamored to be the most right-wing and hard-line opponent of immigration reform and the DREAM Act. In a GOP debate, Romney himself offered the most infamous preferred policy—"self-deportation." The implication was that he favored a policy regime that would make life so miserable and difficult for undocumented immigrants that they would simply choose to leave rather than continue to live under such harsh rules. Most observers assumed that, once the nomination was secure, Romney would tack left on this idea and on other policy issues to appeal to a general election audience. But forces in the party, and indeed his own inner circle, made any such movement impossible.

In spite of all this attention on the immigration front, the economy continued to be the "most important" election issue. So how can we reconcile Latinos' economic fears—supposedly their most critical concern—with their eventual enthusiastic support for the incumbent? Did immigration concerns prevail over the economy in the minds of Latino voters?

To begin, it is critical to understand that many Americans didn't blame President Obama for the crushing economic times and the immigration enforcement efforts and did not lay political responsibility for these issues wholly at the feet of his administration. Conventional accounts of the economic voter insist that "it's the economy" that matters, and that the incumbent presidential candidate gets blamed in poor economic times.[23] It could be that Latinos did not see the economy as particularly bad for themselves (the so-called pocketbook view) or for other Latinos (the sociotropic view). However, survey data indicate that the disproportionate impact of both economic issues and immigration policy on Latinos was not lost on Latinos themselves. Reports from the Pew Hispanic Center in 2011 indicate that a "majority of Latinos (54%) believe that the economic downturn that began in 2007 has been harder on them than on other groups in America."[24]

In other words, the real toll of the economic recession on Latino employment, homeownership, and wealth and the adverse impact on Latinos of border and interior immigration enforcement had not escaped Latino awareness. In sum, it was reasonable to expect that, in November 2012, Latino voters would go to the polls with good reasons to punish Democrats in general, and President Obama in particular.

So why, when Latinos should have been especially prone to retrospective economic voting and when they also had expressed real concern about the immigration enforcement targeting their community, did they support the Democratic ticket? While President Obama was certainly responsible in the minds of Latinos for the historic levels of immigration enforcement, by July 2012 two key developments related to immigration served as correctives to the perceptions among Latinos that Democrats were hostile toward their community. The first was the Supreme Court decision on *Arizona v. United States,* and the second was DACA, the executive order on "Deferred Action for Childhood Arrivals." Latinos credited Obama and the Democrats with both the judicial outcome and the executive order that provided key relief for the Latino community. The shift in the perception of Democrats as hostile to seeing them as "welcoming" sharpened the contrast with the Republican Party. As Mitt Romney called for "self-deportation" and referred to Arizona as a "model" state for immigration policy below the federal level, the hostility they perceived in the Republican "brand" only increased for the Latino community.

Although the Great Recession provided the central backdrop for the 2012 election cycle, the specter of record levels of deportations, coupled with the salience of the Supreme Court case deciding the role of subnational actors in the enforcement of immigration policy, reduced the centrality of economic issues for Latino voters in a way not seen among non-Latino voters.

THE 2012 CAMPAIGN

As campaigns have become more technologically sophisticated, they have fine-tuned the practice of micro-targeting specific messages or appeals to different subgroups of voters. In 2012 targeting Latinos became a significant endeavor for both presidential campaigns: in key battleground states such as Florida, Nevada, Colorado, and Virginia, Obama spent nearly $20 million on outreach to Latino voters, and Romney spent $10 million. Some researchers have found that campaigns that target Latino voters with ethnically salient get-out-the-vote appeals win more Latino votes.[25] Data on campaign advertising also reveal that Spanish-language television and radio advertising can increase Latino turnout.[26] The outreach efforts during the 2012 campaign were hardly "by the book," however, nor were they equal in their effort. To understand why ethnically based messaging mattered so much in 2012, we first take a cursory look at the outreach efforts of the Obama and Romney campaigns.

In direct contrast to the 2008 election, in which Latino voters were fought over state by state in a competitive and long-lasting Democratic primary contest, the 2012 election included a Republican primary contest in which Latinos often felt under attack. Attempting to attract what they perceived as an anti-immigrant voting bloc in the conservative primary elections, the leading Republican candidates took a very hard-line stance against undocumented immigrants, bilingual education, and bilingual voting materials. Most importantly, Mitt Romney, who feared being called a moderate by the more conservative primary candidates, staked out a firm, unwavering, and unforgiving position on immigration. As mentioned earlier, Romney said that he would address the issue of the 11 million undocumented immigrants living in the United States through a policy of "self-deportation." In repeated follow-up interviews and debates, when asked what self-deportation actually meant, Romney explained that he wanted to institute a series of laws that would crack down on unauthorized immigrants by making it so impossible for them to work that, unable to make ends meet, they would have no choice but to "self-deport" to escape their miserable lives in America. While this may have sounded reasonable to some Republican primary voters, Romney's "self-deportation" statement and continued explanations of the policy sounded ridiculous to most Latinos. On November 7, 2012, the day after the election, Latina Republican strategist Ana Navarro quipped via Twitter that looking at the exit poll data for Latinos, "Romney just self-deported himself from the White House."

The "self-deportation" comment was not Romney's only trouble with Latinos. During a presidential debate, he said that he would "veto the DREAM Act." About the same time, Romney named Kris Kobach, the Kansas secretary of state, as his principal adviser on immigration. Kobach was the architect of the Arizona SB 1070 anti-immigrant legislation (see Chapter 7) and had a hand in crafting copycat legislation in Alabama; he is widely despised by Latino activists. In addition to his close connections with Kobach, Romney appeared in photographs alongside Sheriff Joe Arpaio, the law enforcement officer from Maricopa County, Arizona, who perhaps more than other figure today embodies anti-immigrant and anti-Latino policy. Nationally known (and under Justice Department investigation) for his outlandish policies, Arpaio has publicly embraced racial profiling, consistently uses bias in making arrests, persists in using excessive force against Latino inmates, and has failed to investigate more than 400 sex crimes.[27] Besides associating with Arpaio, Romney called the myriad anti-immigrant legislative initiatives in Arizona, during a primary debate in that state, a model for the nation and said that he wanted to implement mandatory "e-verify," a workplace program that would crack down on undocumented immigrant workers.

When Romney finally wrapped up the Republican nomination, the many who predicted that he would moderate his views on immigration pointed to the several high-profile Latino Republicans he appointed to his advisory committee and then dispatched to speak on his behalf. Even these surrogates, however, were often at odds with the official statements issued by Romney or by the Republican Party. Speaking to Univision anchor Jorge Ramos during the Republican National Convention, Romney supporter Carlos Gutierrez, former secretary of the Treasury under George W. Bush, agreed with Ramos that the official Republican platform ratified at the convention was troubling to many Latinos. The platform endorsed more Arizona-style anti-immigrant legislation and called for an end to the Fourteenth Amendment, which affirmed citizenship for anyone born in the United States. Republicans vowed to strip citizenship from children born in the United States if their parents were undocumented immigrants. Gutierrez struggled to explain to Ramos and his viewers that Latinos should pay no attention to the Republican platform—whose positions on immigration he called "minor administrative matters"—and that the real choice was the candidate, Mitt Romney.

Romney had two chances to make inroads with Latinos in 2012, both of which he squandered. First, the US Supreme Court heard arguments on the constitutionality of the Arizona SB 1070 law, which authorized state and local police to ask anyone they suspected of being in the country illegally for proof of citizenship, and which was decried as racial profiling against all Latinos. President Obama spoke out firmly against SB 1070, and in fact it was the Obama Department of Justice that sued the state of Arizona. When the Supreme Court ruled that three of the four provisions in the Arizona law were not constitutional but allowed the fourth provision—the one allowing police to ask for proof of citizenship—Romney issued a statement that he opposed the federal government's interference in states' rights and believed that Arizona should have the freedom to enact its own laws. In contrast, Obama commended the Supreme Court for striking down three-quarters of the Arizona law and vowed that his Department of Justice would continue fighting the fourth provision until it too was overturned. Obama called the law an attack on all Latinos that had to be stopped. Romney continued to refer reporters to his statement that states should be free to pursue their own laws.

As discussed earlier, the final and ultimately most critical moment for Latino outreach was the DACA policy. When Latino registered voters were queried on their social connectedness to undocumented immigrants, a full 60% said that they personally knew someone who was undocumented, and one-sixth of them said that someone in their family was undocumented. While the Obama administration's deferred action policy was greeted with full-throated enthusiasm by Latino voters, Romney opposed it.

Eager to deflect the heat from the immigration issue and salvage any possibility of nudging Latino voters into the Republican column, Romney stressed the connections between the economy under Obama's administration and the financial stress so many Latinos were experiencing. In a preemptive effort to counter President Obama's message to Latino leaders in early June 2012, Romney issued a statement, with accompanying graphics, declaring that Latino economic fortunes had faltered during the president's administration.[28] Romney's strategy was to draw attention to the high unemployment rate, increased poverty levels, and lower median household incomes among Latinos.[29]

OUR SURVEY EXPERIMENT

To test our predictions about the importance of the immigration issue for Latino voters, we fielded a survey experiment during the 2012 presidential election campaign among Latino registered voters in five battleground states. From June 12 to June 21, we asked respondents whether a candidate's position on immigration would make them more or less likely to support that candidate (see Table 8.3).[30]

Although numerous immigration cues have been tested by campaigns and studied by academics, including the effects of using the term "illegal" versus the term "undocumented" and emphasizing cultural threats over economic threats, we focus on generic candidate statements perceived as welcoming or hostile toward immigrants.[31] A large body of research has documented the centrality of emotions in political evaluations.[32] Our manipulation of immigration statements here cuts to the core of the affective dimension of the immigration debate.

The descriptive results of the survey experiment are presented in Table 8.3 with observations for all of the five battleground states combined and also broken down by state. The respondents who received the welcoming immigration message broke three to one toward offering more support for the candidate. At the lower end, in Colorado and Virginia, the welcoming message garnered 56% and 58% "more likely" support, respectively. At the upper end, Arizona candidates with a welcoming message marshaled 65% "more likely" support, and for Florida candidates it was 71%.

In sharp contrast to this pattern, only 17% of Latinos overall were more likely to support a candidate who staked a position hostile to immigrants. While the proportion of Latinos who were "more likely to support" a candidate with a welcoming message ranged from 56% to 71%, the range for a candidate with a hostile message was bracketed by a low of 12% in Arizona and a maximum of 21% in Florida. Assuming voter-candidate congruence on the issue of the economy, a welcoming cue had a net effect

TABLE 8.3 Responses to Candidate Statements on Immigration in Five Battleground States in the 2012 Election

Welcoming cue: "America is a nation of immigrants. We need to treat immigrants with respect and dignity and help them become part of America instead of attacking them."

	Five States Combined	*Arizona*	*Colorado*	*Florida*	*Nevada*	*Virginia*
More likely to support	67	65	56	71	63	58
Don't care what they say	18	21	25	16	20	25
Don't know	10	12	13	10	4	9
Less likely to support	3	2	5	3	10	6
Net effect	**+64**	**+63**	**+51**	**+68**	**+53**	**+52**

Hostile cue: "Illegal immigrants are a threat to America who have committed a crime. We can never support amnesty for illegals."

	Five States Combined	*Arizona*	*Colorado*	*Florida*	*Nevada*	*Virginia*
More likely to support	17%	12%	17%	21%	16%	16%
Don't care what they say	21	20	28	20	25	19
Don't know	12	9	12	15	9	8
Less likely to support	49	59	41	43	50	55
Net effect	**-32**	**-47**	**-24**	**-22**	**-34**	**-39**

Source: Latino Decisions/America's Voice, Five Battleground States Survey, June 2012.

Note: Figures shown are column percentages. Data are weighted to reflect Latino statewide demographics.

of +64 points in mobilizing Latino support (the difference between "less likely to support" and "more likely to support").

Perhaps more telling than the positive mobilizing effect of a welcoming message were the differences we observed in the proportion of Latinos who were less likely to support a candidate. Assuming that the response "less likely to support" is an expression of lower enthusiasm, we note that the divide is especially stark by immigration cue. Among Latinos exposed to the welcoming immigration message, an overall 3% indicated that they were less likely to support the candidate, compared to nearly half of them (49%) who gave this response when cued with a hostile immigration message. In other words, even when a candidate holds a position on the economy shared by the Latino voter, his or her use of a hostile cue on immigration will have a net effect of -32 points.[33]

In short, a welcoming immigration message brings two of three Latino voters into a candidate's fold, but a hostile immigration message leaves a candidate with only one in six Latino voters who are "more likely" to offer support.[34] If turnout from the perspective of a campaign is about rallying voters to the ballot box, then an unwelcoming immigration message is counterproductive to a Latino mobilization strategy because it saps away enthusiasm for the candidate. Based on these data collected in June 2012, we find it remarkably clear that the Republican candidate's strategy as a restrictionist on immigration would be problematic for his prospects in keeping Latino support that November, even assuming that many Latino voters agreed with his solutions for the economy.[35]

We turn next to our attempt to better capture the importance of the economy and immigration to Latinos by using attitudinal measures about key policy statements from the two candidates, incumbent Barack Obama and challenger Mitt Romney.

ANTI- VS. PRO-IMMIGRANT RHETORIC

Starting from the results reported in Table 8.3, we looked to see whether the effect of anti-immigrant rhetoric versus more welcoming messages could be observed in specific subgroups of the Latino electorate. For example, we might have expected that Latinos who said fixing the economy

FIGURE 8.1 The Net Effect of Immigration Statements on Candidate Support, 2012

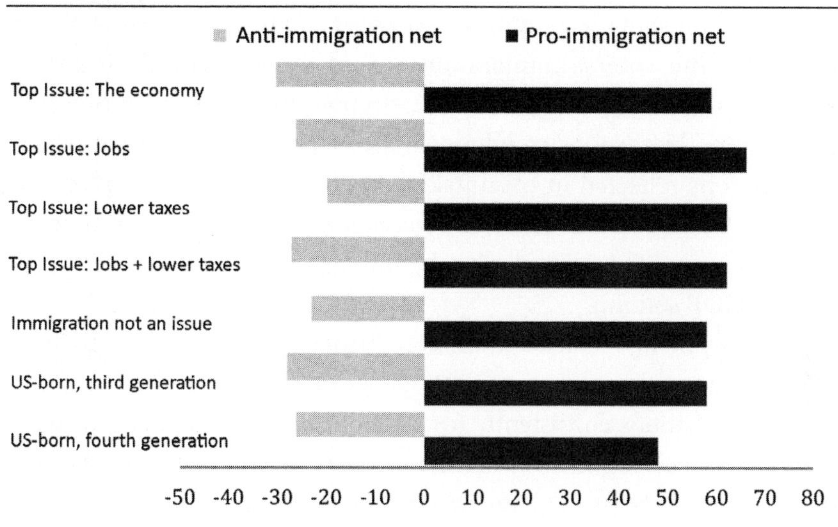

Source: Latino Decisions election eve survey, 2012.

was the number-one issue would be less persuaded by a candidate's rhetoric on immigration policy so long as they agreed with that candidate on the economy. In fact, just the opposite was true. Even for Latinos who said fixing the economy or creating jobs was their top concern in the 2012 election, hearing an anti-immigrant statement made them far less likely to support even a candidate with whom they agreed on the economy. This result is striking because this group of voters just reported at the start of the survey that the economy and jobs were their number-one issue of concern.

The same trend held for Latinos who did not mention immigration as either their first or second most important issue. Yet when confronted with either anti-immigrant or pro-immigrant statements, this group was also strongly responsive to the immigrant messaging.

Finally, we find the same strong trends holding for US-born third- and fourth-generation Latinos—those for whom immigration is not part of their immediate family's Latino identity. Still, these US-born third- and fourth-generation Latinos were very persuaded by what candidates said on immigration in 2012—even beyond the candidates' positions on the economy.

Despite finishing second to the economy as the burning issue of concern to Latino voters, immigration proved to be a critical—if not *the* critical—issue of the November 2012 election. Even years of inaction on immigration by the Obama administration—and worse, years of the adverse actions reflected in breathtaking deportation rates—coupled with a persistently slow recovery from a recession that was devastating in the Latino community were not enough, in the end, to move the Latino vote into the GOP column.

This surprising resilience from the Obama campaign can be credited, in our view, to three key factors. First, as we showed in Chapter 3 and again here, Latinos consistently trust Democrats over Republicans when it comes to securing their economic interests. A year out from the election, in November 2011, Latinos still blamed George W. Bush, not Barack Obama, for their economic troubles. And they placed greater trust in the president and his co-partisans to lead them back to prosperity.

This economic effect was no doubt aided by Latinos' considerable preference for a government that addresses economic trials rather than relying on the free market. That Latinos are progressive and believe that government should solve problems made an economic appeal from the Romney camp that much harder to sell.

Second, despite his administration's terrible record on deportations, Obama took two giant steps toward recovering his position on the issue of immigration. The prosecutorial discretion memos in the summer of 2011 can be understood as the administration finally coming to grips with the importance of the issue to the president's political prospects. Aiding this effort were courageous DREAMers, outspoken and committed immigration activists, and some clever polling. More importantly, further DREAM activism resulted in the more effective DACA program. More than any other event in the 2012 campaign, DACA signaled the turnaround of the Obama relationship with Latino voters.

Finally, the most reliable weapon in any Democratic campaign to mobilize Latinos sprang into action—the Republican Party. Republican primary candidates pushed the party further and further to the right on immigration, to the point that the most moderate candidate in the field—and the eventual nominee—embraced a policy of making 11 million people miserable in hopes of driving them out of the country. How unsurprising that this policy was off-putting to the spouses, children, neighbors, and coworkers of those he hoped to drive away.

MULTIPLE VISIONS OF LATINO VOTING INFLUENCE

As discussed in Chapter 6, asking whether Latinos can "single-handedly" determine an electoral outcome is too stringent a definition of influence. Instead, we have considered three dimensions in measuring Latino electoral influence: state-specific demographics, including group size and growth rate; electoral volatility with respect to registration, partisanship, and turnout; and the degree of resource mobilization. Among the relevant factors are the rates of party registration, the pre-election polls of vote intention, targeted Latino campaign spending, media coverage of Latino voters within a state, estimated turnout rates, the overall size of the Latino population, and the group's growth rate. Taken together, these factors help explain where and when Latinos are influential in presidential politics.

In his 2013 book *Mobilizing Opportunities,* Ricardo Ramírez takes a holistic approach to analyzing the power and influence of the Latino electorate, focusing on state-level context and mobilization efforts and asking about the nature of Latino influence across different states. He asks the basic question: were Latino voters—or some other group of voters—actually influential in the election outcomes? One approach to answering this question has been called the "pivotal vote" thesis; Ramírez rightly takes issue with it for being too results- or outcome-driven. Our view is that, although this may be but one among several important ways to understand group-based political power, the search for "pivotal blocs" will continue to have considerable appeal in media accounts of elections as well as within campaigns themselves. So we consider the pivotal vote thesis here, though we are careful to make some important improvements and caveats, per Ramírez' recommendations in *Mobilizing Opportunities.*

There are two fundamental ways in which a campaign can help its candidate: getting potential voters to actually show up and vote, and convincing likely voters to cast a ballot in favor of their candidate. These tasks are not equivalent in their relative merits, nor do they remain constant throughout a campaign or among different candidates. Candidates spend time and resources reaching out to different subgroups of voters, and they have different approaches in different states. Not only do campaigns take different approaches, but some may go so far as to try to demobilize or suppress the vote. Here we take an expanded view of what it means for Latinos to be influential and provide examples of candidates and campaigns expending significant resources vis-à-vis the Latino electorate.

The fact that some noncompetitive states are Latino-heavy presents an obstacle to effectively assessing Latino voting influence. How could Latinos possibly be so influential in presidential politics if they are concentrated in California, New York, Texas, and Illinois, which are not battleground states? As FiveThirtyEight.com analyst Nate Silver stated in 2012, "Almost 40 percent of the Hispanic vote was in one of just two states—California and Texas—that don't look to be at all competitive this year."[36] However, the question to ask is not what percentage of all Latinos are in competitive states, but rather what percentage of voters in competitive states are Latino and whether the margin of victory is likely to make this group crucial to the outcome. To the extent that many Latinos across the nation share some important concerns, the fact that a growing share of all voters are Latino in Nevada, Colorado, Florida, and even new destinations such as North Carolina, Virginia, Ohio, and Iowa, and therefore could have significant electoral influence, suggests that Latinos do matter—even if Latinos in California, New York, or Illinois do not matter at all.

Louis DeSipio and Rodolfo de la Garza asked how electoral outcomes would differ under alternative scenarios, but this is the wrong approach.[37] Instead, we replace their somewhat narrow, deterministic notions of influence with probability-based assessments for each state and for an election as a whole. Rather than simply asking whether a state's choice for president would have been different in the absence of Latino voters, we ask: how likely is it that a set of states will all have votes close enough that they will fall into a range of plausible Latino influence and so the winner of the election will hinge in turn on these states?

To capture the range of plausible influence in our model, we consider two realistic scenarios that are the best for each candidate. For instance, within each state, what was a plausible level of Latino voter turnout and percentage of Latino votes cast for Romney that would have been optimal from Romney's point of view, and what combination would have been optimal for Obama? Then we determine the probability of an election outcome falling somewhere between these two plausible extremes. Once the election is over, the analysis remains essentially the same, except that instead of asking how likely it is that the election was decided by a set of Latino-influence states, we ask about the probability of such an outcome, in retrospect, given what we know now.

Campaign strategy is driven by a clear assessment of which scenarios are more or less likely, and a post-election reassessment must similarly deal with probabilities. Thus, while some speculate on how different history might have been if the 2000 Gore campaign had expended a little effort to train the elderly Jewish voters of Palm Beach County in how to read the now-infamous "butterfly ballot," few would think of this small group of voters as singularly influential; we recognize the situation in Florida in 2000 as unique, since it arose from the confluence of an enormous number of systematic and random factors.

Using the best information available, the question of group influence becomes: what was the probability that the Electoral College vote and the vote margins within the states would be such that the group of interest might be deemed a decisive factor? When we compare the relative influence of Latinos and African Americans, as well as the combined influence of both groups, in the 2012 presidential election, this is the question we're answering.

To illustrate the dynamic of Latino influence in the 2012 presidential election we created an interactive website that allows users to visualize what Latino influence looks like.[38] Combining real-time weekly polling data from every state for both Latinos and non-Latinos with the estimated share of all voters who will be Latino, website users can see what would have happened if Latino turnout had been somewhat lower or higher than expected, if the candidates had gotten more or less voter support than expected, or both. If Latino turnout had been somewhat low in Colorado, or Latino voters had broken more heavily for Romney in Florida, how would the overall Electoral College have changed? From interacting with this Latino influence map, it becomes quite apparent that the Latino vote had major implications for the outcome of the 2012 Electoral College. Had Latino voter turnout rates been somewhat lower, Virginia and Colorado would have gone to Romney. Had Latinos in Florida or New Mexico leaned more toward Romney, Obama would have lost both states. The Latino vote map at the website shows these different scenarios from the 2012 election.

In many of these same states, African Americans were also a large factor in election outcomes. Had black voter turnout been lower, Obama would have lost Virginia and Pennsylvania. Because both minority groups were targeted extensively by the Obama campaign, we think it makes sense to assess both Latino and black influence in 2012, as well as the combined Latino and black influence.

Given the data populating our Latino vote map, and drawing on the work of the political scientist Andrew Gelman, we have assessed the influence of Latinos and African Americans on the election outcome in every single state; we provide a combined minority influence score for some states in Table 8.4.[39]

Table 8.4 reports our results from 10,000 statistical simulations on the actual outcome of the 2012 election, in selected states, and calculates the proportion of simulations in which each state's voting puts it in the interval of voting power for Latinos, for African Americans, and for Latinos combined with African Americans. Nevada exemplifies the potential synergy between Latinos and African Americans better than any other state: the probability of combined influence is over 90%, well more than the sum of the individual probabilities of influence. We find similar stories of Latino and black influence in Florida, Colorado, North Carolina, and Virginia, where the probability of minorities swinging the state result ranged from 78% to nearly 100%.

In addition to looking at these states individually, we can use the same logic to assess the probability that these Latino and black swing states

TABLE 8.4 State-Level Model Estimates of the Probability that Latino Voters, African American Voters, or Latino and African American Voters Combined Were Pivotal to Battleground State Outcomes in 2012

	Probability of Latino Influence	*Probability of Black Influence*	*Probability of Combined Black-Latino Influence*
Colorado	0.664	0.064	0.835
Florida	0.605	0.778	0.986
Iowa	0.041	0.057	0.112
Michigan	0.013	0.066	0.122
Nevada	0.370	0.095	0.918
New Hampshire	0.040	0.025	0.076
North Carolina	0.237	0.966	0.993
Ohio	0.083	0.486	0.675
Pennsylvania	0.076	0.245	0.403
Virginia	0.125	0.575	0.782
Wisconsin	0.044	0.073	0.183

were critical to the overall presidential election result. Taking these state results together, the probability that Latinos and blacks combined swung the election to Obama in 2012 was 67.5%.

DISCUSSION: EVALUATING LATINO VOTING INFLUENCE ON THE 2012 PRESIDENTIAL ELECTION

Based on the actual election day results we used in our simulation, Florida and Colorado were essential elements of Latino Electoral College voting power. In nearly every one of the simulation runs in which the outcome hinged on a set of states that were each decided within the margin of plausible Latino influence, these two states (worth thirty-eight electoral votes) were in that set. Given how closely contested Florida was, the high percentage of registered Latino voters in the state, the large number of electoral votes at stake there (twenty-nine), and the state's relative heterogeneity in partisanship, it is hardly a surprise that Florida is currently the linchpin of Latino power. Nevada was close behind Florida and Colorado, appearing in over 90% of the simulation runs where the outcome hinged on Latino influence.

The probability of African American influence was about ten points higher than the probability of Latino influence in 2012, according to our measure; several states appeared in the pivotal set (Ohio, Virginia, North Carolina, and Florida) in at least 90% of the simulation runs decided within the margin of plausible variability for black turnout and vote choice. Together with Pennsylvania (88%), these states accounted for nearly one hundred votes in the Electoral College. Other than Florida, there was no overlap between the top Latino-influence states and the top black-influence states in 2012. And yet these results, taken together, point to the possibility of a minority coalition that could swing a presidential election outcome by making far more states potentially pivotal while producing state outcomes driven by a combined Latino and African American turnout and vote choice. In states where the power of African American or Latino voters would become manifest only in the event of a very close contest, it is much more likely that the combined numbers (and any uncertainty over those numbers) would be instrumental in a victory.

A fascinating consequence of the complementary demographic strengths of blacks and Latinos is that their voting power taken together is stronger—potentially quite a bit stronger—than the voting power of each bloc taken alone. As we reported in Table 8.3, in Wisconsin the probability of Latinos swinging the state outcome was around 4% and the same probability for blacks was around 7%, but the probability of blacks' and Latinos' combined influence was 18.3%. In Nevada the results are even more dramatic. While Latinos are estimated to have been pivotal with a probability of 0.37 and blacks with a probability of 0.10, the two groups taken together are far more formidable: the estimated probability that Nevada would be decided by a margin smaller than the combined plausible variability of blacks and Latinos was over 90%! Although Latino and black voters, taken separately, had between a 16% and 34% chance of being instrumental to the outcome of the 2012 presidential election, together they reached over a 60% chance of influence measured in this manner.

LOOKING AHEAD TO 2016

Without question, US Census Bureau data indicate that the population of Latino adult citizens will continue to grow across every state. Accompanying these demographic changes will be political changes as states begin to appear more competitive and attract the interest of the campaign strategists who map out strategies toward collecting 270 Electoral College votes for their candidate. The three-point margin of defeat for Democratic US Senate candidate Richard Carmona in Arizona in 2012, for example, suggests that Arizona is moving from leaning Republican to being a toss-up as 2016 approaches. As that happens, the Latino voters who account for roughly 20% of the electorate will become manifestly relevant. If Latino turnout is high, Democrats may benefit. If the GOP changes course in Arizona and courts the Latino vote with sincerity, the party may be able to keep Arizona a "leans Republican" state. Whatever the outcome, Arizona is a state to watch in 2016 and could be the newest addition to the list of battleground states with sizable Latino electorates.

Another state that has drawn a lot of recent attention because of its Latino electorate is Texas. After twenty-four consecutive years of Republican governors, Texas is emerging as a "pre-battleground" state. Although it is less likely to be competitive in 2016 than Arizona, the demographic changes in Texas are hard to discount. Civic groups that focus on voter registration and voter turnout are flooding the Lone Star State to register the 2 million Latinos who are eligible but not yet registered to vote. If these groups make even a dent in the rate of Latino voter registration, and ultimately the voter turnout rate, Texas could very quickly become fertile ground for Latino influence. In addition to the untapped potential of the Latino electorate, much has been made about the potential mobilizing power of Julian and Joaquin Castro as potential statewide candidates for governor, attorney general, or US senator in future Texas elections. With voter registration drives and a Castro on the ticket, Texas is very likely to be competitive by 2018 or 2020, and the reason will be Latino voters.

Beyond Arizona and Texas, which have quite significant Latino populations, our data suggest that Virginia, North Carolina, Iowa, Ohio, and

Georgia could soon become strongly Latino-influenced. These states are now witnessing very close elections year after year, and all have a Latino citizen adult population that is growing dramatically. The potential for synergistic black-Latino power in new immigrant destination states in the South such as North Carolina, Virginia, and Georgia, as well as states in the Midwest and Mid-Atlantic, such as Ohio, Iowa, and Pennsylvania, may have radical implications for the long-term future of presidential politics in the United States.

As the story of the 2012 election made clear, Republican candidates' rhetoric and policy approaches to immigration, even in a period when economic concerns were dominating the political headlines, pose a nearly insurmountable stumbling block to the ability of the GOP to improve its electoral fortunes. Endorsing "self-deportation," more border spending, the denial of in-state college tuition to undocumented immigrants, and "papers please" laws like SB 1070 and declaring Arizona—ground zero in the anti-immigration movement of the last few years—a "model for the nation" are policy positions that appear highly unlikely to reverse GOP fortunes among Latino voters.

In contrast, Democrats mustered a comparatively aggressive outreach campaign that included advertisements, voter mobilization, and targeted appeals. These efforts were considerably more successful after eleventh-hour changes in policy were made by the Obama administration—specifically, deferred action for DREAM-eligible young people—the Supreme Court issued its mixed ruling on SB 1070, and the Romney campaign reacted to these events. A fair evaluation of the dynamics of the 2012 campaign among Latinos, however, would concede that the GOP push was a much stronger factor than the Democratic pull, and that Latinos have yet to reveal their full political potential.

Latinos—alone and in coalition with African Americans—have gained newfound political power that, to date, has benefited Democrats almost exclusively. How this came to be and the long-term implications of the immigration issue for how Latinos will reshape the American political system are the questions to which we turn next.

Part III

THE LATINO AGENDA

Chapter 9

THE PROP 187 EFFECT: THE POLITICS OF IMMIGRATION AND LESSONS FROM CALIFORNIA

With Elizabeth Bergman, David Damore, and Adrian Pantoja

Attempting to separate "Latino" politics from "immigration" politics is a fool's errand. While Latinos care about the same issues as other Americans (economic opportunity, education, health care), as Table 9.1 illustrates, immigration sits at or near the top of the Latino agenda. The economic collapse of 2008 and its subsequent effects drew attention to economic concerns, but as we approach the 2014 midterm elections it is immigration that is the priority of Latino registered voters.

Repeated polling over the last several years by Latino Decisions and others has made it clear that a large share of Latino registered voters are intimately connected to individuals who are affected by immigration policy. A stunning 67% of Latino registered voters nationwide reported knowing an undocumented person personally. Moreover, most of those connections were familial: 51% of respondents who reported knowing

TABLE 9.1 The Most Important Problems for Latino Registered Voters, 2012 and 2013

	November 2012	*July 2013*
Immigration	35%	53%
The economy and jobs	58	28
Education	20	15
Health care	14	12

Source: Latino Decisions election eve poll, November 2012, and Latino Decisions/America's Voice poll, July 2013.

one or more persons without documentation identified a family member as undocumented.

Yet, despite the intimacy of Latinos' deep and close connections to immigration, both political parties have routinely misunderstood those connections—especially the Republican Party. In fact, over the last decade the GOP's rhetoric has become increasingly hostile toward immigrants, especially Latinos, and its policy prescriptions have moved further and further to the right. As a result, Latinos and other minorities are increasingly casting their ballots for Democrats.

In this chapter, we assess the electoral consequences of anti-immigrant politics. We begin at the national level by contrasting the GOP's present positioning and politics to George W. Bush's handling of immigration, and then we take an in-depth look at California.

GOP IMMIGRATION POLITICS: BEFORE AND AFTER GEORGE W. BUSH

While serving as the governor of Texas between 1995 and 2000, George W. Bush never went down the anti-immigrant path, though it might have been easy for him to do so. Instead, he supported a compromise response to the Fifth Circuit Court's decision in *Hopwood:* pending the re-hearing in *Fisher,* that compromise ensured the continued presence of minority students at the University of Texas after the university's affirmative action policy was struck down.[1] His efforts as president to reach out to Latinos were notable. Bush was the first president in American history to deliver a

FIGURES 9.1 AND 9.2 Types of Interpersonal Connections between Undocumented Immigrants and Latino Registered Voters, June 2013

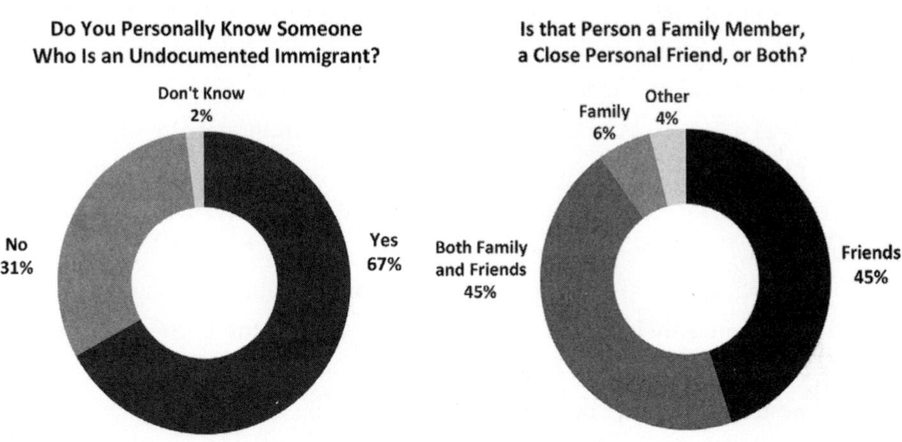

speech (a weekly radio address) entirely in Spanish. He and his chief political adviser, Karl Rove, firmly believed that future GOP growth would be among Hispanics. Bush was rewarded for his efforts in this vein when an estimated 40% of Latinos voted for his reelection in 2004.

However, not all Republicans were supportive of the Bush-Rove strategy of Latino outreach, and soon after the 2004 election, conservative Republicans in the US House of Representatives began to ratchet up their anti-immigration efforts. In December 2005, Congressman James Sensenbrenner, then chair of the House Judiciary Committee, authored HR 4437, which proposed making undocumented status a felony and, by extension, creating a lifetime ban on US citizenship for any individual in the country without proper documentation.

The reaction to HR 4437 was immediate and widespread: the 2006 immigration rights marches turned out more than 3 million people in over 150 American cities and provided some of the impetus for immigration reform efforts in 2006 and 2007. In both years, members of the Senate came close to agreement but were unable to overcome the opposition to move the legislation forward. As a consequence of these failures, the last reform of the country's immigration laws remained the Immigration

Reform and Control Act, which was passed in 1986, during President Ronald Reagan's second term.

Examining Latino participation in the last four national elections captures the electoral repercussions of these legislative failures. While there was a good deal of finger-pointing among both parties and their allied interests as to who was responsible for derailing immigration reform, there was no such equivocation among Latino voters. According to exit polls, Latinos have increasingly and overwhelmingly favored Democratic candidates in the ensuing elections.

Republicans, who once spoke compassionately about immigration reform, forfeited their standing on the issue and left the party with few if any credible immigration advocates.

These dynamics are nothing new. Rather, what is happening nationally for the GOP is essentially a repetition on a grand scale of what occurred in California, beginning in the 1990s. Indeed, focusing on California enables us to observe at a finer level of analysis and over a longer period of time how immigration politics is capable of reshaping the political landscape.

CALIFORNIA THEN AND NOW

California is a Republican state—or at least it *was* a Republican state. From the end of World War II until 1994, Democrats lost every presidential election in the state save two—the Lyndon Johnson landslide over Barry Goldwater in 1964 and Bill Clinton's plurality victory in 1992. The Democrats were two for ten over forty years. In gubernatorial elections, it was little better. Democrats won only four races during this period, to the Republicans' nine.

Moreover, between 1980 and 1994, Republicans were moving Latinos into the party. Field poll data make it clear that Latinos in the state were less Democratic every year between 1980 and 1994.[2] Between 1980 and 1984, former California governor Ronald Reagan raised his share of the Latino vote from 35% to 45% while carrying 59% of the entire state as he cruised to his second term as president. In response to his strong showing, Reagan famously quipped to pollster Lionel Sosa that "Hispanics are Republicans, they just don't know it."

But any movement among Latinos toward the GOP abruptly ended in 1994 with the passage of Proposition 187. That ballot initiative was a critical moment in Latino political development in California: it reversed the decade-plus drift in the state toward the GOP, mobilized over 1 million new Latino voter registrations, and consequently shifted the state firmly to the Democratic column in subsequent elections. Moreover, that shift back to the Democrats among Latinos occurred at precisely the moment when Latino population growth in California exploded.

Today the Democratic Party controls every constitutional office in the state and holds supermajorities in both chambers of the California Legislature. At the federal level, both US senators are Democrats, as are thirty-nine of the state's fifty-three-member delegation to the House of Representatives. The state has voted Democratic in the last six presidential elections, and in 2012 Barack Obama bested Mitt Romney 60% to 37%, with an electoral margin of over 3 million votes (which accounted for more than half of his national margin of 5 million). Although Latinos are not solely responsible for this margin of victory in California, they have proven critical in shifting the state legislature and the congressional delegation to the Democrats.

Proposition 187, which required law enforcement agents to report any arrestee who violated immigration laws to the California Attorney General's Office and to the Immigration and Naturalization Service (INS) and prohibited unauthorized immigrants from accessing government services, including education, was championed by Republican governor Pete Wilson in his 1994 reelection bid. It would also form the cornerstone of his short-lived 1996 presidential bid. Although Proposition 187 passed with 59% of the vote, the bulk of its provisions were ruled unconstitutional in federal court. After an extended legal battle, California withdrew its legal defense in 1999 and that effectively killed the law.

Emboldened by their success at the ballot box in 1994, conservatives qualified two other ballot measures consistent with the spirit of Proposition 187 in the next two elections: Proposition 209 (1996) sought to ban affirmative action in the state, and Proposition 227 (1998) significantly limited the state's bilingual education program. As with Proposition 187, both ballot measures passed. In hindsight, however, it was clear that any

TABLE 9.2 Population and Voter Registration Growth in California, by Race/Ethnicity, 1994–2004

	Total	*Black*	*Latino*	*Asian*	*White*
Population in 1994	31,523,000	2,197,155	9,084,787	3,306,782	16,662,672
Population in 2004	36,144,000	2,240,928	11,891,376	4,192,704	16,843,104
Growth	4,621,000	43,773	2,806,589	885,922	180,432
Growth rate	14.7%	2.0%	30.9%	26.8%	1.1%
Voters registered in 1994	14,723,784	957,046	1,766,854	736,189	11,263,695
Voters registered in 2004	16,557,273	993,436	2,980,309	1,159,009	11,424,518
Growth	1,833,489	36,390	1,213,455	422,820	160,824
Growth rate	12.5%	3.8%	68.7%	57.4%	1.4%

victories achieved by the proponents of these ballot measures and their GOP allies were fleeting at best, while the long-term consequences have been disastrous.

The timing of these ballot measures could hardly have been worse for California Republicans: they coincided with explosive growth in the state's Latino electorate, a trend that has been extensively documented in political science research.[3]

An overview of these trends is offered in Table 9.2, which reports population and voter registration growth in California from 1994 to 2004 broken down by racial and ethnic group. Overall, California grew by nearly 15% (or 4.6 million people) during this period, but this growth was almost entirely driven by Latinos and Asian Americans. Similarly, Latinos and Asian Americans were the primary drivers of growth in voter registration. Between 1994 and 2004, the state of California added an estimated 1.8 million newly registered voters, of which 66% were Latino and 23% were Asian, leaving just 11% of new voters who were either white or black.

Of course, in and of itself, growth in the registration of California's minority population does not explain the state's Democratic shift. For this to be the case, these new voters must not only identify as Democrats but also turn out to vote for Democratic candidates. With respect to the first requirement, the evidence could not be clearer. For instance, in an analysis of voter registration records in Los Angeles County between 1992 and 1998, Matt Barreto and Nathan Woods found that just 10% of new Latino registrants were affiliated with the Republican Party in the aftermath of the three so-called anti-Latino propositions in California.[4]

More importantly, the anti-Latino initiatives motivated many newly registered Latinos to vote. Adrian Pantoja, Ricardo Ramírez, and Gary Segura found that Latinos who naturalized and registered to vote during the 1990s were significantly more likely to turn out.[5] Likewise, Barreto, Ramírez, and Woods found that the best predictor of voter turnout in 1996 and 2000 was whether or not Latinos were newly registered following Proposition 187.[6] The overall result, then, was more Latinos registering than in previous years, and more Latinos voting as Democrats.

The 2000 presidential election provided an opportunity for the GOP to regain its standing with Latinos in California and elsewhere. George W. Bush used his understanding of Latino voters in Texas to rally support for the Republican ticket in the Latino community. However, even as Bush attempted to introduce a new compassionate face to the Republican Party, the Republican brand continued to be problematic for California Latino voters. Most notably, a survey conducted by the Tomás Rivera Policy Institute during the 2000 election revealed that 53% of Latino voters in California still associated the Republican Party with Pete Wilson.[7]

More generally, Figure 9.3 illustrates that as the Latino vote grew California became a more Democratic state. Most notably, the Latino vote became 10% to 13% more Democratic following the anti-immigrant policies endorsed by the GOP in 1994. In 1992 Democrats won 65% of the Latino vote, in 1996 they won 75% of the Latino vote, and by 2012 Democrats were winning 78% of the Latino vote.

In addition to voting in presidential elections, Latinos in California have also become consistent Democratic voters in other statewide elections since the Reagan era. Statewide results indicate that Latinos voted

FIGURE 9.3 California Presidential Vote for the Democratic Candidate, 1980–2012

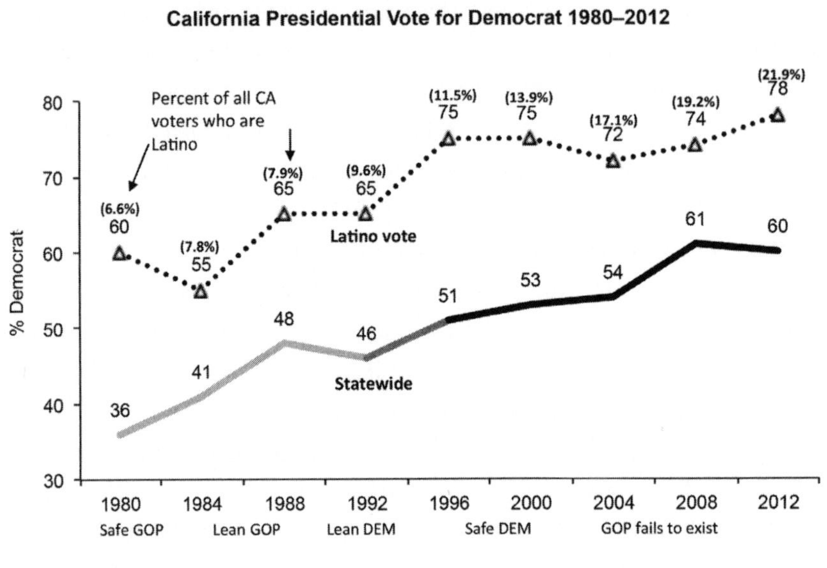

two to one on average in support of Democratic candidates for governor and US senator in every election between 1992 and 2002.[8]

Some observers saw the 2003 gubernatorial recall election as a potential shift away from the Democratic Party.[9] Most analysts now suggest, however, that the circumstances and context of this election were unique and that inferring trends from it is not valid.[10] Still, that election does highlight just how important Latino voters are to the Democratic Party in California: owing in part to the approximately ten-point drop in Latino Democratic support, Democratic governor Gray Davis was recalled from office and replaced with Republican Arnold Schwarzenegger.[11] Had Latinos turned out at slightly greater rates and voted at their average support rate for Democratic candidates, Davis would not have been recalled in 2003.

THE PROPOSITION 187 EFFECT

Research by Shaun Bowler, Stephen Nicholson, and Gary Segura provides perhaps the most comprehensive evidence of the broad and lasting effects of Propositions 187, 209, and 227 and the GOP's embrace of anti-immigrant politics.[12] Specifically, using data from the California field poll from 1980 to 2002, they demonstrate at the individual level of analysis that California's partisan shift represented more than a demographic transition from white Republicans to Latino Democrats.

As noted earlier, Latinos in California had been moving toward the GOP prior to 1994, as was happening in much of the rest of the country. Perhaps because of its role in proposing and passing the Immigration Reform and Control Act of 1986, the Republican Party experienced substantial gains in voter identification among California Latinos.[13] Starting in 1994, however, this trend was reversed as large numbers of California Latinos moved away from the Republican Party and toward the Democratic Party.

Bowler, Nicholson, and Segura's analysis suggests specifically that, prior to the initiatives, there had been a partisan breakdown among Latinos that favored Democrats 38% to 34%, with a substantial number of Latinos registering as independents but largely voting Democratic.[14] After the passage of Proposition 227 in 1998, the Democratic advantage among Latinos increased from four percentage points to fifty-one, while the probability that a Latino would identify as a Republican decreased from 34% to 12%.

Interestingly, their analysis indicates that absent the three ballot propositions, and all other things remaining the same, over the twenty-two years there was an almost 18% increase in the probability of a Latino thinking of himself or herself as a Republican. This, of course, makes the results for the ballot initiatives even more compelling: the propositions effectively eradicated all of the GOP's gains among Latinos between 1980 and 2002. The propositions reversed a trend that had been drawing larger numbers of Latino voters into the GOP fold. Moreover, it was the cumulative effect of the Republicans' sustained support for anti-immigrant policies that made the pro-Democratic shift so sizable.[15]

While the magnitude of these effects may be startling, the general direction of the relationship should not be all that surprising given that Propositions 187, 209, and 227 targeted Latinos. What California Republicans probably did not anticipate, however, was the extension of these effects to other segments of the state's electorate. To this end, research by Tali Mendelberg suggests that when white voters perceive campaign messages as overtly racist, these messages are less likely to activate anti-minority stereotypes or racial resentment and instead may be perceived as violating norms of racial equality.[16] Indeed, the racially charged rhetoric (proponents referred to Proposition 187 as the "Save Our State" initiative and produced messaging that blamed Latinos and immigrants for most of the state's economic and social hardships) combined with the partisan nature of the campaigns surrounding the initiatives created a context that may have caused white voters to question their partisan loyalties.[17]

Consistent with these expectations, Bowler, Nicholson, and Segura found evidence of backlash among white Californians.[18] Prior to Prop 187, Republicans had an eight-point advantage among whites, and the predicted probability that an Anglo Californian would identify as a Republican was 38%, as compared to a 30% probability of identifying as a Democrat, all else remaining the same. After the passage of the three propositions, Democrats had reversed the situation: they held a six-point advantage over Republicans, 37% to 31%, with the largest shifts occurring after the passage of Propositions 187 (in 1994) and 227 (in 1998). Perhaps more importantly, the effect among non-Hispanic whites, though smaller in magnitude as compared to Latinos, erased much of the rightward shift of the white population over the time period studied.

While the GOP may have anticipated, yet underestimated, the political blowback from Latinos, it is unlikely that they expected blowback from Anglo voters. Had this factored into their strategic calculus, it is unlikely that prominent Republicans in the state would have attached their names to the anti-immigrant propositions. As a consequence of this miscalculation, by 2002 both Latinos and non-Hispanic whites were substantially more likely to be Democrats and less likely to be Republicans than before Proposition 187.

Since 2002, there is little evidence suggesting that the trends documented by Bowler, Nicholson, and Segura are abating (see Figure 9.3) or that California Latinos have forgotten what occurred in the 1990s.[19] Even in 2010, when Democrat Jerry Brown squared off against Republican Meg Whitman in the gubernatorial race, 80% of Latino voters were very or somewhat concerned that Whitman had appointed Pete Wilson as a campaign co-chair—twelve years after Wilson left office and sixteen years after the passage of Proposition 187!

HAS THE GOP HIT ROCK BOTTOM IN CALIFORNIA?

Given the Republicans' emaciated standing in the Golden State, it seems hard to believe that the party could become even less of a factor in California politics in coming years. However, with a depleted party organization and no statewide officeholders or prominent mayors around whom the party might rally, it is equally difficult to imagine scenarios that would return the GOP to its prior standing anytime soon. The GOP's best path to relevancy may be slowly and methodically expanding its ranks within the state's delegation to the US House of Representatives and in the California Legislature. Yet even in these more homogenous and geographically concentrated electoral contexts, analysis conducted by Latino Decisions suggests that a number of districts presently held by Republicans are vulnerable to Latino influence and hence are potential Democratic pickups.

California's House Districts

Nationally, there are forty-four Republican-held and sixty-one Democratic-held districts where the 2012 Latino voting-age population was larger than the 2012 margin of victory. Depending on the ratio between the Latino voting-age population and the incumbent's 2012 margin of victory (as well as the district's 2012 presidential vote), these districts can be placed into one of three tiers, as illustrated in Table 9.A1 in the appendix.

Given the growth in California's Latino population, the average Latino voting-age population in California's fifty-three House districts is 34%. This is roughly two and a half times the national average. In thirty-one California House districts, the Latino voting-age population exceeds the 2012 margin of victory. While Democrats represent most of these districts, including six tier 1 districts (see Table 9.A1), in 2012 Republicans did win nine of them. Among these nine districts, three Republican incumbents appear to be particularly susceptible to the politics of immigration and

Latino influence: Jeff Denham (CA-10th) and Gary Miller (CA-31st), who represent tier 1 districts, and Buck McKeon (CA-25th), whose district was classified as tier 2 but will be retained by the GOP.

So while the Republicans' failure to respond constructively to California's changing political demography has cost the party plenty in the last two decades, they could lose yet more seats. The continued vulnerability of California's dwindling number of House Republicans is largely an artifact of the state's 2001 redistricting plan, which was designed to preserve the state's seniority in Congress by protecting incumbents of both parties. As a consequence, just one of California's House seats (the 11th in 2006) changed parties under the old maps—a particularly notable accomplishment given that majority control of the House of Representatives changed parties twice during the decade.

With the passage of Proposition 20 in 2010, however, authority over redistricting was removed from the California Legislature and placed in the hands of a fourteen-member panel of citizens, the Citizens Redistricting Commission (which also oversees state legislative redistricting). As part of this reform, neither incumbency nor partisanship could be considered in the state's new congressional boundaries. Instead, districts were required to follow city and county boundaries and, wherever possible, preserve neighborhoods and communities of interests.

By removing the political machinations that often determine redistricting outcomes, the districts that emerged in California in 2011 are more organic and may allow for a truer expression of voters' political preferences than is the norm in House elections. Unfortunately for Republicans, outside of a few dwindling pockets, the new maps provide another indicator of how little appetite California voters have for the GOP and its policies. Running in unprotected districts, Republicans lost four times as many House seats in 2012 than during the prior five elections combined—not a promising omen for a delegation whose ranks have dwindled to fifteen.

The California Legislature

The dynamics working against Republicans in California are even more visible in the California Legislature, where, since the 2012 election,

Republicans hold a total of 37 of 120 seats—12 in the Senate and 25 in the Assembly. The state legislative context is also where the effects of California's open primary—another reform intended to weaken partisan influences—can be more easily observed. Because of another 2010 ballot measure, California elections are now two-round affairs with all voters and candidates operating in the same pool. The top two vote finishers, regardless of party, move to the second round; this process ensures a majority winner, but not necessarily two-party competition.

As with the state's new redistricting process, its primary reforms offer indirect evidence of the GOP's problems this time in terms of the party's capacity to even field candidates. Specifically, in November 2012, all eighty Assembly seats and half of the state's forty Senate seats were on the ballot. However, just 74% of these contests featured a Republican and Democrat competing on election day. In twenty districts (eleven Democratic and seven Republican Assembly districts and two Democratic Senate districts), two candidates of the same party faced off. In four other contests Democrats defeated minor party opponents, and in two Assembly districts Democrats ran unopposed. Put another way, in nineteen of one hundred state legislative elections, the Republicans did not even have a candidate. If that was not bad enough, the politically neutral district boundaries further exposed the GOP's diminished standing as the Democrats picked up three additional state Senate seats in 2012.

Given the growth in the state's Latino population (as measured in the 2010 census), in forty-nine of the seventy-four state legislative districts that were contested by both parties in 2012, the Latino voting-age population exceeds the margin of victory, and in over half (sixty-four) of the seats in the California Legislature the Latino voting-age population exceeds either the 2012 margin or the party registration difference between Democrats and Republicans (see Table 9.A2 in the appendix). Yet, as is the case with California's US House seats, there remain a handful of competitive state legislative districts where Latino voters are positioned to be influential in coming election cycles.

We applied the methodology used to identify Latino-influence districts in our US House analysis to the California Assembly and Senate, with three differences (see Table 9.A2 for results). First, we did not incorporate information about the 2012 presidential vote. Second, absent election returns, for the twenty Senate seats that will be on the ballot in 2014, we used voter registration data to estimate competitiveness. We consider a district competitive if the difference in Democratic and Republican voter registration is ten points or less (based on the California secretary of state's February 2013 update). Third, because of data limitations, we used the 2010 census, as opposed to the 2012 voting-age population estimates. Thus, if anything, our analysis underestimated Latino voting-age population and overestimated the white electorate.

Across both chambers there are twenty districts—nine in the Senate and eleven in the Assembly—where either the 2012 margin of victory or the two-party voter registration difference is 10% or less and the Latino voting-age population exceeds the difference in support between Democrats and Republicans. In the Assembly, two Democratic-held districts (the 36th and 65th) and two Republican-held districts (the 40th and the 60th) are rated as tier 1 Latino-influence districts, as are two Democratic-held Senate districts (the 5th and the 34th) and three Republican-held Senate districts (the 12th, the 14th, and the 18th). That is, these districts are highly competitive and have significant numbers of voting-age Latinos. The three tier 1 Republican-held Senate seats, all of which will be contested in 2014, appear to be particularly vulnerable owing to the substantial Democratic registration advantages and majority-minority voting-age populations. Indeed, all three have Latino voting-age populations that either exceed or are close to 50%. The other eleven districts are rated as tier 2 districts where Latinos are influential, but these districts are less competitive. In terms of partisanship, Democrats hold seven of the tier 2 districts, including four in the Senate.

The implications of this are at least twofold. Even with the Democrats enjoying supermajority status in both chambers of the California Legislature, the relentlessness of the state's political demography provides additional opportunities for the Democrats to expand their margins. While so much of the increased Democratic support in California stems from the growth in the Latino electorate and these voters' overwhelming support for Democratic candidates, the full consequences of this shift may not yet be fully realized in the California Legislature.

In contrast, even if the GOP were to put forth a less alienating brand of politics, there are few opportunities for the party to improve its standing owing to the limited number of competitive state legislative districts. To this end, even if the GOP were to sweep all tier 1 and tier 2 districts in 2014 and 2016 (while holding all of its present seats), the party would still be a significant minority in both chambers.

Looking back to the mid-1990s and early 2000s in California politics provides many clear lessons for the Republican Party today. The California that delivered 60% of the vote to Obama in 2012 did not occur by happenstance; not long ago, California was a winnable state for Republican presidential candidates.

Today the Republican Party in California is in free fall. Republican presidential candidates have lost the last six elections in California and thus abdicated to the Democrats 20% of the Electoral College votes needed to win the presidency. Presently, there are no Republican statewide officeholders and the party's ranks have fallen below one-third in both chambers of the California Legislature, while Republicans represent just over one-quarter of the state's seats in the House of Representatives. In 2010, when Republicans picked up sixty-three House seats nationally, the party failed to pick up a single seat in California. Running in politically neutral districts in 2012, the GOP lost seven state legislative seats and four congressional seats and is poised to lose additional seats in coming elections. Consistent with these dismal electoral showings, the share of Californians registered as Republican declined from 37% in 1992 to less than 30% in 2012.[20] If these trends continue, by 2020 more Californians will be registered as independents than as Republicans.

To be sure, the GOP's political decline in California is not simply the result of the state's changing political demography—it is more than a matter of Latino and Asian American voters having rapidly replaced white voters. Rather, the data and narrative presented here underscore the importance of immigration politics against the backdrop of a burgeoning minority electorate. Quite simply, the decision of California Republicans to embrace anti-Latino and anti-immigrant policies during the mid-1990s alienated not just the fastest-growing segments of the state's electorate (immigrants, Latinos, Asian Americans, and other minorities) but also many white voters.

Today Arizona, Florida, Texas, and even Virginia and North Carolina are facing their own immigration politics and fast-growing Latino electorates. Already the pattern in California has surfaced in neighboring Nevada to save Democrat Harry Reid's Senate seat in 2010 in what was otherwise a strong Republican electoral cycle. The question is whether Republicans in Washington and in other critical states are willing to learn the lessons of the California GOP in order to remain politically viable, not just in 2014, but in 2016 and beyond.

Chapter 10

IMMIGRATION POLITICS AND THE 2014 ELECTION

With Elizabeth Bergman and David Damore

The decision by many Republicans during the middle part of the last decade to abandon the politics of Latino outreach championed by then-President George W. Bush in favor of messaging and policies reminiscent of Pete Wilson–era Republicanism in California has led Latinos to increasingly cast their ballots for Democrats.* But is this movement away from the GOP and toward the Democrats indicative of a long-term national realignment akin to what occurred in California, or does it reflect responsiveness among Latino voters to short-term political conditions?

Clearly, some Republicans fear that the GOP is on the verge of a national Proposition 187 movement. During an appearance on NBC's *Meet the Press* in June 2013, Senator Lindsey Graham (R-SC) declared that the Republican Party is "in a demographic death spiral as a party and the only

*An earlier version of parts of this chapter appeared as Elizabeth Bergman, Gary Segura, and Matt Barreto, "Immigration Politics and the Electoral Consequences: Anticipating the Dynamics of Latino Vote in the 2014 Election," *California Journal of Politics and Policy* (February 14, 2014), DOI: 10.1515/cjpp-2013-0046, available at: http://www.degruyter.com/view/j/cjpp-ahead-of-print/cjpp-2013-0046/cjpp-2013-0046.xml?format=INT.

way we can get back in good graces with the Hispanic community in my view is to pass comprehensive immigration reform. If you don't do that, it really doesn't matter who we run [in 2016] in my view."[1] Graham's comments came on the heels of a report that was inaugurated by Republican National Committee chair Reince Priebus in the aftermath of the 2012 election. Among the report's chief recommendations was that the Republican Party change its relationship with Latinos for one compelling reason:

> If Hispanic Americans hear that the GOP doesn't want them in the United States, they won't pay attention to our next sentence. It doesn't matter what we say about education, jobs or the economy; if Hispanics think that we do not want them here, they will close their ears to our policies. In essence, Hispanic voters tell us our Party's position on immigration has become a litmus test, measuring whether we are meeting them with a welcome mat or a closed door.[2]

The reasons for such introspection are obvious: during the past decade the country's rapidly changing political demography has shifted a number of states (Colorado, Florida, New Mexico, Nevada, and Virginia) from Republican- to Democratic-leaning, and in coming electoral cycles these same dynamics threaten to put other Republican strongholds, such as Arizona, Georgia, North Carolina, and Texas, into play. Latino political influence is emerging precisely at the moment when the size and voting power of the Republican base is waning. While the GOP continues to receive approximately 90% of its vote from non-Hispanic whites, that share of the population—almost 80% when Ronald Reagan was elected to the presidency in 1980—is now just 63%.

Yet, despite these warnings, many Republicans would prefer to either ignore the immigration issue or, worse, continue down the path that resulted in Mitt Romney winning just 23% of the Latino vote in 2012. As a consequence, today we are witnessing another pivotal movement in immigration politics. The 113th Congress is considering a spate of immigration reform bills, reengaging the failed efforts of 2006 and 2007. Whether or not this latest moment accelerates or reverses the trends begun by Proposition 187 and reinvigorated by the 2006 Sensenbrenner bill

FIGURE 10.1 Share of Latino Voters in 2013 with Past Self-Reported Vote for a GOP Candidate for Any Office

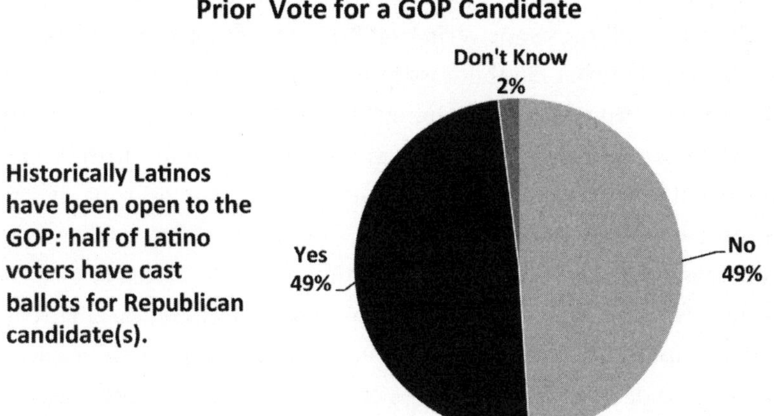

Source: Latino Decisions/Hart Research/SEIU, July 18, 2013 (N = 600).

is the central question. The outcome hinges on the passage (or failure) of comprehensive immigration reform legislation and the degree to which Republicans are allocated a share of the credit (or blame) for the outcome.

What can recent public opinion polling tell us about whether the immigration debate will matter to the future prospects of the Republican Party? The evidence suggests that there are significant political risks for the GOP in 2014 and beyond if comprehensive reform fails, and a substantial opportunity for improvement should the party play a constructive role in bringing such legislation to fruition. Specifically, we draw on recent polling conducted by Latino Decisions to examine Latino attitudes relevant to the debate over immigration reform.

Those who advocate no policy change on the part of the GOP argue that Latinos are not "a natural Republican constituency," as many Republicans claim, but rather are irretrievably Democratic. As a consequence, immigration reform will only make more Democrats, not persuade Latino registered voters to support Republicans. Such a claim is ahistorical and rooted more in the last four election cycles than in any long-term assessment of Latino vote preferences.

Polling data suggest that a sizable number of Latino voters have cast a ballot for a Republican at least once in their life. As we report in Figure 10.1, a poll of registered Latino voters in 2013 showed that approximately half of all those answering (49%) recalled voting for Republican candidates in the past. So there is room for growth.[3] Indeed, the shift in Latino support from Bush to Romney (40% to 23%) represents the largest inter-election movement of any racial and ethnic group during this period—and it's all the more troubling given that Latinos cast roughly 5 million more ballots in 2012 than in 2004. Thus, the evidence suggests that as much as one-fifth of the Latino electorate may be available to a GOP candidate with the right qualities and absent the immigration albatross.

That as many as half of all Latino voters have shown a willingness to vote for candidates of both parties is critical to understanding whether—and how—action on immigration might have political effects. To assess whether Latino voters feel that the immigration issue could shape or reshape their vote intentions, Latino Decisions used a split-sample experiment: we asked respondents how their vote intention might change if Republicans "tried to block" or "worked to pass" comprehensive immigration reform.

The results were striking. When prompted with the possibility that the GOP might work to pass immigration reform, 34% of Latino registered voters said that such an effort would make it more likely that they would vote for a GOP candidate, compared with only 13% reporting that it would make them less likely. About half said that GOP efforts on immigration reform would have no effect on their vote; both loyal Republican and loyal Democratic voters were in this group. By twenty-one percentage points, the movement among Latino voters is decidedly toward the GOP when the party works for comprehensive reform. By comparison, blocking immigration reform has real dangers for the GOP. When prompted with the possibility of this outcome, 59% of Latino voters said that it would make them less likely to support GOP candidates, compared with only 8% who viewed this possibility more positively. Fewer than 30% of our respondents said that such an action would have no effect.

The results illustrate two important points regarding the immigration debate and GOP prospects. First, things could get worse. That is, as bad

FIGURE 10.2 Potential for Growth in GOP Vote Share among Latino Registered Voters, 2013

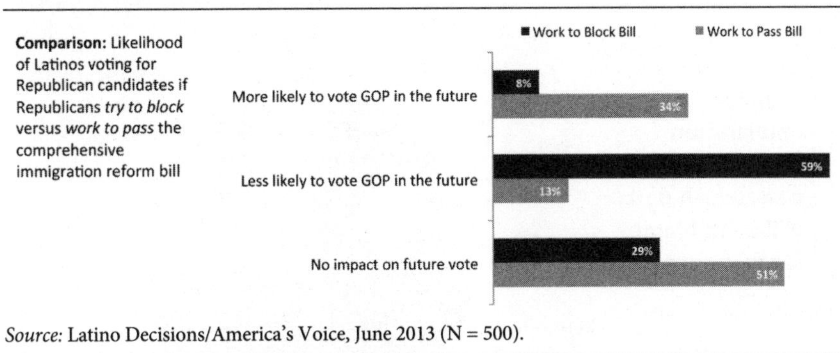

Source: Latino Decisions/America's Voice, June 2013 (N = 500).

as the GOP has performed in recent elections among Latino voters, the party is at risk of further reducing its already dismal standing. It is also worth noting that the party's handling of immigration alienates other growth segments of the electorate, especially younger voters and Asian Americans.[4] Thus, just as we saw in California, immigration politics creates spillover effects that could further hinder the GOP's competitiveness. Second, and perhaps more importantly, the downside from opposition to immigration reform is larger than the upside from taking action. A key conservative talking point in the summer of 2013 was that there was no benefit to GOP candidates for enacting immigration reform. These data suggest that there is certainly a benefit from action, but a more significant cost incurred from inaction.

The GOP's political calculations within the legislative context have sought to manage expectations of what reform might entail (for example, comprehensive versus piecemeal versus maintaining the status quo), while trying to set up the Democrats for the blame should reform fail. To this end, House GOP strategists have repeatedly attempted to construct the terms of the debate around border security and Democrats' insistence on an all-or-nothing approach, in hopes of shifting blame to the Democrats if no bill emerges. There is little evidence in the polling that such an approach would be effective with the Latino electorate, as many see the party's insistence on a "security first" approach as a Republican poison pill to kill reform.

FIGURE 10.3 Partisan Blame Assessment among Latino Voters Should Comprehensive Immigration Reform Fail, 2013

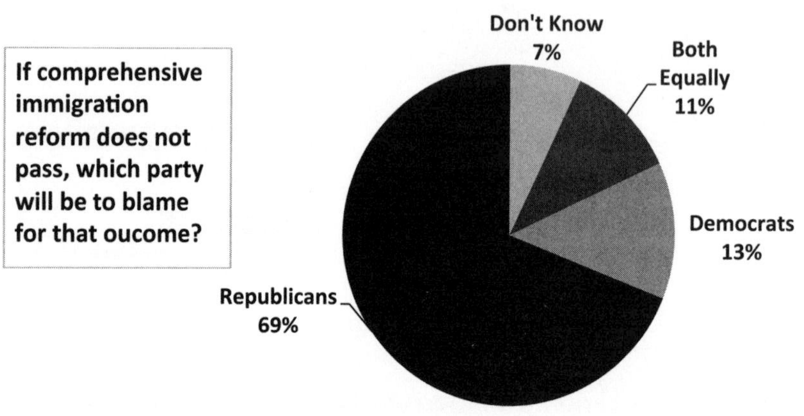

Source: Latino Decisions/Hart Research/SEIU, July 18, 2003 (N = 600).

Figure 10.3 illustrates the potential attribution of blame by Latino registered voters should immigration reform falter. Over two-thirds (69%) of all voters surveyed would hold the GOP responsible for failure, while only 13% would point to the Democrats; another 11% would blame both parties equally. Moreover, the failure of immigration reform would have significant reputational effects on the GOP brand name.

Figure 10.4, which summarizes changes in voters' affective reactions to the GOP under the failure scenario, illustrates three key points. First, the GOP brand is poor among Latino registered voters. The Republican party's net favorability is -27, meaning that the share of voters who view the party positively is twenty-seven percentage points smaller than the share of those who view it unfavorably. Second, when prompted with the possibility of the failure of immigration reform, things got significantly worse for the GOP. The party's favorability dropped eleven percentage points (to 22%), while unfavorable views of the GOP climbed thirteen points, to 73%, creating a net favorability for the GOP of an astonishing -51. Perhaps more telling is the third finding reported in Figure 10.4. In the left-hand block, we report the same figures for respondents who reported having previously voted for GOP candidates; not surprisingly, the

FIGURE 10.4 GOP Reputational Effects among Latino Voters Should Comprehensive Immigration Reform Fail, 2013

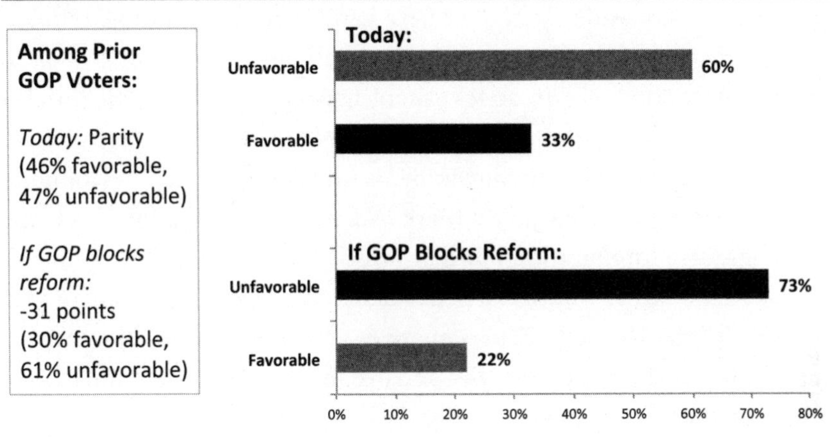

Source: Latino Decisions/Hart Research/SEIU, July 18, 2003 (N = 600).

GOP's reputation among these voters is higher. Unprompted, they had only a -1 net favorability. When prompted with the possibility that the GOP would stop immigration reform, however, even among these former GOP voters net favorability dropped thirty points, to a net -31.

So the polling evidence from the summer of 2013 makes clear that there is substantial opportunity for GOP electoral growth should the party embrace and advance immigration reform. But if the party is seen as the obstacle to enacting that legislation, it would shoulder most of the blame among Latino registered voters, resulting in further reputational and electoral erosion.

PLACING THE 2014 MIDTERM ELECTIONS IN CONTEXT

As informative as these data are, they ultimately are limited by the fact that they come from a national sample. Thus, while we know how Latino voters, in general, perceive the politics of immigration reform, how exactly these attitudes translate into votes and affect electoral outcomes is shaped by at least three considerations.

First and most obviously, elections in the United States are geographically based, and to date much of the evidence capturing the influence of the Latino vote has focused on presidential and, to a lesser extent, statewide elections. In 2014, however, the presidency is not on the ballot, and there are few statewide elections where Latinos are poised to be influential. Specifically, of the thirty-five US Senate seats that will be contested in 2014, only three are in states where Latinos might be influential—Colorado, New Mexico, and perhaps Virginia. Moreover, all three of these elections feature Democratic incumbents (the cousins Udall in Colorado and New Mexico and Virginia's Mark Warner) who voted for S 744 (the comprehensive immigration bill that passed the Senate in 2013), and all three are expected to win. Thus, as detailed in the following section, it is in elections for the House of Representatives where the politics of immigration will be salient and potentially decisive in 2014, but where the impact of Latino voters is less clear.

Second, because 2014 is a midterm election, voter turnout will decline precipitously compared to the 2012 presidential election. Typically, around 60% of eligible voters turn out in presidential elections and just over 40% in midterm elections. Although some think that the incumbent president's party always loses House seats during a midterm election, in fact the party of the president has gained House seats in two of the last four midterms, and in the last two, majority control of the House changed parties.

To be sure, Latino turnout relative to overall population share lags behind other demographic groups. During midterm elections, however, participation by *all* voting blocs declines. Thus, the degree to which "marginal" voters are motivated to turn out overwhelmingly for one party can have outsized effects when the size of the electorate shrinks. For instance, many analysts and prognosticators expect Latinos to vote at low rates in 2014. Thus, if Latinos are mobilized—perhaps frustrated or even angry with House Republicans for blocking an immigration bill—increased Latino turnout in 2014 would undermine the models on which these predictions are based. This is exactly why analysts at the Rothenberg Political Report, the Cook Political Report, and FiveThirtyEight.com all incorrectly predicted that Harry Reid would lose to Sharron Angle in the 2010 midterm. Offended by Angle's harshly anti-Latino messaging, Latino voters in the Silver State constituted the same share of the electorate in 2010 as they did in the general election of 2008, and their 90% support was a key factor in Reid's victory.[5] More generally, given the growth and relative youth of Latino and other minority voters relative to whites, one point is clear: the 2014 midterm election will feature the smallest share of white voters in a nonpresidential election in the country's history.

Third, the competitiveness of a given electoral contest is shaped by factors (such as retirements, divisive primaries, or challenger quality) that, for the most part, are unique to each context. Races that seem like they should be competitive can result in blowouts, while other contests that appear out of reach for one party can become competitive if an incumbent is weakened by a late-breaking scandal or a surprisingly strong challenger emerges. Projecting from 2012 to 2014, two House districts illustrate these dynamics. In Minnesota's 6th District, Republican Michelle Bachmann narrowly won reelection by 1.2% in 2012, while underperforming Mitt Romney by nearly fourteen points. Without the galvanizing Bachmann, who announced her retirement in the spring of 2013, it is unlikely that the Democrats will be able to compete for that seat in 2014 given its underlying Republican tilt. Nevada's 3rd District suggests the opposite. Instead of running against a lackluster opponent in a district that was carried twice by Barack Obama and overshadowed by presidential and US Senate races in 2012, Republican Joe Heck is facing a heavily recruited and funded candidate in what will be the most visible election in Nevada in 2014.

With these considerations in mind, in the following section we present our analysis of the House districts where Latinos are positioned to be influential in 2014. As our analysis indicates, depending on how the legislative debate over comprehensive immigration reform unfolds, there are a sufficient number of districts where the preferences of Latino voters may determine which party controls the House come January 2015.

PROJECTING LATINO INFLUENCE IN THE US HOUSE OF REPRESENTATIVES

The conventional wisdom suggests that because of gerrymandering, Republicans should maintain control of the House of Representatives through the end of the decade. Much of this structural advantage resulted from the party's strong showing during the last midterm election in 2010,

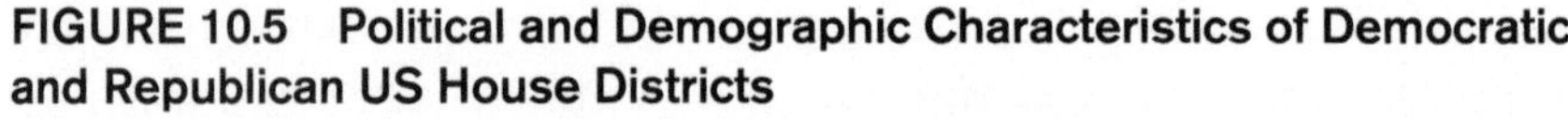

FIGURE 10.5 Political and Demographic Characteristics of Democratic and Republican US House Districts

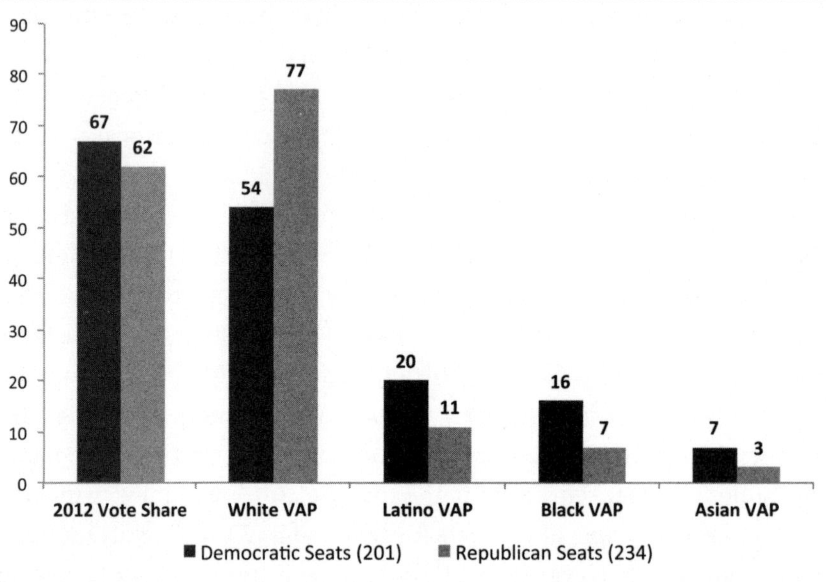

which delivered unified Republican control (both chambers of the statehouse and the governorship) in twenty-one states prior to the legislative sessions that determined redistricting and reapportionment. Across the country, Republicans were able to draw district boundaries favorable to their party even in states that were again carried by President Obama in 2012, such as Ohio, Pennsylvania, and Virginia. As a consequence—or so goes the thinking—most House Republicans have little incentive to address immigration reform or even adapt to the country's changing political landscape.

The data presented in Figure 10.5 succinctly capture the logic underlying these assessments by highlighting the very different worlds that the average House Republican and House Democrat inhabit. Specifically, Figure 10.5 compares the 2012 Democratic and Republican vote shares for all contested House seats, as well as the ethnic and racial composition of the House districts held by Democrats and Republicans in the 113th Congress. By packing partisans of both parties into so many safe districts, the two parties were able to ensure that most House members won their elections with substantial margins. On average, winning Democrats received over two-thirds of the vote in 2012, while winning GOP House members averaged 62% of the vote.

The larger average vote share for Democrats is a key reason why the party gained only eight seats in 2012 despite winning more than 1.5 million more votes nationally than the GOP. Perhaps more significant to the immigration debate, House seats presently held by Republicans have an average voting-age population (VAP) that is over three-quarters white. In contrast, Democratic House seats have on average 30% fewer voting-age whites and over twice as many voting-age African Americans and Asian Americans and nearly twice as many voting-age Latinos as their Republican counterparts.

It is with these data in mind that incumbent House members of both parties often claim to be more concerned about primary challengers than a strong general election opponent from the opposition party. In particular, for Republicans who are concerned about a primary challenge from their right flank, the path of least resistance may be to oppose any legislation that could be depicted either as being weak on security or providing "amnesty" to undocumented immigrants.

However, the pessimism embodied in these predictions overlooks three important points. First, polling suggests that immigration reform is not an animating issue for most Republican primary voters and that most Republican voters generally support the same reforms as Latinos. Second, the Latino population is growing everywhere, including in GOP House districts. Indeed, if anything, these data, which use 2010 US census voting-age estimates, underestimate Latino shares, while overestimating white shares. Third, developing expectations about members' behavior in terms of average district characteristics obscures the individual contexts in which Republican incumbents are vulnerable and Latinos may be influential. So, while voting-age Latinos may have little presence in most Republican-held districts, there are a significant number of districts where Latinos are positioned to affect outcomes in 2014 and, by extension, partisan control of the House of Representatives.

To assess these dynamics, Tables 10.A1 and 10.A2 in the appendix present district-level analyses that examine all seats where the 2010 Latino voting-age population either exceeds or approaches the 2012 margin of victory, as well as districts won by the opposition party's presidential candidate. In total, forty-four Republican (Table 10.A1) and fifty-eight Democratic (Table 10.A2) districts meet these criteria. Each party's seats are then placed into one of three tiers according to their vulnerability and the potential effect of Latino voters in 2014. Tables 10.A1 and 10.A2 also include columns detailing the incumbent's 2012 margin of victory, the difference between President Obama's and Mitt Romney's vote shares in the district, the district's white and Latino voting-age populations, and the member's vote on funding for DACA.[6]

Table 10.A1 indicates that there are fourteen tier 1 and ten tier 2 Republican districts where Latino voters could be decisive in 2014.[7] As a consequence, if House Republicans opt for hard-line immigration policies that are out of step not just with the preferences of Latino voters but with the public more generally, then the party may push already vulnerable incumbents into untenable positions heading into 2014. Given that the Democrats need a net gain of just seventeen seats to secure the majority, failure by the House Republicans to successfully navigate immigration legislation could prove quite costly for the GOP, even if the vast majority of House Republicans win reelection with minimal competition.

As we detailed earlier, a consistent finding in Latino Decisions' polling conducted in 2013 is that the Republican Party has much to lose when it comes to immigration if it chooses to play an obstructionist role. However, by playing a constructive role in passing immigration reform that includes a pathway to citizenship, the GOP would be able to get beyond an issue that makes it nearly impossible for it to make inroads with Latino voters, while at the same time providing valuable political coverage for its most vulnerable House incumbents. If the party instead pushes legislation that focuses only on enforcement or that proposes to make an already cumbersome path to citizenship even more arduous, then Mitt Romney's 2012 performance among Latino voters may be the GOP's high-water mark for quite some time.

As the data in Table 10.A2 make clear, Democrats also have great incentive to act on immigration reform. In fact, there are more Democratic districts where the Latino vote may be influential in 2014. Much of this interparty difference stems, however, from the large number of Democratic seats with majority-minority shares, or near-majority-minority shares. Indeed, many Democratic House members with the largest 2012 margins of victory represent districts where voting-age minorities constitute a majority or a near-majority. Thus, while Latino and minority voters may be "deterministic" in these districts, given the large 2012 margins and the strong Democratic tilt of these voters, it is difficult to think of scenarios in which the outcomes of these 2014 House elections would be affected by short-term political forces to the degree that these districts would swing toward the GOP.

Still, there are a significant number of vulnerable Democrats. Specifically, seventeen Democrats are considered tier 1 targets for Republicans (six from districts carried by Romney), compared to fourteen Republicans (six of whom represent districts that President Obama won). Given that historically the president's party loses on average thirty House seats in a midterm election, Democratic support for comprehensive immigration reform that includes a pathway to citizenship may insulate Democratic incumbents representing marginal seats. Thus, while the Democrats have received strong support from Latino voters in recent election cycles, as polling by Latino Decisions highlights, continued turnout for Democrats depends for many Latinos on the role that Democrats play in immigration reform.

In sum, there are a sufficient number of House seats presently held by both parties where Latino voters could tilt the outcome in 2014 in a manner that determines which party controls the House of Representatives in 2015.

~

Given the analysis in this chapter, we conclude by considering what it will take for the GOP to improve its electoral standing with Latino voters. Any comment on this possibility, however, requires a nuanced understanding of the Latino vote.

We could argue, for instance, that GOP leadership on immigration would immediately move lots of voters. On a political level, however, logical and empirical inconsistencies emerge. For most Latino voters, rewarding Republicans necessarily means punishing Democrats. That is, irrespective of congressional action or inaction on immigration reform, for Latino voters to support Republican House candidates in 2014 (and beyond) would require that they reevaluate and change their extant partisan preferences (and of course, for these votes to "matter" these voters must reside in one of the districts identified in Tables 10.A1 and 10.A2). The vote-switching literature does allow individual preferences to vary across different offices and levels of government.[8] The vote-switching behavior by the most liberal Latinos that is required, however, if the "harm-to-Democrats" theory is going to work is unlikely to occur in the same congressional district.

On the other hand, there are three other paths to electoral influence that could tilt in the GOP's direction. First, there is demonstrably a Latino population that is less predisposed to vote Democratic. These voters have a history of voting for the GOP, may not be as liberal as other Latinos, and find themselves in the Democratic column precisely because of the GOP's rhetoric and positioning on immigration and other Latino policy priorities such as health care and education.

Earlier, we illustrated that almost half of all Latino registered voters have a history of having voted GOP in the past. The existence of a sizable cohort of prior Republican voters among Latinos suggests that there is considerable room for growth absent the party's present handling of immigration. In the simplest terms, if 40% of Latinos voted for George W. Bush and only 23% supported Mitt Romney, the implication is that a significant share—maybe as much as 17% to 20% of the national Latino electorate—is movable, *absent the anti-Latino and anti-immigrant rhetoric and party image.*

Second, there is the issue of abstention. Often less examined in the immigration debate is the peril that the Democrats may face if they fail to act or are perceived to have acted ineffectively. In 2012 President Obama faced a significant uphill climb with Latino voters, whose enthusiasm was low given his administration's record number of deportations and failure even to propose comprehensive immigration reform legislation in his first term. These voters were not anxious to vote Republican, but some might have been contented not to have voted at all in the absence of administrative action on DACA.

Finally, the decline of hostile rhetoric from Republicans may simply result in undermobilization for Democratic-leaning Latinos. The poisonous debate over immigration during the last several election cycles has helped to mobilize a larger share of left-leaning Latino voters to register and turn out. Even if the GOP does not persuade a meaningful share of Latino voters to move to its column and the Democrats do nothing to disappoint Latinos, simply eliminating the negative rhetoric and deemphasizing the issue of immigration could provide space for GOP brand recovery. More importantly, getting immigration off the table would remove the mobilizing effect the issue has had and conceivably reduce the Democratic vote share merely through declining Latino enthusiasm for voting.

There is evidence of this enthusiasm gap in the record of the 2010 election. Latino Decisions' weekly tracking poll showed significant improvement in enthusiasm and intended turnout *after* Senator Harry Reid brought the DREAM Act up for a vote in the Senate. Without action—even unsuccessful action—Latino voters who might otherwise have voted Democratic were less enthused and less likely to turn out. Action motivated enthusiasm. Alternatively, the evidence is also clear that hostile GOP rhetoric motivates Latinos to go to the polls. Less hostility and the passage of immigration reform might demobilize parts of this electorate.

We recognize that handicapping particular elections should always be approached with caution, as the most important long-term factor shaping each party's electoral fortunes is the distribution of partisanship in the electorate. Nevertheless, there are intervening factors and events that can significantly alter the partisan dynamic. In our estimation, comprehensive immigration reform is one such factor that may loom particularly large in November 2014.

Although President Obama's aggregate vote share declined by 2% between 2008 and 2012, his support among Latino voters increased by 4%. How much of that shift was due to the changing composition of the Latino electorate, and how much stemmed from preference changes among the Latinos who voted in both elections? That question has important implications. Our findings indicate that Latinos who supported McCain stuck with Romney only 65% of the time, compared to 84% of non-Hispanic McCain backers. Or put differently, Romney's low levels of Latino support were not simply a function of the changing composition of the electorate, but also resulted from changes in the preferences of Latino voters.[9] For the GOP to fend off the electoral consequences of demographic change, the party must persuade those Latino voters who are open to supporting Republican candidates that the age of hostility is over. The failure of immigration reform would make this all but impossible.

Chapter 11

OBAMACARE FROM THE LATINO PERSPECTIVE

For a number of reasons, the success of the Patient Protection and Affordable Care Act (ACA) lies in its ability to increase health insurance access for groups like the Latino population. With their demographic profile of being generally younger and heavily uninsured, the Latino population in the United States occupies a "sweet spot" for those making projections regarding the potential impact of the ACA. Latinos lack health insurance at the highest rates of any minority group in the nation. In 2010, 30.7% of the Hispanic population was not covered by health insurance, compared to 11.7% of the non-Hispanic white population. Owing to these high rates of non-insurance, the ACA is projected to expand insurance to 9 million Latinos.[1] Since insurance is the primary barrier to health care for Latinos, the new health care reform bill is especially critical for the Latino community.

Access to health care coverage continues to be a major concern for the Latino population. Despite the fact that their employment rate is similar to that of other racial and ethnic groups, Latinos disproportionately lack employer-based insurance. Also, Latinos' access to employer-based insurance has declined in the past decade.[2] Factors such as citizenship requirements, educational attainment, and socioeconomic status help to explain why Latinos disproportionately lack employer-based insurance compared to other racial and ethnic groups.[3] Furthermore, Latinos are more likely to work in industries that do not provide health benefits, such as agriculture and the service, mining, domestic, and construction industries.[4]

Beyond lacking health insurance, Latinos face other barriers to gaining access to health care, including language barriers, a lack of interpreter services, and a lack of Latina/o doctors in the United States.[5] All of these barriers have led to less health care, less utilization of health services, and health care policies that are poorly suited to the needs of the Latino community.[6]

These barriers to health care and Latinos' low levels of health insurance have had a negative impact on their health status. Latinos experience higher mortality rates from diabetes, homicide, chronic liver disease, and HIV infection when compared to the total population and to whites.[7] Also, Latinos have higher rates of stomach cancer, childhood asthma, and obesity than non-Hispanic whites.[8] Moreover, Latinas experience alarmingly high rates of cervical cancer—double those of white women.[9] The disparities in their access to health care clearly has a negative impact on Latinos' health status and is the reason why the ACA's projected positive impact on their access to insurance is so vital to Latinos.

If, for all these reasons, the ACA is vital to Latinos, it is equally true that the support of Latinos is simultaneously important to the successful implementation of the law. Latinos are the youngest population in the United States. As of 2012, the median age of the non-Hispanic white population was 42.3, while the median age for Asian Americans was about nine years younger at 33.2, blacks were over eleven years younger than whites at 30.9, and Latinos were about fifteen years younger, with a median age of 27.6. Given the need for the ACA marketplaces to attract young (and healthy) Americans to enroll to bring down overall costs, Latinos' youthfulness adds to the need for this population to have high enrollment levels.

WHAT DO LATINOS THINK ABOUT HEALTH CARE REFORM?

While the literature on Latinos' health disparities is vast and informative, less is known about their attitudes toward health policy. The limited but growing literature in this area includes some studies on Latinos' attitudes toward health care policy in particular states. For example, Gabriel Sanchez and his co-authors use data from New Mexico to examine differences between Latinos and non-Latino whites in attitudes toward health care policies.[10] They find that Latinos are more likely than non-Latino whites to feel that affordable health care programs are important. Harry Pachon, Matt Barreto, and Frances Marquez have demonstrated that the policy preferences of Latinos in California are different from those of non-Latinos in that state.[11] They find that the health care policy preferences of most people in California center on HMO reform. Latinos' policy preferences for health care reform, however, center on access to affordable health care.

This chapter builds on this work by exploring Latinos' attitudes toward the ACA and federal health care reform more generally. Because Latino Decisions has been tracking the attitudes of the Latino electorate and the overall population toward health care reform since 2009, our research team has more insight than anyone else into how this critical population's views toward the ACA have evolved over time.[12]

The first survey, before the passage of the law, revealed that Latinos supported the expansion of health coverage, and a strong majority (61%) believed that the federal government should ensure that all people have health insurance, even if it meant raising taxes. As reflected in Figure 11.1, this support for universal health coverage among Latinos was higher than it was among the general US population at the time.

Despite their strong support for expansion of coverage, the November 2009 survey revealed that a large segment (44%) of the Latino population felt that public officials did not take their health care needs into account "much" or "at all" during the national health care debate. Why did so many Latinos feel that Congress overlooked their interests when crafting the Affordable Care Act?

FIGURE 11.1 Proportion of Latino Individuals Who Support the Expansion of Health Care Coverage, November 2009

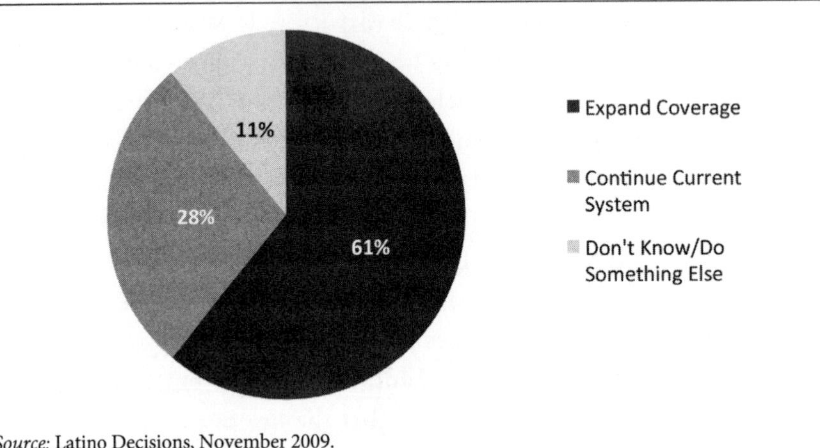

Source: Latino Decisions, November 2009.

Our survey provided some insights into this question. For example, the poll also revealed that Latinos appeared to have a broader definition of *universal* health coverage than Congress did: a majority (67%) of Latinos believed that anyone living in the United States should be eligible to buy or receive health care regardless of citizenship status; the ACA, by contrast, restricts coverage to American citizens. One of the most controversial elements of the congressional reform debates was the potential inclusion of the public option, or a government-run health plan that would compete with private insurance. Our survey indicated that a robust 74% of Latinos—a much larger portion than in the general population—supported the inclusion of the public option in health care reform. In summary, the fact that the majority of Latinos supported two elements of reform that did not make it into the ACA—the inclusion of undocumented immigrants in health reform and the public option—could help explain why so many Latinos believed that their interests were not considered during the reform debates.

We continued to examine the attitudes of Latinos toward the ACA as it developed and found strong support among this population for the law despite tremendous opposition. For example, polling data from March

2010 found that Latino registered voters remained supportive of health care reform even as their support for immigration reform began to take hold. More specifically, when asked in that poll what the single most important issue facing the nation was, health care reform topped the list (32%), followed by jobs and the economy (29%) and then immigration reform (17%). The poll of 500 Latinos fielded in early March 2010, just before the health care vote, found that Latino registered voters remained very strong supporters of health care reform.

The federal health care reform debates captured the nation's attention during President Obama's first year in office. Obama and his fellow Democrats had little time to celebrate their historic policy victory, however, as Republican candidates rode a wave of voter frustration with the economy and the federal government itself to take control of the House of Representatives in the 2010 midterm elections. Making the Affordable Care Act their primary target, the newly installed Republican-majority House wasted little time before passing a symbolic repeal of President Obama's signature domestic policy. Although Republican efforts to repeal this law were stalled quickly in the Democratically-controlled Senate, this legislative action set the stage for a longer-term policy battle over the future of our nation's health care policy.

As the debate heated up in Washington, public opinion polls suggested that efforts to criticize the law moved public opinion. For example, a Gallup poll from January 2010 indicated that 46% of Americans wanted their congressional representative to vote to repeal the health care law, compared to 40% who wanted it to stand.[13] This trend was consistent with other national polls conducted at the time that consistently showed that Americans were divided in their attitudes toward the Affordable Care Act. But did those attitudes match Latinos' views?

A poll conducted in February 2011 by ImpreMedia and Latino Decisions gave us the opportunity to explore how Latinos viewed this issue. Latinos' support for maintaining the law remained higher than the general public's support: 49% of the sample reported that the Affordable Care Act "should be left as law" compared to 31% who believed that "the bill should be repealed." Latinos demonstrated a much lower preference for repeal (31%) in the Gallup poll compared to the general public (46%).

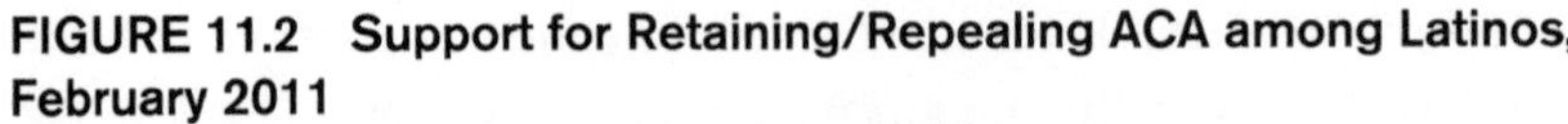

FIGURE 11.2 Support for Retaining/Repealing ACA among Latinos, February 2011

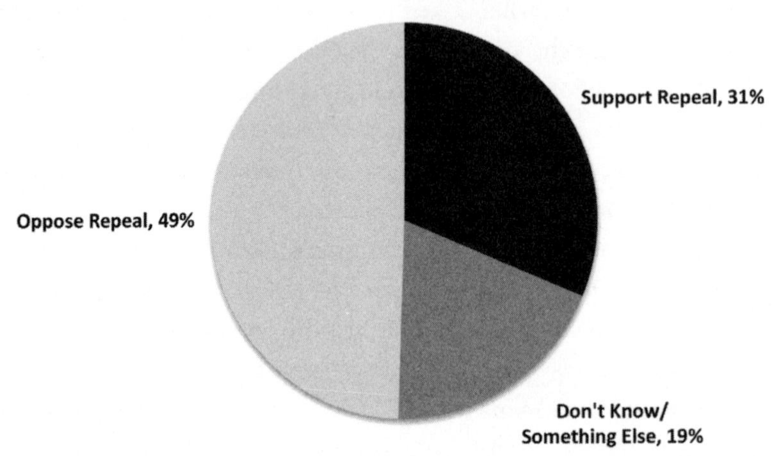

Source: Latino Decisions, February 2011.

However, Latino support for Obama's health care plan dipped over time. At first glance, when we review a figure used in a report based on an ImpreMedia–Latino Decisions survey from November 2009 (see Figure 11.1), it appears that Latino attitudes toward this policy remained surprisingly stable over time. Specifically, just before passage of the Affordable Care Act, 28% of Latinos supported maintaining the current health care system relative to expansion-based reform, a share very similar to the 31% in the more recent (February 2011) poll who supported repeal.

By October 2011, a largely symbolic attempt to repeal the ACA had been passed by the Republican majority in the House of Representatives, a multi-state lawsuit challenging its constitutionality had been filed, and there was widespread speculation that the Supreme Court would rule on the case. Results from a third survey (October 2011) showed that Latino support for the ACA remained relatively high: 50% of the Latino electorate believed that the act should "stand as law," compared to 29% (27% of nonvoters) who felt that it should be repealed. Besides their opinions on the issue of repeal, the attitudes of Latinos toward the ACA itself remained remarkably stable: the trends found in the October 2011 poll were nearly identical to those revealed in a February 2011 survey. When we compare our trends to those from a Kaiser Family Foundation health tracking poll conducted in September 2011, we see again that Latino support for the health care reform legislation remained higher than that of the general population: only 19% of the general population in the Kaiser poll indicated that Congress should "keep the law as is."

Beyond the broad question of whether to keep the law or repeal it, the Latino electorate's very supportive attitude toward most of the landmark legislation had one major exception. When the poll asked respondents to indicate whether "lawmakers should keep or repeal" various aspects of the law, 85% of Latino voters said that they supported providing tax credits for small businesses to provide their employees with coverage, and 80% supported providing financial aid to those with low and moderate incomes to purchase coverage. Only 32% of Latinos, however, supported the "individual mandate"—the requirement that all Americans have health insurance coverage. Furthermore, only 25% of the uninsured in the sample supported keeping the individual mandate.

These trends suggest that what they perceived as the high cost of purchasing health insurance during a period of high economic stress and their lack of confidence in—or awareness about—future financial support for mandatory purchase may have been driving Latino attitudes toward the individual mandate. A robust 52% of respondents who reported that their health care costs had increased over the past year were opposed to the individual mandate. Plus, the extensive efforts of many within the Republican Party to challenge the constitutionality of this aspect of the law may have found traction among Latinos.

The survey also provided an overview of the attitudes of Latino voters toward the perceived benefits of the core goals of the ACA—increasing access to health care, improving the cost of health care, and improving its quality. Across all three of these dimensions, Latino voters ultimately believed that their health care would "stay about the same" with implementation of the ACA. More specifically, when asked about the quality of their care, the same percentage of Latino voters believed that the quality of their health care would "get better" (23%) as believed it would "get worse" (23%). Regarding cost, there were more Latinos who thought that the cost of health care would "get worse" (31%) than those who thought costs would "get better" (24%). In short, a large segment of the Latino electorate seemed to believe that their care would not improve much with implementation of the ACA, and might cost them more.

While these data suggest that Latinos were not very optimistic about the ACA improving health care for their families, 29% of Latino respondents believed that the law would improve their ability to get and keep health insurance, compared to 22% who believed their ability to acquire health insurance would get worse. Finally, results from a post-passage Kaiser Family Foundation tracking poll suggest that Latinos are a bit more optimistic about the law than the general public. For example, responses from the general population in the March 2011 Kaiser Family Foundation tracking poll show that 32% felt that the quality of care would get worse with the implementation of the law, and 42% felt that the costs of care would get worse. Those percentages are significantly higher than what we found for the Latino population: in our polling, 23% believed that the quality of health care would get worse, and 24% believed that health care would become more expensive.

Overall, Latinos were similar to the wider population in having mixed views on the Affordable Care Act following its passage. Although Latinos remained generally positive about the law—as reflected by their support to maintain most of its provisions—they expressed some opposition to the individual mandate to purchase insurance. It also appears that the uncertainties about the implementation of the law and their ongoing experiences over the past two years with lost access to coverage and rising health care costs have weakened Latinos' optimism that the reform legislation will improve their access to health care services.

WITH THE OPENING OF THE ACA MARKETPLACE, HOW MUCH DID LATINOS KNOW ABOUT IT?

Latino Decisions followed up on the 2011 survey by partnering once again with ImpreMedia to conduct a new poll of Latino adults in April 2013.[14] In this study, 800 Latino adults were queried about their knowledge of the new health care law. What we found was a major need not only for more

FIGURE 11.3 Latino Knowledge of, and Familiarity with, the Affordable Care Act

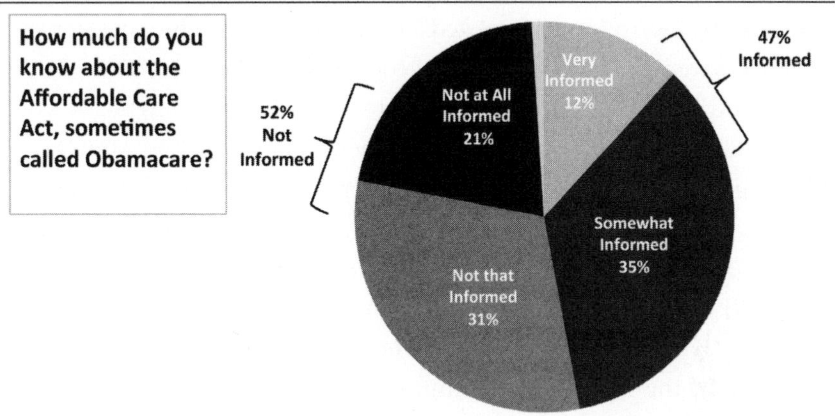

Source: ImpreMedia/Center for Health Policy/Latino Decisions National Health Care Survey, May 1, 2013 (N = 800).

outreach to the Latino community about the new law but for information more directly targeted to this population. In response to our questions, only 12% of Latino adults felt very informed about the ACA, compared to a combined 52% who felt either "not all that informed" or "not that informed" (see Figure 11.3).

This result was reinforced by the overwhelming majority (69%) of Latino adults who said that the ACA was confusing and complicated. Another component of this segment of the survey indicated that only 13% of Latinos thought that public officials in Washington had taken the health needs of the Latino community into account during the ACA debates and bill passage. Finally, when asked to provide the names of different parts of the new law, a robust 71% indicated that they "did not know" any of those subpolicies.

Levels of knowledge about the ACA were higher among those with higher levels of education, with college graduates expressing greater knowledge of the new health care reform law than those with less education. Even 39% of Latino college graduates, however, were either "not at all informed" or "not that informed" about the ACA.

Despite low levels of expressed knowledge, 89% of Latinos said that they were interested in learning more about the ACA, including 56% who said that they were "very interested." Furthermore, after hearing some basic information, 75% believed that the ACA would be good for the Latino community in the long run, compared to only 16% who said that it would be bad for that community. These survey findings provided some reason for optimism that, if properly engaged, the Latino community would be avid consumers of information pertaining to the historic reform legislation, and would enroll in the marketplaces. However, on deadline day—March 31, 2014—Latino subscribership was lagging significantly.

What can be done to increase Latino participation in a program they support? In the April 2013 national survey, we tested a series of messages intended to interest Latinos in learning more about the ACA. Each message was linked with a specific element of the new law, and all of the messages generated a positive response among Latinos, a fact that reveals underlying enthusiasm for the components of the law. However, some messages—such as increasing credits for small businesses, increasing access to health care by expanding the number of community health centers, and improving the availability of medical services such as OB-GYN visits and HIV/AIDS testing—tested better than others. We also included multiple measures of the potential effectiveness of specific messengers in the ACA outreach effort. All of the messengers listed in Figure 11.4 had a lot of traction with the Latino community.

Tapping into social networks for outreach is key, given the high number of Latinos who reported that they would be more likely to enroll if encouraged by family members and friends. Utilizing Latino doctors is also vital: among the messengers tested in the survey, they are outperformed only by family members. One potential group of messengers that is not as obvious as family members and Latino doctors is Latino teachers, who could be very valuable to increasing Latino engagement with the ACA given the trust and respect Latino families accord to teachers.

In another April 2013 poll of Latino adults, this one in the state of Colorado, we found trends very similar to those revealed in the national poll. However, as a final mechanism to assess knowledge of the ACA, we asked respondents in Colorado to indicate whether they believed that

FIGURE 11.4 Effect of Messengers on the Likelihood that Respondents Seek More Information about Obamacare

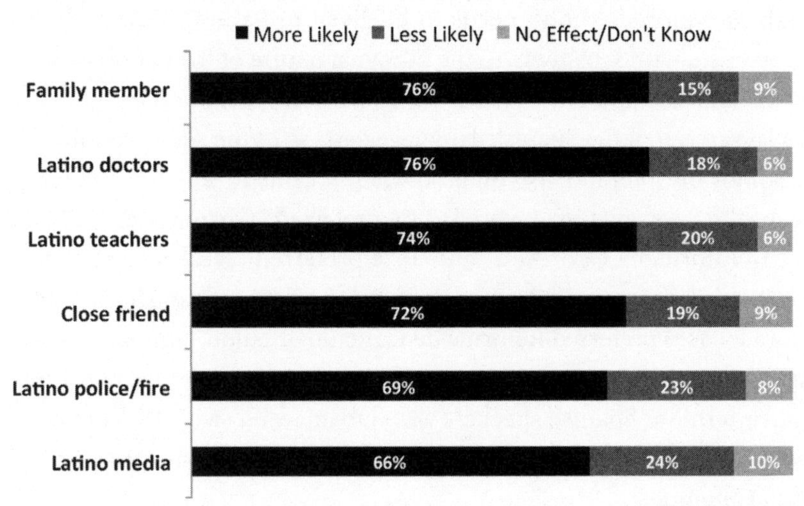

Source: ImpreMedia/RWJ Center for Health Policy/Latino Decisions National Health Care Survey, April 2013 (N = 800).

undocumented immigrants would be able to purchase private health insurance through the state health exchanges. Only 25% of the sample were correct in saying that undocumented immigrants would be "restricted from purchasing insurance through the exchanges," while 50% believed that they would be able to participate in the exchanges and another 25% indicated that they did not know. Interestingly, a strong majority (61%) of Latinos in Colorado believed that regardless of the current structure of the law, undocumented immigrants "should be able to access benefits" through the ACA. During the congressional debates on the law, a vast majority of Latinos nationally expressed support for undocumented immigrants being included in the reform legislation.

A major focus of the Colorado poll was on identifying best practices for those interested in doing ACA outreach. For example, when asked which language they would like to be used to convey information about the ACA, 59% of respondents indicated a preference for English, compared to 14% who preferred Spanish. However, a large segment (27%)

of the Latino population in Colorado preferred to receive information in both languages. This suggests that information about the ACA (and about health care more broadly) needs to be given to Latinos in both English and Spanish, with sensitivity to the bilingual nature of the Latino community in Colorado and other states. This is a troubling finding in light of the very late arrival of the Spanish-language version of the ACA website.

Latinos in Colorado also differed when it came to which name for the new health care law they favored: 38% preferred "Obamacare," 29% preferred "Affordable Care Act," and 14% preferred "Health Care Reform Program." There was similar variation among Latino Spanish speakers in Colorado: 34% preferred Reforma de Cuidado de Salud, compared to 20% who preferred Reforma de Seguro Medico. Interestingly, the third most popular term for Spanish speakers was "Obamacare," with 18% indicating that this term had traction for both English- and Spanish-speaking Latinos in Colorado.

The long-term success of the Affordable Care Act will depend on how well the law performs for Latinos, who all along, according to our data, have supported the law more than non-Latinos, from its inception to the opening of the marketplaces across the nation. Even by the official enrollment deadline of March 31, 2014, the credibility of the law among Latinos remained tenuous owing to a lengthy delay in the provision of Spanish-language tools for enrollment.[15] Uptake among Latinos has been slow—46% of Latinos say they have not enrolled because of the lack of Spanish-speaking materials to aid its implementation in their communities—and states are only now beginning to aggressively market the benefits and communicate information about signing up through the state and federal exchanges.[16] Even if these obstacles do not bode well for the short-term success of the law, however, Latinos remain highly interested in learning more about the ACA since they stand to gain more from its success than any other racial/ethnic population in the nation.

Chapter 12

LATINO ENVIRONMENTAL ATTITUDES

With Adrian Pantoja

In 2010 Vista Valley Services submitted a proposal to the Pomona City Council in California to build a solid-waste transfer station in the city's designated industrial zone.* If approved, the proposed waste transfer station would include a 55,000-square-foot building, sitting on ten to thirteen acres of land, and handle about 1,500 tons of trash per day. Open twenty-four hours a day, the site will process the contents of an estimated 600 garbage trucks daily. Advocates for the waste transfer station claim that it will create fifty permanent, well-paying jobs for a city that has endured decades of economic decline. Opponents, most of whom are Latino, claim that this proposal is the latest manifestation of environmental racism, since over 70% of the city's residents are Latino and the proposed site is within a one-mile radius of nine schools, all of which are majority-Latino.

The Pomona case is not an isolated event. Latinos have mobilized elsewhere to protect their communities from environmental damages. In 1991 grassroots organizations and national environmental groups stopped the building of a hazardous-waste incinerator in Kettleman City, California, a predominantly Latino town. In the 1980s, the "Mothers of East Los Angeles," a group of Latina churchwomen, prevented the building of

*Adrian Pantoja is the lead coauthor of this chapter.

an incinerator in the city of Vernon and later a hazardous-waste treatment plant in the city of Huntington Park. Both Vernon and Huntington Park are largely immigrant Latino cities. Indeed, environmental activism among Latinos can be traced back to the mid-1960s, when opposition to pesticides and other environmental toxins factored prominently in the union organizing of Cesar Chavez and the United Farm Workers.

Of course, protests and activism around environmental matters are frequently carried out by a small group of committed individuals who are willing to spend the time and energy to protect the wider community. Absent in these examples are data documenting the feelings and beliefs of Latinos more generally. In other words, despite these examples and the prevalence of environmental hazards in Latino communities, only a handful of studies have systematically analyzed the environmental attitudes of Latinos.[1] As Latinos gain a meaningful voice in government, they will be in a position to develop and influence public policies. Will environmental issues factor prominently in their policy agenda? How will environmental issues rank for Latinos relative to other issues?

DO LATINOS CARE ABOUT THE ENVIRONMENT?

The dearth of research investigating Latino environmental attitudes suggests that scholars assume that Latinos have other policy priorities, like immigration or education. Indeed, there is a general assumption that concern for the environment is largely a white issue. Early research comparing white and African American environmental attitudes seems to confirm this assumption.[2] The theoretical framework underlying these initial studies draws on Maslow's "hierarchy of needs" theory by essentially arguing that poor and minority populations have more pressing issues like personal security, economic needs, affordable housing, better schools, and affordable day care services and that, compared to these pressing needs, environmental matters are secondary or insignificant.[3] Whites and affluent individuals in the United States and other Western industrialized countries, so the argument goes, have had their basic material needs met and therefore have the time and money to concern themselves with other, more distant matters like environmental conservation.

A counter-hypothesis, the "environmental deprivation" theory, argues that the poor and minorities display greater concern relative to whites because they are directly affected by environmental problems.[4] Direct experience with environmental issues, such as high levels of air pollution, toxic waste, and contaminated water, makes them as important as social issues in these communities, and this direct exposure to environmental problems, the theory argues, leads to more pro-environment attitudes in these communities compared to the attitudes of people with more limited experience or exposure to these problems. Thus, since Latinos and other minorities suffer disproportionate rates of environmentally related morbidity and mortality, these groups are more likely to display awareness of and concern for the environment.

Whether Latinos and other minorities display higher or lower levels of pro-environment attitudes largely depends on the environmental issues being studied. For example, Latinos are likely to display less concern over offshore oil drilling than whites because few Latinos live near coastal areas, especially in California. When it comes to air pollution or the storage of toxic waste, however, Latinos display higher levels of concern because these environmental issues have a disproportionate impact on them.[5]

Using polling data on Latino environmental attitudes from the California field polls from 1980 to 2000, Matthew Whittaker, Gary Segura, and Shaun Bowler laid out six environmental policy issues:

1. Air and water pollution
2. Protecting the state's environment
3. Toxic waste
4. Spending on the environment
5. Self-identifying as an environmentalist
6. Offshore drilling[6]

On the first three issues, Latinos displayed higher levels of concern than whites and African Americans, thus lending support to the environmental deprivation hypothesis. On the last three issues, however, Latinos were no more concerned than whites, and in one instance, offshore drilling, they were less concerned than whites, demonstrating that proximity to an environmental issue influences attitudes. Other studies have produced mixed results when comparing Latinos' environmental attitudes with those of whites. For example, research by Michael Greenberg and by Cassandra Johnson, J. M. Bowker, and Ken Cordell finds that the environmental attitudes of native-born Latinos closely resemble those of whites, while Bryan Williams and Yvette Florez find that perceptions of environmental inequities are higher among Mexican Americans.[7]

Yes, We Care

There is evidence that on some environmental issues Latinos display higher levels of concern than whites.[8] Latinos are particularly concerned about environmental issues that pose an immediate health threat to their families and communities—specifically, brownfields and toxic sites, particulate air pollution from diesel exhaust near industrial zones, and the like. This makes sense in light of other research showing that Latinos react to threatening political issues by taking an interest and participating in politics at higher rates than whites do.[9] Nonetheless, a deficiency of the existing scholarship is that studies of Latino environmental attitudes are limited to studies in a few geographic areas conducted over a decade ago.

Despite their limitations, these studies are significant in that they supplement anecdotal evidence with empirical evidence that the Latinos in their samples displayed pro-environment beliefs. Nonetheless, it's important to go beyond these state-specific investigations and offer a broader and more contemporary view of Latino environmental attitudes. This study fills this gap by drawing on data from focus groups and a unique national survey of Latino environmental attitudes carried out by Latino Decisions on behalf of the Natural Resources Defense Council (NRDC).[10]

Prior to the survey, researchers at Latino Decisions conducted focus groups in Chicago, Illinois; Arlington, Virginia; and Charlotte, North Carolina. Contrary to the stereotype that Latinos are unconcerned about environmental issues, we found that all of the participants were engaged by the topic we presented and quick to offer opinions. We opened the discussion with the broad question: "There are lots of environmental issues facing the country and world. Of all of the environmental issues out there, which are you most concerned about?" Much of the discussion centered on global warming, climate change, and air pollution. The comment of one female respondent from Charlotte is representative: "I would say it's air pollution, air pollution, that worries me the most . . . the kind that comes from factories, you know, the big factories. It bothers me when I'm driving around and I see the smog damaging the air that you breathe every day. That bothers me a lot."

Not only were participants engaged by the topic, but many were strongly supportive of government legislation and policies designed to reduce air pollution and combat climate change. Even when weighing the economic consequences of such programs, Latinos did not back away from protecting the environment. One of the reasons participants gave for favoring environmental action was that they were deeply concerned about the well-being of their children and future generations. And an unanticipated finding from the focus groups was that respondents often discussed environmental issues in their home country and displayed a great deal of concern for their relatives back there. For instance, a female respondent in Arlington said: "Not in my immediate community here but back in my country, I know that the drought season is worse. That the people in the two previous years are dealing more with the lack of water. And the poverty in several areas is increasing because of . . . the crops get withered either because there is lack of water or excess water during the times when it wasn't supposed to be raining."

The focus groups were instrumental in helping us design the survey, which would include many questions on themes drawn from the groups. We included a wide range of policy questions in addition to those designed to provide a social, political, and demographic profile of the respondents.

The survey results revealed that Latinos are very concerned about climate change and air pollution and support government action to remedy these problems. In the survey, Latinos were asked if they favored or opposed the president taking action to fight the carbon pollution that causes climate change. A robust 80% stated that they "somewhat favored" or "strongly favored" presidential action (see Figure 12.1). In a related question, 78% of Latinos agreed ("somewhat" or "strongly") with the more general statement, "We need strong government actions to limit climate

FIGURE 12.1 Support for the President Taking Action to Fight the Carbon Pollution that Causes Climate Change, 2014

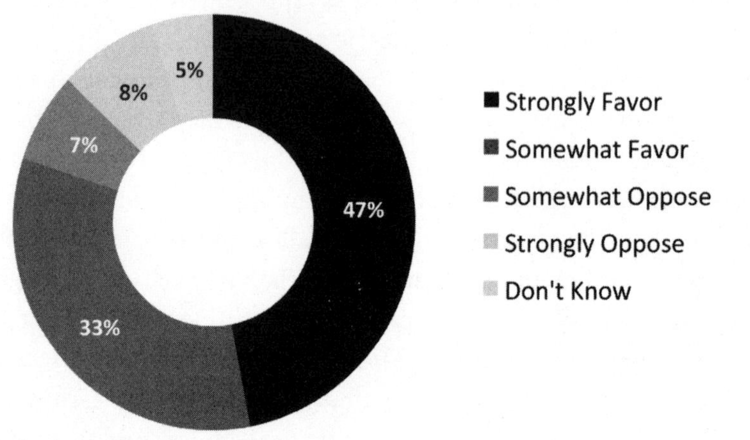

change." In fact, the survey shows, environmental issues come in second only to immigration reform as a top policy issue for Latinos.

Respondents were also asked to state their level of support for five policy ideas proposed by the scientific community for combating climate change:

1. Requiring better gas mileage for automobiles
2. Increasing the use of renewable energy, such as solar and wind
3. Setting limits on the amount of carbon pollution that power plants can discharge into the air
4. Building homes and buildings that are more efficient and use less energy
5. Investing and preparing our communities for future weather events like storms, floods, or hurricanes

Over 90% of Latinos favored ("strongly" or "somewhat") four of these five proposals (Figure 12.2). The only policy idea that fell below 90% was setting limits on the amount of carbon pollution that power plants discharge.

The high levels of pro-environment beliefs were found across most segments of the Latino electorate. We cross-tabulated the responses by a

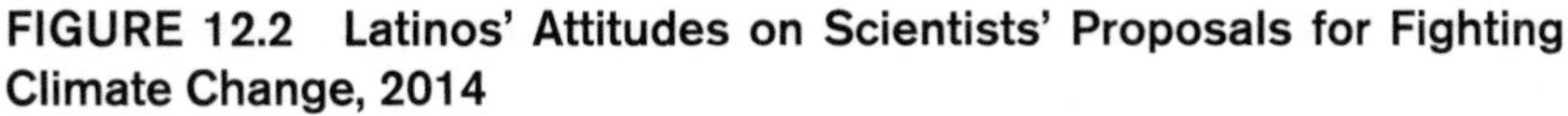
FIGURE 12.2 Latinos' Attitudes on Scientists' Proposals for Fighting Climate Change, 2014

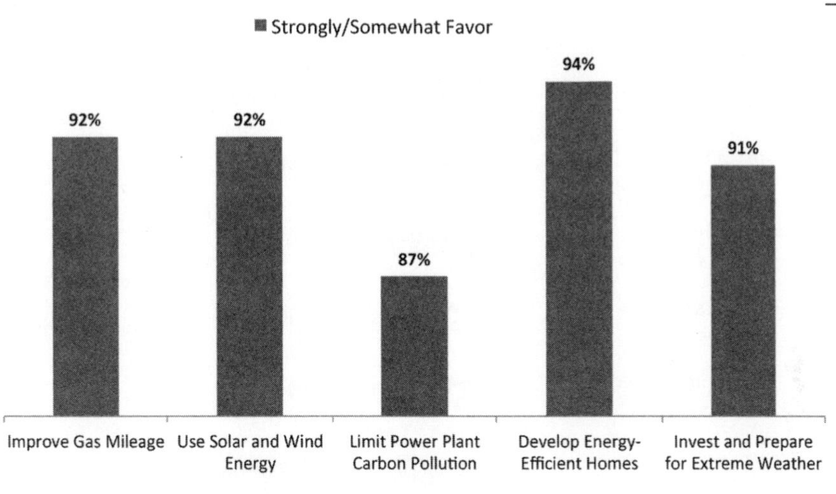

variety of sociodemographic, attitudinal, and political characteristics and found few differences across age groups, nativity, language use, gender, income, education, and other characteristics. The one factor associated with significant differences in attitudes was partisanship; there were significant differences between Latinos who self-identified as Democrats, Republicans, or independents. Of the three groups, Democrats displayed the highest level of pro-environment attitudes, while Republicans displayed the lowest. Independents fell between these two extremes. Figure 12.3 illustrates the partisan divided across the following six questions:

1. "If your member of Congress issued a statement giving strong support to limit the pollution that causes climate change, would that make you feel more favorable or less favorable towards them?" ["Much more likely" and "somewhat more likely" responses are reported in Figure 12.3.]
2. "We need strong government actions to limit climate change." ["Strongly agree" and "somewhat agree" responses are reported in Figure 12.3.]

FIGURE 12.3 A Partisan Divide among Latino Voters Who Self-Identify as Republican, Democrat, or Independent

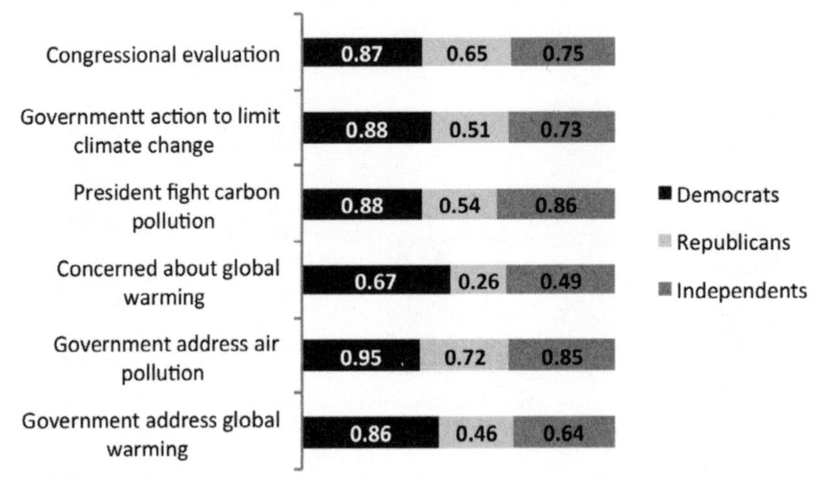

3. "Would you favor or oppose the president taking action to fight the carbon pollution that causes climate change?" ["Strongly favor" and "somewhat favor" responses are reported in Figure 12.3.]
4. "Most scientists say that the Earth is getting warmer and it is human activity that is causing it. They call it 'global warming' or 'climate change.' How concerned are you about global warming or climate change?" ["Extremely concerned" and "very concerned" responses are reported in Figure 12.3.]
5. "Now just thinking about the environment. How important do you think it is for our government to address each of the following issues: air pollution?" ["Extremely important" and "very important" responses are reported in Figure 12.3.]
6. "Now just thinking about the environment. How important do you think it is for our government to address each of the following issues: global warming and climate change?" ["Extremely important" and "very important" responses are reported in Figure 12.3.]

There was a twenty-two-point gap between Democrats and Republicans when it came to supporting a member of Congress for issuing a statement about limiting pollution. There was a thirty-seven-point gap between Democrats and Republicans on government action to limit climate change. Supporting presidential action to fight carbon pollution showed a thirty-four-point gap between Democrats and Republicans. By far the largest gap (forty-one points) was found on the question tapping concerns over global warming. The second-largest gap (forty points) emerged from the question on whether the government should address global warming. Finally, there was a twenty-three-point gap on the question of whether government should address air pollution.

Although the partisan gap is significant, it is politically inconsequential at this point in time given that Latinos overwhelmingly identify as and vote Democratic. Should the Republican Party make significant inroads with the Latino electorate, however, it is likely that their policy priorities will shift. One area that is likely to experience the greatest shift is on policies pertaining to the environment.

WHY DO LATINOS HAVE PRO-ENVIRONMENT BELIEFS?

Having shown that Latinos display high levels of support for environmental policies, we need to explore the factors underlying their concerns. Clearly, there is a significant partisan gap, but are there other factors that may be predictive of Latino environmental beliefs?

If proximity to environmental issues causes Latinos to display high levels of concern, we should see strong support for policies related to air pollution, since this is one of the greatest threats to Latino communities.[11] According to a recent study by the Natural Resources Defense Council, "Nearly one out of every two Latinos lives in the most ozone-polluted cities in the country." Living in cities with high levels of air pollution has a direct effect on Latinos' health outcomes. According to the NRDC report, "Latinos are three times more likely to die of asthma than other racial or ethnic groups."[12] To capture Latino concerns about environmental issues on a local level, the survey asked: "Thinking about the city where you live, would you say that air pollution is a major problem, somewhat of a problem, or not a problem in your city?" Sixty-nine percent of Latinos said that air pollution was a problem ("a major problem" or "somewhat of a problem") in their city. Latinos who see air pollution as a problem in their city display higher levels of pro-environment evaluations relative to Latinos who say air pollution is not a problem. This local environmental concern is a "local motivator."

In our survey, contrary to the findings by Greenberg and by Johnson, Bowker, and Cordell that concern is highest among acculturated English-speaking Latinos, Spanish speakers displayed higher levels of pro-environment attitudes.[13] This is a significant finding considering that over 40% of Latinos are foreign-born—which brings us to our second set of predictors: transnational ties and global orientations.

Latinos are distinct from Anglo Americans in that large numbers have established transnational ties with their home country. Transnational ties are captured with the following question: "Thinking about any family who is living in [country of origin]. How worried are you about environmental problems in their communities?" In the survey, 63% of respondents said that they were "very worried" or "somewhat worried." Finally, the ties that Latinos maintain with their home countries have led to the development of a global orientation. Respondents were asked if they thought about the moral or ethical reasons why the earth should be protected in terms of themselves, their family, their community, their country, or the entire world. Majorities said "the entire world" needs to be protected.

Latinos who have transnational ties and a global orientation display higher levels of pro-environment attitudes than other Latinos. These two additional factors can be characterized as "global motivators."

To assess the impact of local and global motivators on Latino environmental attitudes, these motivators and other demographic factors were cross-tabulated with the following three policy questions:

1. "Would you say it is extremely important, very important, not that important, or not at all important for our government to address air pollution?"

2. "Would you favor or oppose the president taking action to fight the carbon pollution that causes climate change?"
3. "If your member of Congress issued a statement giving strong support to limit the pollution that causes climate change, would that make you feel more favorable or less favorable towards them?"

How did local and global motivators stack up as factors eliciting environmental support from Latinos? If we look at the average response across the three questions, we see that Latinos were strongly supportive of the government combating air pollution (88%) as well as presidential (80%) and congressional (78%) action on climate change. Overall, the respondents who were captured by these seven demographic and attitudinal characteristics (as seen in Tables 12.1, 12.2, and 12.3) scored well above the average response rate. Democrats in particular displayed high levels of pro-environment attitudes. However, the global and local motivators outperform the four demographic factors. For example, in Table 12.1, 99% of respondents who said that air pollution is a problem ("a major problem" or "somewhat of a problem") in their city also said that it is important ("extremely important" or "very important") for the government to address air pollution. On this issue, the local motivator seems to have been underlying Latino support for government action on air pollution. Table 12.1 also shows that global motivators significantly drive Latino attitudes. On the two other questions (Tables 12.2 and 12.3), respondents with global and local motivators were the most supportive of presidential and congressional action. This is not to downplay the significance of the demographic factors, but it does illustrate that they are not as significant as the local and global motivators.

Scholars have largely overlooked the impact of transnational networks in shaping environmental attitudes, primarily because public opinion studies on the environment have explored Anglo American attitudes to a much greater extent, and this group, being so far removed from the immigrant experience, has few ties abroad, if any. Among Latinos, however, transnational networks have a significant impact in shaping environmental attitudes.

~

TABLE 12.1 The Importance of Air Pollution to Latinos

"Would you say it is extremely important, very important, not that important, or not at all important for our government to address air pollution?"	
Local motivator: Air pollution is a problem in Latino communities	99%
Global motivator: "Entire world" response	95
Democrats	95
Spanish speakers	94
Global motivator: Worried about environment/family in Latin America	91
Foreign-born	90
Eighteen- to thirty-nine-years-old	89
Average response ("extremely important" and "very important")	88

TABLE 12.2 Support among Latinos for Action to Fight Climate Change

"Would you favor or oppose the president taking action to fight the carbon pollution that causes climate change?"	
Global motivator: Worried about environment/family in Latin America	92%
Global motivator: "Entire world" response	90
Local motivator: Air pollution is a problem in Latino communities	89
Democrats	88
Foreign-born	79
Eighteen- to thirty-nine-years-old	79
Spanish speakers	78
Average response ("strongly favor" and "somewhat favor")	80

TABLE 12.3 Latinos' Approval of Members of Congress Who Speak Out on Carbon Limits

"If your member of Congress issued a statement giving strong support to limit the pollution that causes climate change, would that make you feel more favorable or less favorable towards them?"	
Global motivator: "Entire world" response	93%
Global motivator: Worried about environment/family in Latin America	92
Local motivator: Air pollution is a problem in Latino communities	91
Democrats	87
Spanish speakers	85
Eighteen- to thirty-nine-years-old	83
Foreign-born	82
Average response ("much more favorable" and "somewhat more favorable")	78

Source for Tables 12.1–12.3: Latino Decisions Climate Change Survey, December 2013.

It is a false assumption that Latinos neglect environmental issues because they are preoccupied with other, more pressing issues, such as immigration reform. Many Latinos live in communities plagued by high levels of air pollution, toxic and industrial waste, and contaminated water. The adverse health consequences of living in such environmental hot spots are well documented.

Latinos of all sociodemographic groupings displayed pro-environment attitudes, but certain segments stood out as having higher levels of support for environmental issues. Specifically, pro-environment sentiment is higher among Democrats, younger Latinos (eighteen- to thirty-nine-year-olds), Spanish speakers, and the foreign-born. Still, local and global motivators were even more significant. Latinos who worried about the environment and their family in Latin America, who had a global orientation, and who were concerned about air pollution in their cities displayed the highest levels of pro-environment beliefs. These are not small segments of the Latino population: about two-thirds of our respondents could be classified as possessing local and global motivators.

This chapter began with the political battle over a solid-waste transfer station in Pomona, California. Whether the city council ultimately approves the building of this facility remains an open question at the time of this writing. Given the prevailing stereotypes about Latinos and their environmental attitudes, proponents of the waste transfer station may not have anticipated the fierce Latino opposition. Perhaps one reason why Pomona was selected for the facility rather than its wealthier neighbor Claremont was precisely because most of its residents are low-income immigrants. Claremont is a wealthy Anglo American city that prides itself on its environmental consciousness. Our survey shows, however, that Latinos also care deeply about the environment and have much to say about air pollution, climate change, and other environmental issues. Latinos are determined to take part in politics and engage in national debates on a wide range of issues. When it comes to protecting the environment, Latinos are eager to have their voices heard, even if some Americans seem unaware that Latinos have something to say at all.

Chapter 13

SOME FINAL THOUGHTS

We have made the case in these last pages that Latinos have the capacity to reshape the American political system and in fact have begun to do so. As a consequence of both their growing numbers and the ability (or inability) of the political parties to accommodate them, Latinos have completely reshaped California politics, begun to have a national impact in Senate elections and the presidential popular vote, and become politically engaged in a widening variety of issues.

Almost without exception, the majority of Latino political attitudes fall on the side of collectivism and mutual responsibility—the belief that government can and should act to improve the lives of citizens. Latinos have not shown themselves to be a monolithic bloc—there are too many differences among them to expect lockstep unity. For instance, though they vote overwhelmingly and increasingly Democratic, more than half of all Latino voters have cast at least one GOP vote in an election. Nevertheless, recent elections have revealed a growing Democratic unity among Latino voters, and recent polls on Latino views of pan-ethnicity highlight a sense of group identity, across nationality groups, that is strong and growing stronger. Not only are Latinos an electoral group, but they are having a systematic impact on the electoral arena.

We are cautious, of course, about oversimplifying the positions of Latinos. Even today, one-quarter of the Latino electorate remains reliably

Republican, and there is every reason to expect that should the GOP revise and improve its outreach and messaging to Latinos—and get the issue of immigration reform off the table—the party could easily recover and collect one-third of Latino votes, or maybe more.

Moreover, politics sometimes changes. One hundred years ago, African Americans were understood as a Republican constituency group, which is hardly imaginable today. African Americans shifted in their ideological and partisan preferences over the years, however, as events and new issues arose, and the same could happen with Latinos. Indeed, we already have an example of a Latino electorate moving right—the Latinos of California prior to the passage of Proposition 187.[1]

On the other hand, it is hard for us to conceive of a set of circumstances that would shift Latinos to the GOP in large numbers anytime soon, and we have three reasons for thinking so. First, the role of race in the GOP coalition is profound and dates back to Richard Nixon's "Southern Strategy," if not earlier. The GOP collects a hefty share of white working-class votes in the South. Racial diversification of the party might win Republicans some new nonwhite voters, but it could very well cost them votes among poor whites; deprived of race as a reason to vote Republican, this constituency might rethink its political allegiance to a party that has never represented it economically.

Second, the religious engine of evangelical Christianity and Mormonism, which has played a powerful role in the GOP for so long, has proved far less effective at recruiting and retaining Latino voters. Latinos are deeply religious on average and attend church more often than non-Hispanic whites. But for Latinos, as we showed in Chapter 3, religion has little to do with voting, and even hot-button social issues do not appear to sway their political thinking.

Finally, it is difficult to know who would lead such an outreach effort in the Republican Party. George W. Bush, with support from longtime adviser Karl Rove, made Latino outreach one of his priorities, giving speeches in Spanish and publicly embracing comprehensive immigration reform. For his efforts, he received a strong 40% of the Latino vote in 2004. But Bush's outreach to Latinos and his immigration reform efforts were also repudiated by his party; when GOP legislators, rather than assisting Bush in his efforts, passed legislation declaring undocumented immigrants to be felons, they sent millions of people into the streets and into the voting booths. As the party has gotten more, rather than less, conservative on immigration issues, the question of who will lead the effort to improve the party's relationship with Latinos remains unanswered.

Political scientists, by and large, are loath to make predictions. The social world and human behavior are filled with way too many variables for them to be comfortable making predictions—and the further off in the future a prediction is, the worse it is apt to be. We cannot say for sure that the GOP will lose races in 2014 because of the growth in Latino voting power. But we would be comfortable betting that Republicans will lose races, in part because that outcome would be consistent with every national election in the last decade. We cannot say that the GOP is on its way to defeat in 2016. The right GOP candidate and the wrong Democratic candidate could combine to sway enough Latino voters and moderate whites to elect a Republican president. But we wouldn't bet on it. In fact, barring an invasion or a profound economic collapse, both of us have a very difficult time seeing a Democrat lose the race for the White House in 2016.

Demography may not be destiny, but it dramatically constrains the range of the possible. In 2012 the Democratic incumbent president was African American, presided during a period of nearly 8% unemployment, and—as a consequence—managed to poll only 39% of the white non-Hispanic vote. And he still won by more than 5 million votes! Latinos played a role in that victory—as did Asian Americans and most importantly African Americans. A lot would have to change in the thinking of those electorates for the GOP to prevail in a national election anytime soon.

Limited time and space have prevented us from addressing here countless other aspects of Latino life in America. We have not been able to speak authoritatively about all of the social trends that affect Latinos, and apart from illustrating Latino disadvantages in education, we have said little about that area, knowing that there are volumes of good work on Latinos in the educational system. We have not offered a comprehensive overview of Latino opinion on all other issues—sometimes because their opinions were not important to their electoral behavior, and other times because their opinions were not meaningfully distinct from those of other Americans. In liking jobs, hating criminals, and knowing very little about international diplomacy, Latinos are exactly like most other Americans.

In the coming years, Latinos will exert greater electoral and policy influence in states and communities across the country and in national politics as well. They have come to prominence in the American political realm as many before them have done—by making their way down a difficult path and going against the occasionally active resistance of the existing majority. What sets Latinos apart is their rapid rate of growth, which has led them to surpass all previous newcomer populations in size and, by extension, potential for political and social influence. The spasms of racial and xenophobic antagonism toward Latinos can in some ways be better understood if viewed from a perspective that accounts for how rapidly this population has changed socially and demographically.

Latino Decisions has devoted the last seven years to watching these political developments, and all our polling suggests that major political change will follow from the demographic changes we have observed. In California such change is already a reality, and as Latinos across the country continue to show up at the polls in ever greater numbers, the rest of America, we believe, will quickly catch up.

ACKNOWLEDGMENTS

First and foremost, we want to express our thanks and friendship to our partners in Latino Decisions, Mark Rosenkranz and Andrew Rosenkranz. The four of us have worked together since 2007 to build Latino Decisions from the ground up and we would not have succeeded without their partnership. We first hatched the idea of Latino Decisions with Mark and Andrew at Agua Verde, a restaurant near the University of Washington, when all four of us lived in Seattle. The research presented and analyzed in these pages is truly a joint effort with Mark and Andrew and would not be possible without their hard work and dedication to Latino Decisions.

Second, Sylvia Manzano—now our third principal at Latino Decisions—came to work with us over three years ago after having started by relying on Latino Decisions' data in her academic research and scholarship. In fact, Sylvia commissioned one of the earliest Latino Decisions studies—a poll of Latino voters in Texas during the March 2008 Obama–Clinton primary. As she likes to say, she was a customer before she became a team member. Sylvia has a very accomplished record as a social scientist, having published numerous research articles in academic journals and books, and also has a very accomplished record as a political consultant and pollster, having directed some of Latino Decisions' largest projects during the 2012 election. Her work is pivotal to the growth and reach of Latino Decisions, and she co-authored several chapters in this book.

Gabriel Sanchez, a nationally recognized political scientist at the University of New Mexico, was our very first employee and founder of the LD blog. Gabe has been a critical contributor since the earliest days of LD and much of the research and analysis presented in this book is a result of projects Gabe has been heavily involved with for more than five years during his collaboration with LD.

Latino Decisions, like this book, represents a collection of smart and accomplished people, some of whom are contributors here and are rightfully listed as coauthors in many chapters. Our team of analysts and contributors amaze us with their insights and thoughtful, skilled, analysis. We are in their debt.

The data collection team of Jessie (J-Loba) Wolf, Dan Fleetwood, Mike Nagai, Natalie Lutz, Juan Corona, Chelsea Benning, Phil Styf, Christine Jones, and dozens of skilled interviewers do an outstanding job of producing the raw material on which all LD analyses are based. We are particularly in debt to J-Loba, who has programmed (and/or copy-pasted) late into the night on too many occasions to help get us into the field in a timely and effective manner. Living the LD dream, Jessie, living the LD dream!

Over the last seven years, we have had the privilege to work with, and for, some of the nation's most effective advocates of Latinos and their full incorporation into American society. We are deeply in the debt of Lynn Tramonte, Clarissa Martinez de Castro, Evan Bacalao, Cristobal Alex, Adriana Quintero, Lourdes Torres, Rosalina Cardenas, Monica Lozano, Angie Kelly, Marshall Fitz, and Christopher Calhoun. To Ben Monterroso, who supported and believed in us from our very first days—before he even knew us yet!—thank you, Ben. An extra-special thanks to our friends and confidants Frank Sharry and Arturo Vargas, for being among our most enthusiastic clients, whose daily fight on behalf of Latinos—citizens and non-citizens alike—inspires us profoundly.

Over the years, several people have taught us a great deal about how to navigate the waters of DC and have supported our growth and efforts as friends and clients. We owe great thanks to Joe Sudbay, Dina Siegal Vann,

Maria Meier, Angela Arboleda, Jose Parra, Maria Cardona, Ruy Teixeira, Vanessa Cardenas, Marcelo Gaete, Tom Schaller, David Ayon, David Lublin, Cara Morris Stern, Alex Nogales, Mike Podhorzer, and Pili Tobar. Thank you.

Chapter 4, on unengaged voters, benefitted greatly from the thinking of Arturo Vargas and Evan Bacalao, both of the National Association of Latino Elected and Appointed Officials, who commissioned the original project.

The book benefitted greatly from the able research assistance of Kassra Oskooii at the UW. We thank the helpful folks at PublicAffairs, especially Clive Priddle for his encouragement and patience in extracting the final manuscript, and his very smart suggestions on improving the research and findings presented in this book. Maria Goldverg and Melissa Raymond exhibited great energy and enthusiasm in the assembly and editing stage and improved the book significantly.

Finally, Latino Decisions would not be able to function without the support of our families and friends who have stepped in on countless occasions when we have had to take redeye flights to DC on a moment's notice, or shouldered the parenting burdens when our conference calls went hours long—through the dinner hour—and supported our endeavors in countless other ways that have allowed us to make LD a success. We are in great debt to our families and closest friends—including Samy Alim, for his love and support, Tom Menendez and Claudio Yerahian, who are the worlds' greatest substitute Papás; Nathan Woods and Blanca Guillen-Woods, who have welcomed us into their home to drink wine and recount our days on the mean streets (and offices) of the nation's capital on too many occasions to count; and finally, and especially, we thank Julie Barreto.

APPENDIX

TABLE 9.A1 Latino Influence in US House Districts in California

Tier	*Member*	*District*	*2012 Margin*	*Obama–Romney*	*White VAP*	*Latino VAP*
(Republican Held Districts)						
1	Denham	10	5.4	3.6	51.8	34.9
1	Miller	31	10.0	16.6	34.4	44.4
2	McKeon	25	9.6	-1.9	50.3	31.5
3	Valadao	21	16.0	11.1	23.3	65.8
3	Royce	39	16.0	-3.7	37.1	28.9
3	Issa	49	16.0	-6.7	65.6	22.2
3	Cook	8	15.0	-13.9	56.0	30.3
3	Nunes	22	24.0	-15.0	48.1	39.3
3	Calvert	42	21.0	-15.1	50.8	32.1

(continues on following page)

TABLE 9.A1 Latino Influence in US House Districts in California (continued)

Tier	*Member*	*District*	*2012 Margin*	*Obama–Romney*	*White VAP*	*Latino VAP*
(Democratic Held Seats)						
1	Peters	52	2.4	6.4	64.6	11.5
1	Bera	7	3.4	4.0	61.2	13.7
1	Swalwell	15	4.2	38.2	40.9	21.0
1	Brownley	26	5.4	10.3	50.8	38.5
1	Ruiz	36	5.8	3.2	51.9	39.4
1	Waxman	33	8.0	23.8	70.3	10.3
2	Garamendi	3	8.4	11.2	55.1	23.6
2	Capps	24	10.0	11.0	62.0	29.0
2	McNerney	9	11.0	17.7	42.0	32.7
2	Negrete McLeod	35	12.0	36.8	19.3	64.7
3	Lowenthal	47	13.0	22.5	38.5	29.6
3	Costa	16	15.0	19.2	30.2	52.8
3	Roybal-Allard	40	18.0	65.0	6.6	84.3
3	Takano	41	18.0	25.2	30.9	50.2
3	Hahn	44	20.0	71.1	9.0	64.5
3	Sherman	30	21.0	33.2	56.7	24.0
3	Davis	53	23.0	25.0	48.0	27.7
3	Sanchez	46	28.0	25.2	22.5	60.9
3	Napolitano	32	31.0	32.7	21.1	57.8
3	Sanchez	38	35.0	31.9	21.9	57.0
3	Vargas	51	43.0	40.5	17.6	63.9
3	Cardenas	29	48.0	56.5	21.8	64.1

TABLE 9.A2 Latino Influence in California Legislative Districts

Tier	Member	District	2012 Margin	Dem–Rep Registration	White VAP	Latino VAP
(Republican Held Districts)						
1	Morrell	Assembly 40	0.80	1.59	40.50	37.45
1	Linder	Assembly 60	3.60	-4.68	35.96	47.49
1	Fuller	Senate 18	–	35.31	33.12	51.50
1	Cannella	Senate 12	–	15.79	30.32	59.14
1	Berryhill	Senate 14	–	17.78	21.93	66.27
2	Gorell	Assembly 44	5.80	1.97	49.59	38.15
2	Nestande	Assembly 42	9.40	-8.17	65.78	24.50
2	Nielsen	Senate 4	–	-6.40	70.39	16.37
2	Huff	Senate 29	10.20	-3.95	35.17	32.36
3	Logue	Assembly 3	11.20	-7.18	70.00	18.30
3	Mansor	Assembly 74	13.20	-12.85	65.87	13.39
3	Wilk	Assembly 38	13.80	-6.07	58.65	23.19
3	Donnelly	Assembly 33	18.00	-5.71	51.38	33.74
3	Hagman	Assembly 55	19.40	-8.32	36.52	26.86
3	Olsen	Assembly 12	21.20	-5.71	58.31	29.45
3	Achadjian	Assembly 35	22.60	-5.22	61.13	30.05
3	Wagner	Assembly 68	21.60	-16.38	52.30	24.73
3	Waldron	Assembly 75	25.40	-19.78	56.47	30.83
3	Conway	Assembly 26	35.00	-10.21	41.51	51.16
3	Knight	Senate 21	15.20	-1.16	45.00	36.31
3	Emmerson	Senate 23	12.60	-6.69	51.04	32.82
3	Walters	Senate 37	14.00	-14.53	59.45	18.77
3	Wyland	Senate 38	–	-14.78	63.16	23.30
3	Anderson	Senate 36	–	-16.01	67.04	20.63
3	Vidak	Senate 16	–	-16.16	57.41	30.82
(Democratic Held Districts)						
1	Fox	Assembly 36	1.10	0.32	42.87	37.21
1	Quirk-Silva	Assembly 65	4.00	0.78	35.23	33.94
1	Correa	Senate 34	–	2.64	33.22	41.48
1	Galgiani	Senate 5	1.00	5.41	45.49	32.93
2	Salas	Assembly 32	5.80	19.55	23.46	63.64
2	Fong	Assembly 8	8.60	4.57	65.54	14.73
2	Muratsuchi	Assembly 66	9.60	5.76	49.30	18.59
2	Pavley	Senate 27	7.20	7.95	61.19	22.20
2	Yee	Senate 8	–	-8.69	61.24	24.02

(continues on following page)

TABLE 9.A2 Latino Influence in California Legislative Districts (continued)

Tier	*Member*	*District*	*2012 Margin*	*Dem–Rep Registration*	*White VAP*	*Latino VAP*
2	Lieu	Senate 28	–	-8.12	53.53	35.32
2	Roth	Senate 31	10.60	2.37	33.16	47.15
3	Jackson	Senate 19	11.40	12.17	47.65	42.49
3	Chau	Assembly 49	12.80	17.19	13.90	29.45
3	Holden	Assembly 41	15.40	11.24	49.52	27.17
3	Gray	Assembly 21	16.40	10.91	39.20	48.47
3	Jones-Sawyer	Assembly 9	17.80	14.66	38.90	22.66
3	Hernandez	Assembly 48	18.80	19.29	22.66	59.25
3	Gatto	Assembly 43	20.40	20.15	58.18	21.31
3	Williams	Assembly 37	20.80	15.61	58.57	33.02
3	Medina	Assembly 61	22.00	8.69	30.35	46.81
3	Weber	Assembly 79	23.40	14.83	38.02	29.69
3	Calderon	Assembly 57	25.00	20.41	21.26	63.19
3	Vacant	Assembly 45	26.80	23.54	53.18	27.11
3	Perea	Assembly 31	28.00	18.72	21.52	63.74
3	Eggman	Assembly 13	30.80	18.17	32.59	36.35
3	Alejo	Assembly 30	30.80	29.22	29.39	61.20
3	Lowenthal	Assembly 70	31.60	27.20	40.12	33.62
3	Rodriguez	Assembly 52	32.00	20.76	20.66	63.08
3	Perez	Assembly 56	32.20	19.71	27.03	66.08
3	Daly	Assembly 69	35.20	27.23	15.36	71.14
3	Gonzalez	Assembly 80	39.20	27.76	17.76	62.90
3	Garcia	Assembly 58	43.60	31.81	15.66	63.26
3	Rendon	Assembly 63	49.00	40.01	13.52	70.88
3	Liu	Senate 25	21.60	10.50	55.22	23.12
3	Padilla	Senate 20	–	22.48	19.06	63.78
3	Torres	Senate 32	–	22.51	22.27	56.53
3	Hueso	Senate 40	–	22.84	19.56	57.90
3	DeLeon	Senate 22	–	23.70	14.15	48.90
3	Hernandez	Senate 24	–	46.94	14.15	61.91

TABLE 10.A1 Tier 1 Latino Influence House Seats Held by Republicans (14 seats)

Tier	Member	State	Seat	2012 Margin	Obama–Romney	White VAP	Latino VAP	Defund DACA
1	Walorski	IN	2	1.4	-14.0	85.2	6.3	Yes
1	Coffman	CO	6	2.0	4.1	67.3	16.7	Yes
1	Webster	FL	10	3.4	-7.7	69.9	14.2	Yes
1	Reed	NY	23	3.8	-1.2	91.1	2.6	Yes
1	Denham	CA	10	5.4	3.6	51.8	34.9	No
1	Southerland	FL	2	5.4	-5.8	68.5	4.8	Yes
1	Grimm	NY	11	5.4	4.3	66.9	13.9	No
1	Gibson	NY	19	5.8	6.2	87.9	5.4	Yes
1	Pittenger	NC	9	6.1	-13.4	76.6	6.6	-
1	Buchanan	FL	16	7.2	-9.3	83.5	8.8	Yes
1	Heck	NV	3	7.5	0.8	64.4	13.5	Yes
1	Weber	TX	14	8.9	-19.8	56.9	19.2	Yes
1	Miller	CA	31	10.0	16.6	34.4	44.4	Yes
1	Tipton	CO	3	12.0	-6.0	75.6	20.6	Yes

TABLE 10.A2 Tier 2 Latino Influence House Seats Held by Republicans (10 seats)

Tier	Member	State	Seat	2012 Margin	Obama–Romney	White VAP	Latino VAP	Defund DACA
2	Davis	IL	13	0.3	-0.3	83.4	2.6	Yes
2	Benishek	MI	1	0.5	-8.3	93.2	1.1	Yes
2	Bachmann	MN	6	1.2	-15.0	93.0	1.8	Yes
2	Collins	NY	27	1.6	-12.4	93.5	1.8	Yes
2	Renacci	OH	16	4.0	-8.2	94.0	1.5	Yes
2	Johnson	OH	6	6.6	-12.5	95.7	0.7	Yes
2	Rigell	VA	2	7.6	1.5	66.5	5.7	Yes
2	Runyan	NJ	3	8.8	4.6	80.0	5.6	Yes
2	McKeon	CA	25	9.6	-1.9	50.3	31.5	Yes
2	King	NY	2	17.0	4.4	68.8	18.6	Yes

TABLE 10.A3 Tier 3 Latino Influence House Seats Held by Republicans (20 seats)

Tier	*Member*	*State*	*Seat*	*2012 Margin*	*Obama–Romney*	*White VAP*	*Latino VAP*	*Defund DACA*
3	Valadao	CA	21	16.0	11.1	23.3	65.8	No
3	LoBiondo	NJ	2	17.0	8.1	71.0	12.2	Yes
3	Ros-Lehtinen	FL	27	23.0	6.7	17.5	75.0	No
3	Latham	IA	3	12.0	4.2	88.6	4.7	Yes
3	Reichert	WA	8	19.0	1.6	79.5	7.7	Yes
3	Young	FL	13	15.0	1.5	83.5	7.2	Yes
3	Paulsen	MN	3	16.0	0.8	84.3	3.0	Yes
3	Kline	MN	2	8.2	0.1	87.1	4.3	Yes
3	Diaz-Balart	FL	25	60.0	-2.1	21.2	70.7	–
3	Royce	CA	39	16.0	-3.7	37.1	28.9	Yes
3	Issa	CA	49	16.0	-6.7	65.6	22.2	Yes
3	Pearce	NM	2	18.0	-6.8	45.3	46.9	Yes
3	Amash	MI	3	8.4	-7.3	83.5	5.4	Yes
3	Cook	CA	8	15.0	-13.9	56.0	30.3	Yes
3	Nunes	CA	22	24.0	-15.0	48.1	39.3	No
3	Calvert	CA	42	21.0	-15.1	50.8	32.1	Yes
3	Sessions	TX	32	19.0	-15.5	58.0	21.9	–
3	DeSantis	FL	6	14.0	-16.3	82.8	5.7	Yes
3	Culberson	TX	7	24.0	-21.3	50.9	27.0	Yes
3	Farenthold	TX	27	18.0	-22.3	47.2	45.1	Yes

TABLE 10.A4 Tier 1 Latino Influence House Seats Held by Democrats (17 seats)

Tier	*Member*	*State*	*Seat*	*2012 Margin*	*Obama–Romney*	*White VAP*	*Latino VAP*	*Defund DACA*
1	McIntyre	NC	7	0.2	-19.3	72.5	7.3	Yes
1	Matheson	UT	4	0.3	-37.0	79.0	14.0	No
1	Murphy	FL	18	0.6	-4.1	74.7	12.1	No
1	Barber	AZ	2	0.8	-1.5	69.2	21.7	No
1	Schneider	IL	10	1.2	16.4	65.0	18.1	No
1	Tierney	MA	6	1.2	10.8	87.1	6.0	No
1	Owens	NY	21	1.9	6.1	92.1	2.4	No
1	Peters	CA	52	2.4	6.4	64.6	11.5	No
1	Esty	CT	5	2.6	8.3	76.6	13.1	No
1	Bera	CA	7	3.4	4.0	612.0	13.7	No
1	Kirkpatrick	AZ	1	3.7	-2.5	56.2	18.1	No
1	Maloney	NY	18	3.8	4.3	74.3	13.1	No
1	Sinema	AZ	9	4.1	4.5	64.4	22.4	No
1	Gallego	TX	23	4.7	-2.6	28.9	65.8	No
1	Bishop	NY	1	4.8	0.5	80.0	11.2	No
1	Brownley	CA	26	5.4	10.3	50.8	38.5	No
1	Ruiz	CA	36	5.8	3.2	51.9	39.4	No

TABLE 10.A5 Tier 2 Latino Influence House Seats Held by Democrats (8 seats)

Tier	*Member*	*State*	*Seat*	*2012 Margin*	*Obama–Romney*	*White VAP*	*Latino VAP*	*Defund DACA*
2	DelBene	WA	1	7.8	10.8	80.4	6.7	No
2	Horsford	NV	4	8.0	10.7	54.8	22.9	No
2	Garamendi	CA	3	8.4	11.2	55.1	23.6	No
2	Frankel	FL	22	9.2	9.5	69.4	17.7	No
2	Duckworth	IL	8	9.4	16.5	60.5	22.1	No
2	Capps	CA	24	10.0	11.0	62.0	29.0	No
2	McNerney	CA	9	11.0	17.7	42.0	32.7	No
2	Garcia	FL	26	11.0	6.7	20.2	68.9	No

TABLE 10.A6 Tier 3 Latino Influence House Seats Held by Democrats (33 seats)

Tier	Member	State	Seat	2012 Margin	Obama–Romney	White VAP	Latino VAP	Defund DACA
3	Bustos	IL	17	6.6	17.0	81.7	6.4	No
3	Barrow	GA	12	7.4	-11.8	59.9	4.5	Yes
3	Rahall	WV	3	8.0	-32.2	94.1	0.7	Yes
3	Schrader	OR	5	12.0	3.4	81.7	11.7	No
3	Cicilline	RI	1	12.0	34.0	75.6	11.9	No
3	Lowenthal	CA	47	13.0	22.5	38.5	29.6	No
3	Perlmutter	CO	7	13.0	14.8	71.0	22.6	No
3	Costa	CA	16	15.0	19.2	30.2	52.8	No
3	Foster	IL	11	17.0	17.2	59.7	21.8	No
3	Roybal-Allard	CA	40	18.0	65.0	6.6	84.3	No
3	Takano	CA	41	18.0	25.2	30.9	50.2	No
3	Lujan Grisham	NM	1	18.0	15.7	46.9	43.5	No
3	Hahn	CA	44	20.0	71.1	9.0	64.5	No
3	Grijalva	AZ	3	21.0	24.5	34.6	55.2	No
3	Sherman	CA	30	21.0	33.2	56.7	24.0	No
3	Davis	CA	53	23.0	25.0	48.0	27.7	No
3	Hinojosa	TX	15	24.0	15.9	19.4	77.2	No
3	Grayson	FL	9	25.0	24.7	42.9	41.4	No
3	Peterson	MN	7	26.0	-9.8	92.9	2.7	No
3	Lujan	NM	3	26.0	18.8	43.7	36.4	No
3	Vela	TX	34	26.0	22.5	18.6	79.0	No
3	Sanchez	CA	46	28.0	25.2	22.5	60.9	No
3	Wasserman-Schultz	FL	23	28.0	23.6	49.2	36.7	No
3	Castro	TX	20	30.0	19.2	26.3	64.9	No
3	Napolitano	CA	32	31.0	32.7	21.1	57.8	No
3	Titus	NV	1	32.0	33.2	42.2	36.6	No
3	Doggett	TX	35	32.0	28.4	29.4	58.3	No
3	O'Rourke	TX	16	33.0	29.7	17.0	77.6	No
3	Sanchez	CA	38	35.0	31.9	21.9	57.0	No
3	Cuellar	TX	28	38.0	21.6	21.1	72.7	No
3	Vargas	CA	51	43.0	40.5	17.6	63.9	No
3	Veasey	TX	33	47.0	44.9	18.4	61.3	No
3	Cardenas	CA	29	48.0	56.5	21.8	64.1	No

NOTES

All credits are to Latino Decisions unless otherwise cited.

CHAPTER 1

1. Barreto, Segura, and Woods (2004).

CHAPTER 2

1. Gutiérrez (2004).
2. Bowler and Segura (2011).
3. US Census Bureau (2012).
4. Hamilton and Chinchilla (2001).
5. Pantoja, "Transnational Ties and Immigrant Political Incorporation" (2005).
6. Brown and Lopez (2013).
7. Ennis, Ríos-Vargas, and Albert (2011).
8. Sawyer (2005).
9. Stokes-Brown (2009).
10. Lopez and Dockterman (2011).
11. Segura and Rodrigues (2006).
12. DeSipio (2006), 463.
13. For data on nativity and age, see US Census Bureau, American FactFinder, "Sex by Age by Citizenship Status (Hispanic or Latino): 2010 American Community Survey 1-Year Estimates," available at: http://factfinder2.census.gov/faces/tableservices/jsf/pages/productview.xhtml?pid=ACS_10_1YR_B05003I&prodType=table (accessed February 29, 2012).
14. DeSipio (1996).

15. Pantoja, Ramírez, and Segura (2001).

16. Wals (2011).

17. Michelson, "The Corrosive Effect of Acculturation" (2003); see also Pedraza, Bowler, and Segura (2011).

18. Hajnal and Lee (2011).

19. Santoro and Segura (2011).

20. Bowler, Nicholson, and Segura (2006).

21. Fraga et al. (2012).

22. The LNPS was confined to Cuban, Mexican, and Puerto Rican residents of the United States.

23. Fraga et al. (2012).

24. Dawson (1994).

25. Padilla (1985).

26. Beltran (2011).

CHAPTER 3

1. Exit polls suggesting that the number was closer to 44% have been widely discredited. For more on this debate, see Barreto, Guerra, Marks, Nuño, and Woods (2006), and Pedraza and Barreto (2008).

2. Kinder and Winter (2001).

3. Bowler and Segura (2011).

4. Since the CPS reports income in ranges with the final range unbounded at the upper end, we have to estimate mean incomes by extrapolating categorical mean incomes within these ranges; given the absence of an upper bound on the last category, we probably underestimate (slightly) the actual medians. For all data estimates we use sample weights provided by the Census Bureau.

5. On subprime mortgage loans to Latinos, see National Low Income Housing Coalition (2013).

6. See, for example, Glink (2013).

7. See Latino Decisions–ImpreMedia, "Tracking Poll Results—February 2011," available at: http://faculty.washington.edu/mbarreto/ld/Feb_banners.htm.

8. Abrajano, Alvarez, and Nagler (2008).

9. Jones-Correa and Leal (2001).

10. Lopez and Cuddington (2013).

CHAPTER 4

1. For the lower figure, see Lopez and Gonzalez-Barrera (2013); for the higher figure, see National Association of Latino Elected and Appointed Officials (NALEO) Education Fund (2012).

2. Verba, Schlozman, and Brady (1995), 15.

3. See, for example, DeSipio (1996) and McClain and Stewart (1995).

4. Dawson (1994).

5. Although we have used pseudonyms to protect the identities of our informants, we have not changed any details about the particular focus groups in which they participated and we quote their actual words here.

6. Apart from a handful of jurisdictions that allow noncitizen voting at the local or school-district level.

7. DeSipio (1996).

8. Pantoja, Ramírez, and Segura (2001).

9. Bowler and Segura (2011).

10. Rosenstone and Hansen (1993/2003), 227.

11. Break points were selected to create an approximately normal distribution using quartiles and natural break points in the data.

CHAPTER 5

1. Bartels (1988) and Abramson, Aldrich, Paolino, and Rohde (1992).

2. US Census Bureau, Current Population Survey, 2009.

3. Norrander (2000).

4. On the seriousness of both the Clinton and Obama campaigns, see Heilman (2008). On the Latino campaign staffs, see Langley (2007). On the endorsements sought from Latino public figures, see Zeleny (2008) and Barreto and Ramírez (2008). On efforts to maximize Latino outreach, see Teinowitz (2008).

5. These estimates are taken from entrance and exit polls, conducted during the 2008 primary contests, that reported the percentage of Democratic voters in each state who were Latino. See "ElectionCenter2008: Results," CNNPolitics .com, August 20, 2008, available at: http://www.cnn.com/ELECTION/2008/primaries/results/scorecard/#D.

6. NBC News (2008). The Texas outcome was determined by the number of pledged delegates, based on both a primary and a caucus. Clinton won the primary with 51% of the vote, and Obama won the caucus portion with 56%. In total, Obama narrowly won Texas, with ninety-nine delegates (*New York Times* 2008); Clinton picked up ninety-four. Caucus results were not known until a few days after the election, however, and so Clinton's win at the polls became the prevailing media and campaign narrative (Malcom 2008).

7. Bartels (1988), Abramowitz (1989), and Abramson et al. (1992).

8. Gurian and Haynes (1993) and Mutz (1995).

9. Smith, "Clinton 'Nuestra Amiga'" (2008).

10. Norrander (1993) and Stone, Rapoport, and Atkeson (1995).

11. Nuño (2007) and Barreto, DeFrancesco, and Merolla (2011).

12. Nagourney and Steinhauer (2008), Goldstein (2008), and Judis (2007).
13. Smith, "McAuliffe: Obama Has Latino 'Problem'" (2008).
14. Contreras (2008).
15. Hero and Preuhs (2009).
16. Gay (2006), McClain et al. (2007), and Vaca (2004).
17. McClain et al. (2007) and Kaufmann (2006).
18. Barreto (2007) and Segura and Rodrigues (2006).
19. Segura and Valenzuela (2010).
20. Latino Decisions interviewed a total of 7,500 Latino voters over the course of the entire primary season, the general election, and the president's first 100 days in office. This sample included Latinos who voted in Republican or Democratic primaries and general election voters who may have skipped their state primary.
21. Segal (2008).
22. Smith, "Clinton 'Nuestra Amiga'" (2008).
23. On Clinton's voter registration work in Mexican American neighborhoods, see *Washington Post* (2008). On her familiarity with Hispanic culture, see Nagourney and Steinhauer (2008).
24. Heilman (2008).
25. Pierson (1975); Basinger and Lavine (2005).
26. Nuño and Guerra (2008).
27. Nevada's caucus was held January 19, California's primary was on February 5, and Texas went to the polls on March 4. The Nevada and California surveys were administered six months prior to the election. The Texas survey was conducted a week prior to election day.
28. Clinton won even larger shares of the Latino vote in all three of these races because the "other" and "undecided" share largely broke her way on election day.
29. On driver's licenses for undocumented immigrants, see Elmore (2009).
30. Pew Research Hispanic Trends Project (2003, 2004).

CHAPTER 6

1. All of the results presented here are the result of statistical analysis performed on the 2008 American National Election Study. For both Latinos and whites, we examined the factors that were positively or negatively associated with voting for Obama in 2008. In doing so, we used conventional social science regression and maximum likelihood estimation models in which we could account for many important and relevant factors at the same time, such as party affiliation, religiosity, and socioeconomic status. With respect to Latinos, we were also interested in de-

mographics such as place of birth, country of ancestry, language preference, and degree of shared ethnic identity and how each of these related to vote choice in 2008. We also employed three different measures of racial sentiment.

2. Leal (2005).

3. Leal (2003).

4. Amaya (2007).

5. Reyes (2007).

6. Pew Research Hispanic Trends Project (2005).

7. Barreto and Leal (2007).

8. Pew Hispanic Center (2007).

9. Latino Decisions, "November 2008 Presidential Election Poll of Latino Voters" (2008).

10. Latino Decisions, "New Poll Suggests Latino Voters May Make the Difference in Four Key States" (2008).

11. Lopez, Livingston, and Kochhar (2009).

12. Hajnal and Lee (2010).

13. On Republican partisanship among Cubans, see Barreto, de la Garza, Lee, Ryu, and Pachon (2002).

14. Dawson (1994).

15. Segura and Rodrigues (2006).

16. Beltran (2011).

17. Fraga et al. (2010).

18. Sanchez, "The Role of Group Consciousness in Latino Public Opinion" (2006), and "The Role of Group Consciousness in Political Participation among Latinos in the US" (2006); Segura (2009).

19. McClain et al. (2006), Lopez and Pantoja (2004), and Pantoja, "More Alike than Different" (2005).

20. Stereotyped beliefs included: whites are lazier *and* less intelligent than blacks (-2); whites are lazier *or* less intelligent than blacks (-1); whites and blacks are equal on work ethic and intelligence, or one group is superior to the other on one dimension each (0); blacks are lazier *or* less intelligent than whites (1); and blacks are lazier *and* less intelligent than whites (2). Using a simple dichotomous measure rather than the index has no appreciable effect on our findings.

21. Respondents were asked how strongly they agreed or disagreed with the following: (1) "Irish, Italians, Jewish, and many other minorities overcame prejudice and worked their way up. Blacks should do the same without any special favors" ("special favors"); (2) "It's really a matter of some people not trying hard enough; if blacks would only try harder, they could be just as well off as whites" ("try harder"); (3) "Generations of slavery and discrimination have created conditions that make it difficult for blacks to work their way out of the lower class"

("generations of slavery" [reverse]); and (4) "Over the past few years, blacks have gotten less than they deserve" ("less than deserve" [reverse]). Two antagonistic questions, "special favors" and "try harder," were coded 0 (strongly disagree) to 4 (agree strongly) on degree of symbolic racism. Two sympathetic questions, "generations of slavery" and "less than deserve," were reverse-coded 0 (agree strongly) to 4 (strongly disagree) on degree of symbolic racism. The two antagonistic measures were summed to form a single "negatively valenced RR [racial resentment]" scale (two-item alpha = 0.69), and the two sympathetic measures were summed to form a single "positively valenced RR" scale (two-item alpha = 0.73).

22. The computer-based AMP implicitly primes affective responses by momentarily flashing images of black or white faces on the computer screen. The brief facial image is followed by a display of unrelated Chinese characters that respondents are asked to evaluate as either pleasant or unpleasant. To the extent that individuals rate Chinese characters negatively following the display of a black face we can infer a negative reaction to blacks. Negative assessments of ostensibly random symbols represent a kind of affective misattribution that has been amply documented in psychological studies (see, for example, Payne et al. [2005]).

23. Nicholson, Pantoja, and Segura (2006).

24. Yanez (2008).

25. De la Garza and DeSipio (1992, 1996, 1999, 2005).

26. Burden (2006) and Kaufmann (2006).

27. Leal et al. (2005) and Guth et al. (2006).

28. Leal et al. (2005).

29. Barreto, Manzano, and Sanchez (2009) and Barreto et al. (2008).

30. Franklin (2004).

31. *New York Times*/TNS Media (2009).

32. Ceci and Kain (1982) and McAllister and Studlar (1991).

33. Green and Gerber (2004).

34. DeFrancesco-Soto and Merolla (2006), Ramírez (2005, 2007), and Nuño (2007).

35. García-Castañon and Collingwood (2009).

36. De la Garza and DeSipio (1992, 1996, 1999, 2005).

CHAPTER 7

1. Barreto and Segura (2011).

2. Judis (2010).

3. Ibid.

4. Bowler, Nicholson, and Segura (2006).

5. Berman (2010).

CHAPTER 8

1. This estimate is from the Latino Decisions election eve poll. It differs from the NEP exit poll estimates of 71%. Elsewhere, we have demonstrated the significantly superior estimate quality of the Latino Decisions approach (see Barreto and Segura 2011).

2. Foley (2012).

3. ImpreMedia/Latino Decisions, "National Dataset Crosstabs: ImpreMedia–Latino Decisions Election Eve Poll 2012," available at: http://www.latinodecisions.com/files/9313/5233/8455/Latino_Election_Eve_Poll_-_Crosstabs.pdf.

4. Latino Decisions/NALEO/ImpreMedia, "National Post-Election Survey—November 2008," available at: http://www.latinodecisions.com/files/2913/3749/5067/NALEO.Nov08.pdf.

5. Ross (2012) and Quinton (2012).

6. Bennett (2011).

7. Uhlaner and Garcia (2005), Alvarez and Garcia-Bedolla (2003), Bowler, Nicholson, and Segura (2006), Hero and Tolbert (2001), and Pantoja, Ramírez, and Segura (2001).

8. Verba and Nie (1972) and Rosenstone and Hansen (1993/2003).

9. Garofoli (2012).

10. Lopez and Taylor (2012).

11. Chait (2011).

12. Le (2012).

13. Campbell et al. (1960) and Lewis-Beck et al. (2008).

14. Dawson (1994).

15. Barreto and Pedraza (2009), Barreto and Segura (2010), and Dahl (1961).

16. Nuño (2007) and Barreto and Nuño (2011).

17. Ramírez (2005) and Michelson, "Getting Out the Latino Vote" (2003).

18. In general, African American and Latino unemployment rates exceed those of non-Hispanic whites, and this gap has widened in every postwar recession (Bureau of Labor Statistics 2012).

19. Lopez, Livingston, and Kochhar (2009).

20. Taylor, Kochhar, and Fry (2011).

21. Passel, Cohn, and Lopez (2011) and Lopez and Velasco (2011).

22. Golash-Boza (2012).

23. Markus (1988), Lewis-Beck (1988), and Lewis-Beck and Stegmaier (2000).

24. Taylor, Lopez, Velasco, and Motel 2012, 4.

25. Nuño (2007), Abrajano (2010), and Abrajano and Panagopoulos (2011).

26. Barreto, DeFrancesco, and Merolla (2011) and Panagopoulos and Green (2011).

27. *New York Times* (2011).

28. Camia (2012).

29. Romney cited Bureau of Labor Statistics reports that, for example, the Latino unemployment rate had risen to 11% since January 2009, the beginning of President Obama's first term.

30. We crafted a statement asking respondents to suppose that they supported a hypothetical candidate's plan for the economy. We varied randomly whether respondents received a hostile or welcoming cue, approximating actual candidate positions on immigration during the 2012 campaign. The question wording and weighted distribution are detailed in Table 8.3.

31. On "illegal" versus "undocumented," see Merolla, Ramakrishnan, and Haynes (2013). On cultural threats versus economic threats, see Brader, Valentino, and Suhay (2008). In our survey experiment, we used a hypothetical candidate without specifying the candidate's partisan affiliation. This strategy—which is also used by others—represents a trade-off between controlling for the independent effect of partisanship and the cost of doubling the number of treatment cells. We address this strategy in further detail in our evaluative discussion in McGraw, Hasecke, and Conger (2003).

32. See, for example, Marcus (2000).

33. After offering respondents the choice "Don't care what they say," we found that 21% of them said "Don't care" in response to the hostile message and 18% responded this way to the welcoming message. The simplest interpretation is that one in five Latinos say they don't care because they are genuinely not interested in the candidate's immigration views and care only about whether they agree with the candidate's plan for the economy. In some states, the share of "don't care" responses was twice as large as the share of "don't know" responses. Assessed as a dichotomous indicator (i.e., as a "don't care" response versus otherwise), the overall difference is statistically significant using a t-test that assumes unequal variance ($p < 0.03$).

34. Overall, Latino support for a candidate with a welcoming immigration message (mean = 2.55) is statistically different from the distribution of support for a candidate with a hostile message (mean = 1.73; student's t = 27.22; $p < 0.000$).

35. Our experiment was limited in two important respects. First, we did not manipulate the candidate's economic cues, so in this exercise we were unable to evaluate or assign a weight to the relative impact of issues on candidate preference. Second, actual Latino candidate preferences in 2012 were formed in response to candidate statements and policy developments that took place over the course of the Republican primary and general contest.

36. Silver (2012).

37. DeSipio and de la Garza (2005).

38. Latino Decisions/America's Voice Education Fund, "Latino Influence on 2012 Election: President" (vote map), available at: www.latinovotemap.org.

39. Gelman, Katz, and Tuerlinckx (2002).

CHAPTER 9

1. *Hopwood v. Texas,* 78 F.3d 932 (5th Cir. 1996); *Fisher v. University of Texas* (2013).
2. Bowler, Nicholson, and Segura (2006).
3. See Segura, Falcon, and Pachon (1997), Ramírez (2002), Barreto and Woods (2005), and Barreto, Ramírez, and Woods (2005). The non-Hispanic white population declined from 69.9% in the 1980s to 42.8% in 2010, while its share of the electorate declined from 83% to 65% (DiCamillo and Field 2009). During the same period, Latinos' share of the California population grew from 19% in 1980 to 38% in 2010, while its electorate increased from 8% in the 1980s to 26% in 2010. Today one in four Californians is an immigrant. Among the 18 million registered voters in the state, 28.9% are "New Americans" (Immigration Policy Center 2013).
4. Barreto and Woods (2005).
5. Pantoja, Ramírez, and Segura (2001).
6. Barreto, Ramírez, and Woods (2005).
7. Tomás Rivera Policy Institute (2000).
8. Barreto and Ramírez (2004).
9. Marinucci (2003).
10. Kousser (2006).
11. DeSipio, Masuoka, and Stout (2006).
12. Bowler, Nicholson, and Segura (2006).
13. Jacobson (2004).
14. Bowler, Nicholson, and Segura (2006).
15. See Hero and Tolbert (2001).
16. Mendelberg (2001).
17. See Nicholson (2005).
18. Bowler, Nicholson, and Segura (2006).
19. Ibid.
20. Nagourney (2012).

CHAPTER 10

1. Sarlin (2013).
2. Republican National Committee (2012), 15.

3. The National Exit Pool survey estimated that 27% of Latino ballots were cast for Romney in 2012. Latino Decisions' estimate was 23%, based on our election eve survey, which has better sample properties and bilingual interviewing.

4. See, for instance, Smith (2013) and Chen (2013).

5. See Damore (2011).

6. On June 6, 2013, the House of Representatives, on a largely party-line vote, supported defunding President Obama's Deferred Action for Childhood Arrivals (DACA) program.

7. During the summer of 2013, the Democratic Congressional Campaign Committee (DCCC) identified twenty-three Republican districts "where constituents will demand progress on immigration, and where those pressures could persuade our Republican colleagues to support true comprehensive immigration reform." All but four of these districts are included in our analysis. We exclude the 6th (Jim Gerlach), 7th (Patrick Meehan), and 8th (Michael Fitzpatrick) Districts in Pennsylvania and the 14th District in Ohio (David Joyce) because those districts were easily carried in 2012 (with the House Republicans running much stronger than Mitt Romney, who narrowly won each district) and because they contain small Latino voting-age populations. In other instances, members identified by the DCCC may be supportive of a compromise immigration bill but are not in particularly competitive electoral contexts, such as Florida's Mario Diaz-Balart (25th), Ileana Ros-Lehtinen (27th), and David Jolly (13th), as well as California's David Valadao (21st), New Mexico's Steve Pearce (2nd), and New Jersey's Frank LoBiondo (2nd). As a consequence, we place these districts in tier 3.

8. For an overview, see Carrubba and Timpone (2005).

9. See Hopkins (2012).

CHAPTER 11

1. Sanchez (2012).

2. Cooper and Schone (1997) and Sanchez and Medeiros (2012).

3. Carrillo et al. (2011).

4. Ibid.

5. Ibid.; Pitkin-Derose and Baker (2000), Weinack and Kraus (2000), Fiscell et al. (2002), and Betancourt et al. (2001).

6. Carrillo et al. (2011) and Pitkin-Derose and Baker (2000).

7. Carter-Pokras and Zambrana (2001).

8. Ibid.; see also Rumbaut, Escarce, and Morales (2006).

9. Ramírez et al. (2000).

10. Sanchez and Medeiros (2012).

11: Pachon, Barreto, and Marquez (2004).

12. The first poll conducted by Latino Decisions was done in partnership with Robert Wood Johnson Foundation Center for Health Policy at the University of New Mexico and with ImpreMedia. We surveyed 1,000 Latino registered voters during the period November 1–16, 2009, on their views about the nation's health care debate, the administration (at the time), and politics more generally.

13. Jones (2011).

14. Barreto and Sanchez (2013).

15. Vega et al. (2013).

16. Gans et al. (2012).

CHAPTER 12

1. See, for example, Whittaker, Segura, and Bowler (2005), Greenberg (2005), Johnson, Bowker, and Cordell (2004), and Williams and Florez (2002).

2. Hershey and Hill (1977) and Douglas and Wildavsky (1983).

3. Maslow (1970).

4. Mohai and Bryant (1998) and Mohai (2003).

5. Quintero-Somaini and Quirindongo (2004).

6. Whittaker, Segura, and Bowler (2005).

7. Greenberg (2005), Johnson, Bowker, and Cordell (2004), and Williams and Florez (2002).

8. Whittaker, Segura, and Bowler (2005).

9. Pantoja, Ramírez, and Segura (2001) and Pantoja and Segura (2003).

10. The survey is based on a national sample of 805 Latino registered voters, carried out November 27–December 3, 2013. Respondents were interviewed in English or Spanish by fully bilingual interviewers. The overall survey contains a margin of error of +/-3.5%, and on split-sample items the margin of error is +/-4.9%. Respondents were reached using a blended sample of landline telephones, cell phones, and the Latino Decisions online web panel.

11. Quintero et al. (2011).

12. Ibid., 9, 10.

13. Greenberg (2005) and Johnson, Bowker, and Cordell (2004).

CHAPTER 13

1. Bowler, Nicholson, and Segura (2006).

BIBLIOGRAPHY

Abrajano, Marisa. 2010. *Campaigning to the New American Electorate: Advertising to Latino Voters*. Palo Alto, CA: Stanford University Press.

Abrajano, Marisa A., R. Michael Alvarez, and Jonathan Nagler. 2008. "The Hispanic Vote in the 2004 Presidential Election: Insecurity and Moral Concerns." *Journal of Politics* 70, no. 2: 368–382.

Abrajano, Marisa, and Costas Panagopoulos. 2011. "Does Language Matter? The Impact of Spanish versus English-Language GOTV Efforts on Latino Turnout." *American Politics Research* 39, no. 4: 643–663.

Abramowitz, Alan. 1989. "Viability, Electability and Candidate Choice in a Presidential Primary Election: A Test of Competing Models." *Journal of Politics* 51: 977–992.

______. 1995. "It's Abortion, Stupid: Policy Voting in the 1992 Presidential Election." *Journal of Politics* 57, no. 1: 176–186.

Abramson, Paul, John Aldrich, Phil Paolino, and David Rohde. 1992. "Sophisticated Voting in the 1988 Presidential Primaries." *American Political Science Review* 86: 55–69.

Alvarez, R. Michael, and Lisa Garcia-Bedolla. 2003. "The Foundations of Latino Voter Partisanship: Evidence from the 2000 Election." *Journal of Politics* 65, no. 1: 31–49.

Alvarez, R. Michael, and Jonathan Nagler. 1998. "Economics, Entitlements, and Social Issues: Voter Choice in the 1996 Presidential Election." *American Journal of Political Science* 42, no. 4 (October): 1349–1363.

Amaya, Hector. 2007. "Dying American or the Violence of Citizenship: Latinos in Iraq." *Latino Studies* 5, no. 1: 3–24.

Banzhaf, John F., III. 1964. "Weighted Voting Doesn't Work: A Mathematical Analysis." *Rutgers Law Review* 19: 317.

______. 1966. "Multi-Member Electoral Districts: Do They Violate the 'One Man, One Vote' Principle." *Yale Law Journal* 75, no. 8: 1309–1338.

———. 1968. "One Man, 3.312 Votes: A Mathematical Analysis of the Electoral College." *Villanova Law Review* 13: 304.

Barreto, Matt A. 2007. "!Sí Se Puede! Latino Candidates and the Mobilization of Latino Voters." *American Political Science Review* 101, no. 3: 425–441.

Barreto, Matt, Victoria DeFrancesco, and Jennifer Merolla. 2011. "Multiple Dimensions of Mobilization: The Impact of Direct Contact and Political Ads on Latino Turnout in the 2000 Presidential Election." *Journal of Political Marketing* 10, no. 4: 303–327.

Barreto, Matt, Rodolfo de la Garza, Jongho Lee, Jaesung Ryu, and Harry Pachon. 2002. "Latino Voter Mobilization in 2000: A Glimpse into Latino Policy and Voting Preferences." Claremont, CA: Tomás Rivera Policy Institute.

Barreto, Matt, Luis Fraga, Sylvia Manzano, Valerie Martinez-Ebers, and Gary Segura. 2008. "Should They Dance with the One Who Brung 'em? Latinos and the 2008 Presidential Election." *PS: Political Science and Politics* 41 (October).

Barreto, Matt, Fernando Guerra, Mara Marks, Stephen Nuño, and Nathan Woods. 2006. "Controversies in Exit Polling: Implementing a Racially Stratified Homogenous Precinct Approach." *PS: Political Science and Politics* 39 (July).

Barreto, Matt, and David Leal. 2007. "Latinos, Military Service, and Support for Bush and Kerry in 2004." *American Politics Research* 35, no. 2 (March): 224–251.

Barreto, Matt, Sylvia Manzano, and Gabriel Sanchez. 2009. "En Fuego: Latino Voters in the 2008 Primaries." Paper presented at the annual meeting of the Midwest Political Science Association.

Barreto, Matt A., and Stephen Nuño. 2011. "The Effectiveness of Coethnic Contact on Latino Political Recruitment." *Political Research Quarterly* 64, no. 2: 448–459.

Barreto, Matt A., and Francisco Pedraza. 2009. "The Renewal and Persistence of Group Identification in American Politics." *Electoral Studies* 28, no. 4 (December): 595–605.

Barreto, Matt, and Ricardo Ramírez. 2004. "Minority Participation and the California Recall: Latino, Black, and Asian Voting Trends 1990–2003." *PS: Political Science and Politics* 37 (January): 11–14.

———. 2008. "The Latino Vote Is Pro-Clinton, Not Anti-Obama" (opinion). *Los Angeles Times*, February 7.

Barreto, Matt A., Ricardo Ramírez, and Nathan D. Woods. 2005. "Are Naturalized Voters Driving the California Latino Electorate? Measuring the Effect of IRCA Citizens on Latino Voting." *Social Science Quarterly* 86, no. 4: 792–811.

Barreto, Matt A., and Gary M. Segura. 2010. "Do NES Models of Voting Apply to Blacks and Latinos? Results of the 2008 NES Oversample." Paper presented at the annual meeting of the Western Political Science Association. San Francisco.

Barreto, Matt, and Gary Segura. 2012. "How the Exit Polls Misrepresent Latino Voters, and Badly." Latino Decisions, November 1. Available at: http://www.latinodecisions.com/blog/2012/11/01/how-the-exit-polls-misrepresent-latino-voters-and-badly/.

Barreto, Matt A., Gary M. Segura, and Nathan Woods. 2004. "The Mobilizing Effect of Majority-Minority Districts on Latino Turnout." *American Political Science Review* 98, no. 1: 65–75.

Barreto, Matt, and Nathan Woods. 2005. "The Anti-Latino Political Context and Its Impact on GOP Detachment and Increasing Latino Voter Turnout in Los Angeles County." In *Diversity in Democracy: Minority Representation in the United States,* ed. Gary Segura and Shawn Bowler. Charlottesville: University of Virginia Press.

Bartels, Larry M. 1988. *Presidential Primaries and the Dynamics of Public Choice.* Princeton, NJ: Princeton University Press.

Basinger, Scott, and Howard Lavine. 2005. "Ambivalence, Information, and Electoral Choice." *American Political Science Review* 99, no. 2: 169–184.

Beltran, Cristina. 2011. *The Trouble with Unity: Latino Politics and the Creation of Identity.* Oxford: Oxford University Press.

Bennett, Brian. 2011. "Obama Administration Reports Record Number of Deportations." *Los Angeles Times,* October 18.

Berman, Ari. 2010. "Anti-Immigrant Zealot Becomes GOP's Colorado Senate Nominee." *The Nation,* August 11.

Betancourt, Joseph R., Alexander R. Green, J. Emilio Carrillo, and Owusu Ananeh-Firempong II. 2001. "Defining Cultural Competence: A Practical Framework for Addressing Racial/Ethnic Disparities in Health and Health Care." *Public Health Reports* 118 (July–August): 293–303. Available at: http://www.ncbi.nlm.nih.gov/pmc/articles/PMC1497553/.

Bowler, Shaun, Stephen P. Nicholson, and Gary M. Segura. 2006. "Earthquakes and Aftershocks: Race, Direct Democracy, and Partisan Change." *American Journal of Political Science* 50, no. 1 (January): 146–159.

Bowler, Shaun, and Gary M. Segura. 2011. *"The Future Is Ours": Minority Politics, Political Behavior, and the Multiracial Era of American Politics.* Washington, DC: Congressional Quarterly Press.

Brader, Ted, Nicholas A. Valentino, and Elizabeth Suhay. 2008. "What Triggers Public Opposition to Immigration? Anxiety, Group Cues, and Immigration Threat." *American Journal of Political Science* 52, no. 4: 959–978.

Brown, Anna, and Mark Hugo Lopez. 2013. "II. Ranking Latino Populations in the States." Pew Research Hispanic Trends Project. August 29. Available at: http://www.pewhispanic.org/2013/08/29/ii-ranking-latino-populations-in-the-states.

Burden, Barry. 2006. "A Tale of Two Campaigns: Ralph Nader's Strategy in the 2004 Presidential Election." *PS: Political Science and Politics* 39, no. 4: 871–874.

Camia, Catalina. 2012. "Romney Taps Ex-Commerce Leader for Hispanic Team." *USA Today,* June 6.

Campbell, Angus, Philip E. Converse, Warren E. Miller, and Donald E. Stokes. 1960. *The American Voter.* Ann Arbor: University of Michigan Press.

Carrillo, J. Emilio, Victor A. Carrillo, Hector R. Perez, Debbie Salas-Lopez, Ana Natale-Pereira, and Alex T. Byron. 2011. "Defining and Targeting Health Care Access Barriers." *Journal of Health Care for the Poor and Underserved* 22, no. 2: 562–575.

Carrubba, Cliff, and Richard J. Timpone. 2005. "Explaining Vote Switching Across First- and Second-Order Elections Evidence from Europe." *Comparative Political Studies* 38, no. 3: 260–281.

Carter-Pokras, Olivia, and Ruth Enid Zambrana. 2001. "Latino Health Status." In *Health Issues in the Latino Community* 8, no. 23. New York: John Wiley & Sons.

Ceci, Stephen J., and Edward L. Kain. 1982. "Jumping on the Bandwagon with the Underdog: The Impact of Attitude Polls on Polling Behavior." *Public Opinion Quarterly* 46, no. 2: 228–242.

Chait, Jonathan. 2011. "Obama's Latino Strategy Takes Shape." *The New Republic,* May 12. Available at: http://www.newrepublic.com/blog/jonathan-chait/88173/obamas-latino-strategy-takes-shape.

Chen, Lanhee. 2013. "How Republicans Can Win over Asian-Americans." Bloomberg News, April 18. Available at: http://www.bloomberg.com/news/2013-04-18/how-republicans-can-win-over-asian-americans.html.

Contreras, Raoul Lowery. 2008. "The Bradley Effect Is Still in Effect." *Los Angeles Times,* February 5.

Cooper, Philip F., and Barbara Steinberg Schone. 1997. "More Offers, Fewer Takers for Employment-Based Health Insurance: 1987 and 1996." *Health Affairs* 16: 142–149.

Dahl, Robert A. 1961. *Who Governs? Democracy and Power in an American City.* New Haven, CT: Yale University Press.

Damore, David F. 2011. "Reid vs. Angle in Nevada's Senate Race: Harry Houdini Escapes the Wave." In *Cases in Congressional Campaigns: Storming the Hill,* 2nd ed., eds. David Dulio and Randall Adkins. New York: Routledge.

Dawson, Michael. 1994. *Behind the Mule.* Princeton, NJ: Princeton University Press.

DeFrancesco-Soto, Victoria, and Jennifer Merolla. 2006. "Vota por Tu Futuro: Partisan Mobilization of Latino Voters in the 2000 Presidential Election." *Political Behavior* 28 (December): 285–304.

De la Garza, Rodolfo, and Louis DeSipio. 1992. *From Rhetoric to Reality: Latino Politics in the 1988 Elections*. Boulder, CO: Westview Press.

______ . 1996. *Ethnic Ironies: Latino Politics in the 1992 Elections*. Boulder, CO: Westview Press.

______ . 1999. *Awash in the Mainstream: Latino Politics in the 1996 Elections*. Boulder, CO: Westview Press.

______ . 2005. *Muted Voices: Latinos and the 2000 Elections*. Boulder, CO: Rowman & Littlefield.

DeSipio, Louis. 1996. *Counting on the Latino Vote: Latinos as a New Electorate*. Charlottesville: University of Virginia Press.

______ . 2006. "Latino Civic and Political Participation." In *Hispanics and the Future of America*, eds. Marta Tienda and Faith Mitchell. Washington, DC: National Academies Press.

DeSipio, Louis, Natalie Masuoka, and Christopher Stout. 2006. "The Changing Non-Voter: What Differentiates Non-Voters and Voters in Asian American and Latino Communities?" Working paper. Irvine: University of California, Center for the Study of Democracy (September 19).

DiCamillo, Mark, and Mervin Field. 2009. "Field Poll: The Changing California Electorate, Part I: Large Scale Demographic Changes in California from What It Was 30 Years Ago." Yubanet.com, August 4. Available at: http://yubanet.com/california/Field-Poll-The-Changing-California-Electorate-Part-1.php#.U3tRCt7D_IU.

Douglas, Mary, and Aaron Wildavsky. 1983. *Risk and Culture: An Essay on the Selection of Technical and Environmental Dangers*. Berkeley: University of California Press.

Elmore, Michael. 2009. "Obama Defends Driver's License for Illegals in Interview." ABC News, February 2. Available at: http://abcnews.go.com/blogs/politics/2008/02/obama-defends-d/.

Ennis, Sharon R., Merarys Ríos-Vargas, and Nora G. Albert. 2011. "The Hispanic Population, 2010." *2010 Census Briefs* (May). Available at: www.census.gov/prod/cen2010/briefs/c2010br-04.pdf.

Felsenthal, Dan S., and Moshé Machover. 2004. "A Priori Voting Power: What Is It All About?" *Political Studies Review* 2, no. 1: 1–23.

Fiscell, Kevin, Peter Franks, Mark P. Doescher, and Barry G. Saver. 2002. "Disparities in Health Care by Race, Ethnicity, and Language among the Insured: Findings from a National Sample." In *Race, Ethnicity, and Health*, ed. Thomas A. Laveist. San Francisco: Jossey-Bass & Sons.

Foley, Elise. 2012. "Latino Voters in Election 2012 Help Sweep Obama to Reelection." Huffington Post. November 7. Available at: http://www.huffingtonpost

.com/2012/11/07/latino-voters-election-2012_n_2085922.html (accessed April 2, 2014).

Fraga, Luis, John Garcia, Rodney Hero, Michael Jones-Correa, Valerie Martinez-Ebers, and Gary Segura. 2010. *Latino Lives in America: Making It Home.* Philadelphia: Temple University Press.

Fraga, Luis R., Rodney E. Hero, John A. Garcia, Michael Jones-Correa, Valerie Martinez-Ebers, and Gary M. Segura. 2012. *Latinos in the New Millennium: An Almanac of Opinion, Behavior, and Policy Preferences.* New York: Cambridge University Press.

Franklin, Mark. 2004. *Voter Turnout and the Dynamics of Electoral Competition in Established Democracies since 1945.* New York: Cambridge University Press.

Gans, Daphna, Christina M. Kinane, Greg Watson, Dylan H. Roby, J. Needleman, Dave Graham-Squire, Gerald F. Kominski, Ken Jacobs, David Dexter, and Ellen Wu. 2012. "Achieving Equity by Building a Bridge from Eligible to Enrolled." Los Angeles: UCLA Center for Health Policy Research and California Pan-Ethnic Health Network.

García-Castañon, Marcela, and Loren Collingwood. 2009. "Talking to Latinos: Obama's 2008 Latino Targeted Speeches." Paper presented at the annual meeting of the Western Political Science Association. Vancouver, BC.

Garofoli, Joe. 2012. "Latinos' Enthusiasm Gap Worries Dems." *San Francisco Chronicle,* September 5.

Gay, Claudine. 2006. "Seeing Difference: The Effect of Economic Disparity on Black Attitudes toward Latinos." *American Journal of Political Science* 50, no. 4: 982–997.

Gelman, Andrew, Jonathan N. Katz, and Joseph Bafumi. 2004. "Standard Voting Power Indexes Do Not Work: An Empirical Analysis." *British Journal of Political Science* 34, no. 4: 657–674.

Gelman, Andrew, Jonathan N. Katz, and Francis Tuerlinckx. 2002. "The Mathematics and Statistics of Voting Power." *Statistical Science* 17, no. 4: 420–435.

Glink, Ilyce. 2013. "Foreclosure Crisis Not over for Minorities." CBSMoneyWatch, June 25. Available at: http://www.cbsnews.com/news/foreclosure-crisis-not-over-for-minorities/ (accessed April 2, 2014).

Golash-Boza, Tanya Maria. 2012. *Immigration Nation: Raids, Detentions, and Deportations in Post-9/11 America.* Boulder, CO: Paradigm Publishers.

Goldstein, Amy. 2008. "Democrats' Votes Display Racial Divide." *Washington Post,* February 6.

Green, Donald P., and Alan S. Gerber. 2004. *Get Out the Vote! How to Increase Voter Turnout.* Washington, DC: Brookings Institution Press.

Greenberg, Michael R. 2005. "Concerns About Environmental Pollution: How Much Difference Do Race and Ethnicity Make? A New Jersey Case Study." *Environmental Health Perspectives* 113: 369–374.

Guerra, Fernando, Jennifer Magnabosco, and Brianne Barclay. 2008. "LCSLA 2008 Exit Polls of the Presidential Primary and National Elections in the City of Los Angeles Results of the LCSLA National Election Exit Poll: All City, Valley, and Non-Valley." Los Angeles: Center for the Study of Los Angeles (November 6).

Gurian, Paul-Henri, and Audrey Haynes. 1993. "Campaign Strategy in Presidential Primaries, 1976–1988." *American Journal of Political Science* 37: 335–341.

Guth, James, Lyman Kellstedt, Corwin Smidt, and John Green. 2006. "Religious Influences in the 2004 Presidential Election." *Presidential Studies Quarterly* 36, no. 2: 223–242.

Gutiérrez, David G. 2004. *The Columbia History of Latinos in the United States since 1960*. New York: Columbia University Press.

Hajnal, Zoltan L., and Taeku Lee. 2010. "Race, Immigration, and (Non)Partisanship in America." Working paper. San Diego and Berkeley: University of California.

______ . 2011. *Why Americans Don't Join the Party: Race, Immigration, and the Failure of Political Parties to Engage the Electorate*. Princeton, NJ: Princeton University Press.

Hamilton, Nora, and Norma Stoltz Chinchilla. 2001. *Seeking Community in a Global City: Guatemalans and Salvadorans in Los Angeles*. Philadelphia: Temple University Press.

Heilman, John. 2008. "The Evita Factor." *New York*, February 1.

Hero, Rodney E., and Robert R. Preuhs. 2009. "Beyond (the Scope of) Conflict: National Black and Latino Advocacy Group Relations in the Congressional and Legal Arenas." *Perspectives on Politics* 7, no. 3: 501–517.

Hero, Rodney E., and Caroline J. Tolbert. 2001. "Dealing with Diversity: Racial/Ethnic Context and Social Policy Change." *Political Research Quarterly* 54, no. 3: 571–604.

Hershey, Marjorie, and David Hill. 1977. "Is Pollution 'a White Thing'? Racial Differences in Preadults' Attitudes." *Public Opinion Quarterly* 41: 439–458.

Hopkins, Dan. 2012. "Shifting Voter Support, 2008–2012." The Monkey Cage, November 7. Available at: http://themonkeycage.org/2012/11/07/shifting-voter-support-2008-to-2012/ (accessed April 22, 2013).

Immigration Policy Center. 2013. "New Americans in California: The Economic Power of Immigrants, Latinos, and Asians in the Golden State." Washington, DC: Immigration Policy Center (July).

Jacobson, Gary C. 2004. "Partisan and Ideological Polarization in the California Electorate." *State Politics and Policy Quarterly* 4, no. 2: 113–139.

Jacoby, William G. 2009. "Ideology and Vote Choice in the 2004 Election." *Electoral Studies* 28 (December): 584–594.

Johnson, Cassandra Y., J. M. Bowker, and H. Ken Cordell. 2004. "Ethnic Variation in Environmental Belief and Behavior: An Examination of the New Ecological Paradigm in a Social Psychological Context." *Environment and Behavior* 36: 157–186.

Jones, Jeffrey M. 2011. "In US, 46% Favor, 40% Oppose Repealing Healthcare Law; Three-quarters of Republicans favor repeal; 64% of Democrats oppose it." Gallup Politics, January 7. Available at: http://www.gallup.com/poll/145496/favor-oppose-repealing-healthcare-law.aspx (accessed February 7, 2014).

Jones-Correa, Michael, and David Leal. 2001. "Political Participation: Does Religion Matter?" *Political Research Quarterly* 54, no. 4: 751–770.

Judis, John B. 2007. "Hillary Clinton's Firewall." *The New Republic*, December 18.

______. 2010. "Brown Knows." *The New Republic*, October 18.

Kaufmann, Karen. 2006. "The Gender Gap." *PS: Political Science and Politics* 39, no. 3: 447–453.

Kinder, Donald, and D. Roderick Kiewiet. 1981. "Sociotropic Politics: The American Case." *British Journal of Political Science* 11 (April): 129–161.

Kinder, Donald R., and Nicholas Winter. 2001. "Exploring the Racial Divide: Blacks, Whites, and Opinion on National Policy." *American Journal of Political Science* 45, no. 2: 439–456.

Kousser, Thad. 2006. "The Limited Impact of Term Limits: Contingent Effects on the Complexity and Breadth of Laws." *State Politics and Policy Quarterly* 6, no. 4: 410–429.

Langley, Monica. 2007. "Clinton's Right-Hand Woman Scrambles." *Wall Street Journal*, December 26.

Latino Decisions. 2008. "November 2008 Presidential Election Poll of Latino Voters." November. Available at: http://www.latinodecisions.com/files/2913/3749/5067/NALEO.Nov08.pdf.

______. 2008. "New Poll Suggests Latino Voters May Make the Difference in Four Key States." October 7. Available at: http://www.latinodecisions.com/blog/2008/10/07/new-poll-suggests-latino-voters-may-make-the-difference-in-four-key-states/ (accessed April 4, 2014).

Le, Van. 2012. "How Latino Voters Annihilated Romney and the Republicans." America's Voice. November 7. Available at: http://americasvoiceonline.org/blog/how-latino-voters-annihilated-romney-and-the-republicans-2/.

Leal, David L. 2003. "The Multicultural Military: Military Service and the Acculturation of Latinos and Anglos." *Armed Forces and Society* 29, no. 2: 205–226.

______ . 2005. "American Public Opinion toward the Military: Differences by Race, Gender, and Class?" *Armed Forces and Society* 32, no. 1: 123–138.

Leal, David, Matt Barreto, Jongho Lee, and Rodolfo de la Garza. 2005. "The Latino Vote in the 2004 Election." *PS: Political Science and Politics* 38, no. 1 (January): 41–49.

Lewis-Beck, Michael S. 1988. "Economics and the American Voter: Past, Present and Future." *Political Behavior* 10, no. 1: 5–21.

Lewis-Beck, Michael S., Helmut Norpoth, William G. Jacoby, and Herbert F. Weisberg. 2008. *The American Voter Revisited.* Ann Arbor: University of Michigan Press.

Lewis-Beck, Michael S., and Mary Stegmaier. 2000. "Economic Determinants of Electoral Outcomes." *Annual Review of Political Science* 3, no. 1: 183–219.

Lopez, Linda, and Adrian D. Pantoja. 2004. "Beyond Black and White: General Support for Race-Conscious Policies among African Americans, Latinos, Asian Americans and Whites." *Political Research Quarterly* 57, no. 4: 633–642.

Lopez, Mark Hugo, and Danielle Cuddington. 2013. "Latinos' Changing Views of Same-Sex Marriage." Pew Research Center. June 19. Available at: http://www.pewresearch.org/fact-tank/2013/06/19/latinos-changing-views-of-same-sex-marriage/ (accessed January 16, 2014).

Lopez, Mark Hugo, and Daniel Dockterman. 2011. "US Hispanic Country of Origin Counts for Nation, Top 30 Metropolitan Areas." Pew Research Hispanic Trends Project. May 26. Available at: http://www.pewhispanic.org/2011/05/26/country-of-origin-profiles/.

Lopez, Mark Hugo, and Ana Gonzalez-Barrera. 2013. "Inside the 2012 Latino Electorate." Pew Research Hispanic Trends Project. June 3. Available at: http://www.pewhispanic.org/2013/06/03/inside-the-2012-latino-electorate/.

Lopez, Mark Hugo, Gretchen Livingston, and Rakesh Kochhar. 2009. "Hispanics and the Economic Downturn: Housing Woes and Remittance Cuts." Pew Research Hispanic Trends Project. January 8. Available at: http://www.pewhispanic.org/2009/01/08/hispanics-and-the-economic-downturn-housing-woes-and-remittance-cuts/ (accessed April 4, 2014).

Lopez, Mark Hugo, and Paul Taylor. 2012. "Latino Voters in the 2012 Election." Pew Research Hispanic Trends Project. November 7. Available at: http://www.pewhispanic.org/2012/11/07/latino-voters-in-the-2012-election/.

Lopez, Mark Hugo, and Gabriel Velasco. 2011. "The Toll of the Great Recession: Childhood Poverty among Hispanics Sets Records, Leads Nation." Washington DC: Pew Hispanic Center.

Marcus, George E. 2000. "Emotions in Politics." *Annual Review of Political Science* 3, no. 1: 221–250.

Markus, Gregory B. 1988. "The Impact of Personal and National Economic Conditions on Presidential Vote: A Pooled Cross-sectional Analysis." *American Journal of Political Science* 32 (February).

Markus, Greg, and Philip E. Converse. 1979. "A Dynamic Simultaneous Equation Model of Electoral Choice." *American Political Science Review* 73 (December): 1055–1070.

Maslow, Abraham. 1970. *Motivation and Personality.* New York: Viking Press.

McAllister, Ian, and Donley T. Studlar. 1991. "Bandwagon, Underdog, or Projection? Opinion Polls and Electoral Choice in Britain, 1979–1987." *Journal of Politics* 53 (August): 720–741.

McClain, Paula D., et al. 2006. "Racial Distancing in a Southern City: Latino Immigrants' Views of Black Americans." *Journal of Politics* 68, no. 3: 571–584.

McClain, Paula D., Monique L. Lyle, Niambi M. Carter, Victoria M. DeFrancesco Soto, Gerald F. Lackey, Kendra Davenport Cotton, Shayla C. Nunnally, Thomas J. Scotto, Jeffrey D. Grynaviski, and J. Alan Kendrick. 2007. "Black Americans and Latino Immigrants in a Southern City: Friendly Neighbors or Economic Competitors." *Du Bois Review* 41, no. 1: 97–117.

McClain, Paula D., and Joseph Stewart Jr. 2013. *"Can We All Get Along?" Racial and Ethnic Minorities in American Politics.* 6th ed. Boulder, CO: Westview Press.

McGraw, Kathleen M., Edward Hasecke, and Kimberly Conger. 2003. "Ambivalence, Uncertainty, and Processes of Candidate Evaluation." *Political Psychology* 24, no. 3: 421–448.

Mendelberg, Tali. 2001. *The Race Card: Campaign Strategy, Implicit Messages, and the Norm of Equality.* Princeton, NJ: Princeton University Press.

Merolla, Jennifer, S. Karthick Ramakrishnan, and Chris Haynes. 2013. "'Illegal,' 'Undocumented,' or 'Unauthorized': Equivalency Frames, Issue Frames, and Public Opinion on Immigration." *Perspectives on Politics* 11, no. 3: 789–807.

Michelson, Melissa. 2003. "Getting Out the Latino Vote: How Door-to-Door Canvassing Influences Voter Turnout in Rural Central California." *Political Behavior* 25, no. 3: 247–263.

———. 2003. "The Corrosive Effect of Acculturation: How Mexican Americans Lose Political Trust." *Social Science Quarterly* 84, no. 4: 918–933.

Miller, Warren E., and J. Merrill Shanks. 1996. *The New American Voter.* Cambridge, MA: Harvard University Press.

Mohai, Paul. 2003. "Dispelling Old Myths: African-American Concern for the Environment." *Environment* 45: 11–26.

Mohai, Paul, and Bunyan Bryant. 1998. "Is There a 'Race' Effect on Concern for Environmental Quality?" *Public Opinion Quarterly* 62: 475–505.

Mutz, Diana. 1995. "Effects of Horse-Race Coverage on Campaign Coffers: Strategic Contributing in Presidential Primaries." *Journal of Politics* 57: 1015–1042.

Nagourney, Adam. 2012. "Republican Party in California Is Caught in Cycle of Decline." *New York Times,* July 23.

Nagourney, Adam, and Jennifer Steinhauer. 2008. "In Obama's Pursuit of Latinos, Race Plays Role." *New York Times,* January 15.

National Association of Latino Elected and Appointed Officials (NALEO) Education Fund. 2012. *"Early Results Demonstrate Electoral Clout of Latino Voters."* Available at: http://www.naleo.org/latinovote.html.

National Low Income Housing Coalition. 2013. "Foreclosure Crisis Causes Disproportionate Loss of Wealth among Communities of Color." May 31. Available at: http://nlihc.org/article/foreclosure-crisis-causes-disproportionate-loss-wealth-among-communities-color (accessed April 2, 2014).

NBC News. 2008. "Clinton Revives Campaign in Ohio, Texas." March 5. Available at: http://www.nbcnews.com/id/23463159/#.Uv3bkLTEHVG.

New York Times. 2008. "Election Guide 2008: Texas Nominating Contest Results." Available at: http://politics.nytimes.com/election-guide/2008/results/states/TX.html.

______. 2011. "The Case against Sheriff Arpaio" (editorial). December 16.

Nicholson, Stephen P. 2005. *Voting the Agenda: Candidates, Elections, and Ballot Propositions.* Princeton, NJ: Princeton University Press.

Nicholson, Stephen P., Adrian Pantoja, and Gary M. Segura. 2006. "Political Knowledge and Issue Voting Among the Latino Electorate." *Political Research Quarterly* 59, no. 2: 259–272.

Nie, Norman H., Sidney Verba, and John R. Petrocik. 1979. *The Changing American Voter.* Cambridge, MA: Harvard University Press.

Norrander, Barbara. 1993. "Nomination Choices: Caucuses and Primary Outcomes, 1976–1988." *American Journal of Political Science* 37: 343–364.

______. 2000. "End-Game in Post-Reform Presidential Nomination." *Journal of Politics* 62: 999–1013.

Nuño, Stephen A. 2007. "Latino Mobilization and Vote Choice in the 2000 Presidential Election." *American Politics Research* 35, no. 2: 273–293.

Nuño, Stephen, and Fernando Guerra. 2008. "City of Los Angeles Primary Election Exit Poll." Los Angeles: Loyola Marymount University, Center for the Study of Los Angeles (February 5).

Pachon, Harry, Matt Barreto, and Frances Marquez. 2004. "Latino Politics Comes of Age in the Golden State." In *Muted Voices: Latino Politics in the 2000 Election,* eds. Rodolfo de la Garza and Louis DeSipio. New York: Rowman & Littlefield.

Padilla, Felix M. 1985. *Latino Ethnic Consciousness: The Case of Mexican Americans and Puerto Ricans in Chicago.* Notre Dame, IN: University of Notre Dame Press.

Page, Benjamin I., and Calvin C. Jones. 1979. "Reciprocal Effects of Policy Preferences, Party Loyalty, and the Vote." *American Political Science Review* 73, no. 4 (December): 1071–1089.

Panagopoulos, Costas, and Donald P. Green. 2011. "Spanish-Language Radio Advertisements and Latino Voter Turnout in the 2006 Congressional Elections Field Experimental Evidence." *Political Research Quarterly* 64, no. 3: 588–599.

Pantoja, Adrian D. 2005. "Transnational Ties and Immigrant Political Incorporation: The Case of Dominicans in Washington Heights, New York." *International Migration* 43: 123–146.

———. 2005. "More Alike Than Different: Explaining Political Knowledge among African Americans and Latinos." In *Diversity in Democracy: Minority Representation in the United States,* eds. Gary M. Segura and Shaun Bowler. Charlottesville: University of Virginia Press.

Pantoja, Adrian, Ricardo Ramírez, and Gary M. Segura. 2001. "Citizens by Choice, Voters by Necessity: Patterns in Political Mobilization by Naturalized Latinos." *Political Research Quarterly* 54, no. 4: 729–750.

Pantoja, Adrian D., and Gary M. Segura. 2003. "Fear and Loathing in California: Contextual Threat and Political Sophistication among Latino Voters." *Political Behavior* 25: 265–286.

Passel, Jeffrey S., D'Vera Cohn, and Mark Hugo Lopez. 2011. "Census 2010: 50 Million Latinos: Hispanics Account for More Than Half of Nation's Growth in Past Decade." Washington, DC: Pew Hispanic Center (March 24). Available at: http://pewhispanic.org/files/reports/140.pdf.

Payne, Keith, Clara Cheng, Olesya Govorun, and Brandon Stewart. 2005. "An Inkblot for Attitudes: Affect Misattribution as Implicit Measure." *Journal of Personality and Social Psychology* 89, no. 3: 277–293.

Pedraza, Francisco, and Matt Barreto. 2008. "Exit Polls and Ethnic Diversity: How to Improve Estimates and Reduce Bias Among Minority Voters." In *Elections and Exit Polling,* eds. Wendy Alvey and Fritz Scheuren. Hoboken, NJ: Wiley and Sons.

Pedraza, Francisco, Shaun Bowler, and Gary M. Segura. 2011. "The Efficacy and Alienation of Juan Q. Public: The Immigration Marches and Orientations toward American Political Institutions." In *Rallying for Immigrant Rights,* eds. Irene Bloemraad and Kim Voss. Berkeley: University of California Press.

Penrose, L. S. 1946. "The Elementary Statistics of Majority Voting." *Journal of the Royal Statistical Society* 109, no. 1: 53–57.

Petrocik, John Richard. 1974. "An Analysis of Intransitivities in the Index of Party Identification." *Political Methodology* 1: 31–47.

______. 2009. "Measuring Party Support: Leaners Are Not Independents." *Electoral Studies* 28 (December): 562–572.

Pew Hispanic Center. 2007. "Fact Sheet: Latinos and the War in Iraq." January 4. Available at: http://pewhispanic.org/files/factsheets/27.pdf (accessed April 4, 2014).

Pew Research Hispanic Trends Project. 2003. "Question Search: Hispanic Trends Project Poll Database." Available at: http://www.pewhispanic.org/question-search/?qid=510111&pid=54&ccid=54#top.

______. 2004. "Question Search: Hispanic Trends Project Poll Database." Available at: http://www.pewhispanic.org/question-search/?qid=511400&pid=54&ccid=54#top.

Pew Research Hispanic Trends Project. 2005. "Survey on Latino Attitudes on the War in Iraq." February 7. Available at: http://www.pewhispanic.org/2005/02/07/survey-on-latino-attitudes-on-the-war-in-iraq/ (accessed April 4, 2014).

Pierson, James E. 1975. "Presidential Popularity and Midterm Voting at Different Electoral Levels." *American Journal of Political Science* 19, no. 4: 683–694.

Pitkin-Derose, Kathryn, and David W. Baker. 2000. "Limited English Proficiency and Latinos' Use of Physician Services." *Medical Care Research and Review* 57, no. 1: 76–91.

Quintero, Adrianna, Valerie Jaffee, Jorge Madrid, Elsa Ramirez, and Andrea Delgado. 2011. *US Latinos and Air Pollution: A Call to Action.* Washington, DC: Natural Resources Defense Council.

Quintero-Somaini, Adrianna, and Mayra Quirindongo. 2004. *Hidden Danger, Environmental Health Threats in the Latino Community.* Washington, DC: Natural Resources Defense Council.

Quinton, Sophie. 2012. "Hispanic Vote Not the Game Changer You Might Think It Is." *National Journal,* March 7.

Ramirez, A. G., L. Suarez, L. Laufman, C. Barroso, and P. Chalela. 2000. "Hispanic Women's Breast and Cervical Cancer Knowledge, Attitudes, and Screening Behavior." *American Journal of Health Promotion* 14, no. 5 (May–June): 292–300.

Ramírez, Ricardo. 2002. "Getting Out the Vote: The Impact of Non-Partisan Voter Mobilization Efforts in Low Turnout Latino Precincts." Presented at the annual meeting of the American Political Science Association, Boston.

______. 2005. "Giving Voice to Latino Voters: A Field Experiment on the Effectiveness of a National Nonpartisan Mobilization Effort." *Annals of the American Academy of Political and Social Science* 601, no. 1: 66–84.

______. 2007. "Segmented Mobilization: Latino Nonpartisan Get-Out-the-Vote Efforts in the 2000 General Election." *Peace Research Abstracts Journal* 44, no. 3: 155–175.

Republican National Committee. 2012. *Growth and Opportunity Project: RNC Report.* December. Available at: http://growthopp.gop.com/rnc_growth_opportunity_book_2013.pdf (accessed August 15, 2013).

Reyes, Raul. 2007. "Latinos Know Up Close the Cost of Iraq War." *USA Today,* January 18. Available at: http://usatoday30.usatoday.com/news/opinion/editorials/2007-01-18-opcom_x.htm (accessed April 4, 2014).

Rosenstone, Steven J., and John Mark Hansen. 2003. *Mobilization, Participation, and Democracy in America.* New York: Longman. (Originally published in 1993 by Macmillan.)

Ross, Janell. 2012. "Latino Voters 2012: Sleeping Giant Unlikely to Turn Population Growth into Political Power in November." Huffington Post. September 8.

Rumbaut, Rubén G., Jose Escarce, and Leo Morales. 2006. "The Health Status and Health Behaviors of Hispanics." In *Hispanics and the Future of America,* eds. Marta Tienda and Faith Mitchell. Washington, DC: National Academies Press.

Sanchez, Gabriel R. 2006. "The Role of Group Consciousness in Latino Public Opinion." *Political Research Quarterly* 59, no. 3: 435–446.

______. 2006. "The Role of Group Consciousness in Political Participation among Latinos in the US." *American Politics Research* 34, no. 4: 427–450.

______. 2012. "How the Supreme Court's Health Reform Ruling May Affect the Latino Population." Robert Wood Johnson Foundation, Human Capital Blog (July 20).

Sanchez, Gabriel, and Matt Barreto. 2013. "National Latino Health Care Survey." Latino Decisions (May 1).

Sanchez, Gabriel R., and Jillian Medeiros. 2012. "Tough Times, Tough Choices: The Impact of the Rising Medical Costs on the US Latino Population's Health Care Seeking Behaviors." *Journal of Health Care for the Poor and Underserved* 23, no. 4: 1383–1398.

Santoro, Wayne A., and Gary M. Segura. 2011. "Generational Status and Mexican American Political-Participation: The Benefits and Limitations of Assimilation." *Political Research Quarterly* 64, no. 1: 172–184.

Sarlin, Benjy. 2013. "Sen. Graham: GOP in 'Demographic Death Spiral' Absent Immigration Reform." MSNBC, June 17. Available at: http://tv.msnbc.com/2013/06/17/lindsey-graham-gop-faces-demographic-death-spiral-without-immigration-reform/.

Sawyer, Mark Q. 2005. *Racial Politics in Post-Revolutionary Cuba*. New York: Cambridge University Press.

Segal, Adam. 2008. "Obama/DNC to Invest $20 Million in Hispanic Outreach." Baltimore: Johns Hopkins University, Hispanic Voter Project.

Segura, Gary M. 2009. "Identity Research in Latino Politics. " Paper presented at the annual meeting of the American Political Science Association, Toronto, Ontario. September 2–6.

______ . 2012. "Latino Public Opinion and Realigning the American Electorate." *Daedalus* 141, no. 4 (fall): 98–113.

Segura, Gary M., Dennis Falcon, and Harry Pachon. 1997. "Dynamics of Latino Partisanship in California: Immigration, Issue Salience, and Their Implications." *Harvard Journal of Hispanic Politics* 10: 62–80.

Segura, Gary M., and Helena Alves Rodrigues. 2006. "Comparative Ethnic Politics in the United States: Beyond Black and White." *Annual Review of Political Science* 9: 375–395.

Segura, Gary, and Ali Valenzuela. 2010. "Hope, Tropes, and Dopes: Hispanic and White Racial Animus in the 2008 Election." *Presidential Studies Quarterly* 40, no. 3: 497–514.

Shapley, L. S., and Martin Shubik. 1954. "A Method for Evaluating the Distribution of Power in a Committee System." *American Political Science Review* 48, no. 3: 787–792.

Silver, Nate. 2012. "Hispanic Voters Less Plentiful in Swing States." FiveThirtyEight .com. *New York Times*, June 19.

Smith, Ben. 2008. "Clinton 'Nuestra Amiga.'" *Politico*, January 29.

______ . 2008. "McAuliffe: Obama Has Latino 'Problem.'" *Politico*, June 1.

Smith, Raymond A. 2013. "Immigration Reform and the Growing Asian -American Vote." *Washington Monthly*, June 12. Available at: http://www .washingtonmonthly.com/ten-miles-square/2013/06/immigration_reform_ and_the_gro045259.php.

Stokes-Brown, Atiya Kai. 2009. "The Hidden Politics of Identity: Racial Self-Identification and Latino Political Engagement." *Politics and Policy* 37: 1281–1305.

Stone, Walter J., Ronald Rapoport, and Lonna Rae Atkeson. 1995. "A Simulation Model of Presidential Nomination Choice." *American Journal of Political Science* 39: 135–161.

Taylor, Paul, Rakesh Kochhar, Richard Fry, Gabriel Velasco, and Seth Motel. 2011. "Wealth Gaps Rise to Record Highs between Whites, Blacks, and Hispanics." Washington, DC: Pew Research Center, Social and Demographic Trends (July 26). Available at: pewsocialtrends.org/files/2011/07/SDT-Wealth-Report _7-26-11_FINAL.pdf.

Taylor, Paul, Mark Hugo Lopez, Gabriel Velasco, and Seth Motel. 2012. "Hispanics Say They Have the Worst of a Bad Economy." Washington, DC: Pew Hispanic Center (January 26). Available at: http://www.pewhispanic.org/2012/01/26/hispanics-say-they-have-the-worst-of-a-bad-economy.

Teinowitz, Ira. 2008. "Hispanic Spending in Texas to Surpass $2 Million." *AdAge*, February 25.

TNS Media. 2008. "TNS Media Intelligence/CMAG with Analysis by the Wisconsin Advertising Project." Madison: University of Wisconsin Advertising Project (October 31).

Tomás Rivera Policy Institute. 2000. "Statewide Poll of Latino California Voters in 2000." Los Angeles: University of Southern California, Sol Price School of Public Policy.

Uhlaner, Carol J., and C. F. Garcia. 2005. "Learning Which Party Fits: Experience, Ethnic Identity, and the Demographic Foundations of Latino Party Identification." In *Diversity in Democracy: Minority Representation in the United States*, eds. Gary M. Segura and Shaun Bowler. Charlottesville: University of Virginia Press.

US Bureau of Labor Statistics 2012. "The African-American Labor Force in the Recovery." Washington, DC: US Department of Labor. Available at: http://www.dol.gov/_sec/media/reports/blacklaborforce/.

US Census Bureau. 2012. "The Foreign-Born Population in the United States: 2010." American Community Survey Reports (May). Available at: www.census.gov/prod/2012pubs/acs-19.pdf.

Vaca, Nicolas C. 2004. *The Presumed Alliance: The Unspoken Conflict between Latinos and Blacks and What It Means for America*. New York: HarperCollins.

Vega, Rodolfo, Manuela McDonough, Clancey Bateman, and Jim Maxwell. 2013. "Outreach and Enrollment Strategies for Latinos under the Affordable Care Act." National Council of La Raza. Available at:

http://www.nclr.org/images/uploads/pages/Outreach%20&%20Enrollment%20Strategies%20for%20Latinos%20under%20the%20ACA%20-%20NCLR%20and%20JSI.pdf (February 07, 2014).

Verba, Sidney, and Norman H. Nie. 1972. *Participation in America: Political Democracy and Social Equality*. New York: Harper & Row.

Verba, Sidney, Kay Lehman Schlozman, and Henry E. Brady. 1995. *Voice and Equality: Civic Voluntarism in American Politics*. Cambridge, MA: Harvard University Press.

Wals, Sergio C. 2011. "Does What Happens in Los Mochis Stay in Los Mochis? Explaining Postmigration Political Behavior." *Political Research Quarterly* 64, no. 3: 600–611.

Washington Post. 2008. "Hillary Clinton's Remarks." February 12.

Whittaker, Mathew, Gary M. Segura, and Shaun Bowler. 2005. "Racial/Ethnic Group Attitudes toward Environmental Protection in California: Is 'Environmentalism' Still a White Phenomenon?" *Political Research Quarterly* 58: 435–447.

Wienack, R. M., and N. A. Kraus. 2000. "Racial/Ethnic Differences in Children's Access to Care." *American Journal of Public Health* 90: 1771–1774.

Williams, Bryan L., and Yvette Florez. 2002. "Do Mexican Americans Perceive Environmental Issues Differently than Caucasians? A Study of Cross-Ethnic Variation in Perceptions Related to Water in Tucson." *Environmental Health Perspectives* 110: 303–310.

Yanez, Alonso. 2008. "Myth of the Latino Vote." *Hispanic Link News,* October 29.

Zeleny, Jeff. 2008. "Richardson Endorses Obama." *New York Times,* March 21.

INDEX

DANIEL JAVIER BARRETO

STANFORD NEWS SERVICE

Dr. Matt Barreto and **Dr. Gary M. Segura** are widely published scholars, researchers, and professors at the University of Washington and Stanford University, respectively. They are the founders of Latino Decisions, a leading public opinion and research firm that specializes in issues pertinent to the Latino electorate. Their work is regularly cited by Univision, the *New York Times*, ABC News, National Public Radio, impreMedia, NBC News, the *Wall Street Journal*, CNN, and many others.

PublicAffairs is a publishing house founded in 1997. It is a tribute to the standards, values, and flair of three persons who have served as mentors to countless reporters, writers, editors, and book people of all kinds, including me.

I. F. Stone, proprietor of *I. F. Stone's Weekly*, combined a commitment to the First Amendment with entrepreneurial zeal and reporting skill and became one of the great independent journalists in American history. At the age of eighty, Izzy published *The Trial of Socrates*, which was a national bestseller. He wrote the book after he taught himself ancient Greek.

Benjamin C. Bradlee was for nearly thirty years the charismatic editorial leader of *The Washington Post*. It was Ben who gave the *Post* the range and courage to pursue such historic issues as Watergate. He supported his reporters with a tenacity that made them fearless and it is no accident that so many became authors of influential, best-selling books.

Robert L. Bernstein, the chief executive of Random House for more than a quarter century, guided one of the nation's premier publishing houses. Bob was personally responsible for many books of political dissent and argument that challenged tyranny around the globe. He is also the founder and longtime chair of Human Rights Watch, one of the most respected human rights organizations in the world.

• • •

For fifty years, the banner of Public Affairs Press was carried by its owner Morris B. Schnapper, who published Gandhi, Nasser, Toynbee, Truman, and about 1,500 other authors. In 1983, Schnapper was described by *The Washington Post* as "a redoubtable gadfly." His legacy will endure in the books to come.

Peter Osnos, *Founder and Editor-at-Large*